Contagion

Contagion

*The Financial Epidemic
That Is Sweeping the Global Economy . . .
and How to Protect Yourself from It*

John R. Talbott

WILEY

John Wiley & Sons, Inc.

For general information on our other products and services or for technical support, please contact our Customer Care Department within the United States at (800) 762-2974, outside the United States at (317) 572-3993 or fax (317) 572-4002.

Wiley also publishes its books in a variety of electronic formats. Some content that appears in print may not be available in electronic books. For more information about Wiley products, visit our web site at www.wiley.com.

ISBN-13: 978-0-470-44221-0

Printed in the United States of America

10 9 8 7 6 5 4 3 2 1

Jesus left there and went to his hometown, accompanied by his disciples. When the Sabbath came, he began to teach in the synagogue, and many who heard him were amazed.

"Where did this man get these things?" they asked. "What's this wisdom that has been given him, that he even does miracles! Isn't this the carpenter? Isn't this Mary's son and the brother of James, Joseph, Judas and Simon? Aren't his sisters here with us?" And they took offense at him.

Jesus said to them, "Only in his hometown, among his relatives and in his own house is a prophet without honor." He could not do any miracles there, except lay his hands on a few sick people and heal them. And he was amazed at their lack of faith.

Then Jesus went around teaching from village to village. Calling the Twelve to him, he sent them out two by two and gave them authority over evil spirits.

These were his instructions: "Take nothing for the journey except a staff—no bread, no bag, no money in your belts. Wear sandals but not an extra tunic. Whenever you enter a house, stay there until you leave that town. And if any place will not welcome you or listen to you, shake the dust off your feet when you leave, as a testimony against them."

They went out and preached that people should repent. They drove out many demons and anointed many sick people with oil and healed them.

Mark 6:1–13

Contents

CONTENTS

Preface

I have a good friend in New York, Raphael, who co-owns a wonderful steak house on 110th Street and 2nd Avenue named Ricardo's. Somewhat as a joke, he has begun introducing me to his friends as Johnny Nostradamus. He then proceeds to tell them about my string of accurate predictions regarding housing, the mortgage markets, and the general economy over the past decade.

Facts are facts. I have had a fairly incredible run of accurate predictions, knock on wood. In 1999 I published a book that predicted the collapse of the Internet and high-tech bubble. In 2003 I published *The Coming Crash of the Housing Market,* which not only predicted the housing price decline, but said that it would be severe and national in scope, not local like all other real estate declines had been to date. Entire chapters were dedicated to the problems that Fannie Mae and Freddie Mac and the commercial banking system would have to endure in the future. In February 2006 the release of my new book, *Sell Now! The End of the Housing Bubble* coincided almost exactly with the peak of the housing market. In that text, I was able to show that the problem was much more serious than people realized and that it would not just be national in scope but international. I was able to identify the loose lending practices of the banks as the primary cause of the bubble and explained that lobbying pressures had prevented the government from not having done a better job regulating them. In early 2008, when most everyone was convinced that Hillary Clinton would be the Democratic nominee for president and that the major issue of the general campaign would be the war in Iraq, I wrote *Obamanomics,* not only identifying Barack Obama as the eventual winning Democratic nominee, but successfully identifying economic policy, and specifically the financial crisis, as the most important issue to Americans in the general election.

Now with *Contagion,* I am continuing the challenge of trying to foresee the future. It's not a steady job, but it's all I know. There have been books written that have attempted to explain what has happened in the past with regard to the subprime crisis and the housing price decline to date. Very few professional economists are willing to put their reputations at risk and make a prediction of what happens next. But, for investors and businesspeople and concerned citizens, that is exactly what they want to know. They want some idea from a credible person as to what might happen in the future based on the extent of the crisis to date. I am certain there are some historians and economists who would like to read a capsulation of what is happening, but that is not my intention. I want to, to the best of my abilities, try to help the reader understand where this country is going from here. I cannot guarantee the future, but by explaining the severity of the problems Americans face and the logic behind my argument I just may convince you to take action to better protect your assets, your livelihood and your country.

So how do I do it? How is it that I seem to be able to predict the future? Do I have a crystal ball or a divine talent like Nostradamus himself? Am I the smartest guy in the world? No, I am not the world's smartest man. I'm not stupid, but smarts are not the great competitive advantage I have relative to my peers.

My great competitive advantage in predicting economic events and consequences in the future is my independence. Decades ago, I left behind my job on Wall Street and the world of bosses and committees and boards and groupthink and toeing the party line. I wake up each day not knowing what problem I will attack, but simply knowing that my only objective is to uncover the truth. I have no business, commercial, or monetary incentive to promote anyone's agenda but my own, and I have chosen as my agenda to simply find the truth.

No one likes being lied to. The reason I was attracted to writing in the first place is that I felt the world, in general, was telling too many lies. Through writing, I hoped I might help the world uncover real truths. Business leaders, government leaders, and even friends and relatives had decided that lying was a victimless crime. A primary cause of the entire financial crisis today is due to the corruption and lies that were allowed to enter the sacred halls of our government. There is no such thing as a victimless lie. It is wrong, not only because it is hurtful, but as people in this country are so painfully learning, because as a society, it is unproductive and destructive.

Anyone who thinks, like Alan Greenspan suggests, that the housing, mortgage and banking events this country has suffered through are some kind of random elements that occurred naturally due to general business cycles similar to a hundred year flood needs to read this book. The suffering happening today was preordained years ago when U.S. citizens allowed the Congress and President to accept large campaign contributions from big business and Wall Street in order to avoid any new regulation and the proper enforcement of current laws on the books.

Unfortunately, the worst is not over. As the title of this book implies, this problem is not just going to stop with the decline in U.S. house prices. Residential real estate in the United States is such a large market, and had increased in value so tremendously during the boom years, that a readjustment in its pricing downward cannot help but have significant impacts in not only the United States, but in the world.

I want to thank Bill Falloon and the entire gang at John Wiley & Sons who supported my efforts at getting this important story into print. It is a real risk in the publishing industry to publish a book about current events, especially one that tries to predict future events. It is a testimony to their confidence in me as an author that they took this bet. I also want to thank my friends in Mexico; Peter, Elena, Harold, and Boca and Solovena. Without their support and long walks on the beach I could never have made it through this effort. The cervezas helped also.

■ ■ ■

I sincerely hope that this is the last book I have to write speaking of crashes or recessions or collapses. I hope that the American people wake up and demand better government from their elected representatives and stop the corrupting influence of lobbyists and corporate campaign contributions. And I hope that Americans emerge from the difficult days ahead with a new awareness of what really constitutes a full and meaningful life and never again let rampant consumerism and materialism so distort the direction of their lives.

JOHN R. TALBOTT

johntalbs@hotmail.com

Chapter 1

Bamboozled

con·ta·gion [kuhn-tey-juhn] – *noun*

1. the communication of disease by direct or indirect contact.
2. a disease so communicated.
3. the medium by which a contagious disease is transmitted.
4. harmful or undesirable contact or influence.
5. the ready transmission or spread as of an idea or emotion from person to person: a contagion of fear.

Each of the five preceding definitions of contagion could be appropriate to the current economic and societal circumstances occurring around the world. Although not exactly a disease, the greed, outsized consumerism, and virulent self-centeredness certainly appear to have devastating symptoms associated with them. The current illness is not transmitted directly by contact, but it certainly seems to have the capacity to spread broadly, especially through harmful or undesirable contact. And it really was just an idea that spread, the idea that life is only about wealth accumulation and that men and women can be judged by some sort of bottom-line measurement system that ignores any sense of proper or ethical behavior in one's lifetime. People cared more about the ends than the means to reach those ends.

I don't remember who caught the greed bug first. I'm sure somewhere there were businesspeople who were rather unscrupulous and would sell any product for profit, usually on late night television. The politicians weren't far behind as it is difficult to be a politician without being ego-centric, which always seems to be one step away from unethical. I can still recall the first commercials I saw on television for lawyers offering their services to the recently injured. I remember when doctors and dentists became more interested in profits than patients. Everyone can name televangelists who were caught preaching the gospel more for profits than converts.

Of course, Wall Street has always been greedy. That is what they do. But, even on Wall Street things have deteriorated. Twenty years ago on Wall Street your word was your bond and the reputation of your firm was sacrosanct and to be protected at all times. You made money the old-fashioned way, by out-thinking and out-hustling your competitors and delivering a product or service to your clients that created real value for them.

Since then, trading and principal investing has turned Wall Street into a den of whores. There is no value in something other than what you can convince someone to pay for it. It is a reason to celebrate if you can mislead an investor and get him to pay more than what an asset or business is worth. If you can hide liabilities off the balance sheet and stick them with the customer, all the more reason for merriment.

But I don't want to give the impression that this current crisis started or ended on Wall Street. Wall Street could never have pulled this off on its own. Remember, this all began with an unsustainable housing boom and eventual housing market collapse. Home realtors pushed their clients into ever-bigger homes based on phony high appraisals from non-independent appraisers with the money from mortgage brokers who fraudulently changed qualifying income amounts on mortgage applications, and all contributed to the dramatic boom in house prices. The commercial banks offered such aggressive terms for mortgages and knew full well they wouldn't sit on their balance sheet for long. Then the investment banks packaged these mortgages and sold them to unsuspecting institutional investors, such as pension funds and sovereign wealth funds. It may not have been ethical, but they paid the rating agencies hundreds of millions of dollars to rate much of this junk AAA. Even the dupes who ended up buying this junk were not without fault. They sought out the greater yield these investments returned, but the extent of their due diligence and credit analysis was to ask only about its credit rating. It leaves a lot of hours in the day to go golfing if your entire job consists of just investing in AAA securities with no further homework being done on the credit front.

But the real reason why this disaster was allowed to occur was that the U.S. government had been co-opted. None of this could have been accomplished without significant deregulation of the financial industry and the avoidance of previous regulation and of required supervision in many cases. It was the mantra of the American government for 30 years that less government and less regulation would lead to lower taxes and a stronger economy. Well, today, the United States has higher spending, higher taxes, more government, but a lot less regulation of the largest companies and banks.

Listen to your congressperson today say how surprised they are about the current crisis. Nothing could be further from the truth. They have been warned time and time again about this impending crisis, not only in home prices and in the mortgage market, but also about the high debt leverage of Fannie Mae and Freddie Mac as well as the entire commercial banking and investment banking and hedge fund industry. This crisis was no accident. It was just a matter of time until this entire house of cards fell. Fannie Mae and Freddie Mac are the proper names of these large institutions that used to be abbreviations for their longer names, the Federal National Mortgage Association, for example, for Fannie Mae. They were put in business to buy existing mortgages from banks and to package them and to sell them as securities to investors, basically to turn mortgages into securities that looked more like traditional bonds.

So to understand the real reason why this occurred, you can't just stop at deregulation as an explanation. You have to ask why the deregulation was allowed to occur by our Congress and our President. The simple answer is that they were paid to deregulate industry. Our Congress and our President take billions of dollars each year from business and banks and Wall Street in the form of campaign contributions. They are by far the largest contributors to our national elections. Do you think a for-profit business would make a donation to a congressman unless they were getting something in return? John McCain admits taking money from the telecommunications companies that his committee regulates, but his defense is that it does not influence his voting. If this were true, it would certainly make the for-profit businesses that are handing him the money look awfully stupid for wasting their assets. No, just the opposite is true. A recent study on www.publiccampaign.org showed that for every one dollar in campaign contributions a typical American business makes, it gets back more than $400 in tax benefits, tax deductions, and tax credits from the American government. Certainly a 400 to 1 return on your investment beats any of the alternative investments a company might have in its base operating business. And this does not measure the total benefit corporations receive from

> *Our Congress and our President take billions of dollars each year from business and banks and Wall Street in the form of campaign contributions.*

lobbying. In addition to tax benefits, generous lobbying corporations also receive help in protecting their domestic turf from foreign competitors, union busting with their workforces, price supports for their products, and taxpayer assistance in opening international markets.

Here is some evidence. Senator Charles Schumer, a Democrat from New York, has as his top 10 contributors the biggest financial institutions he is supposed to regulate on the Senate Banking Committee. The list of the top 10 campaign contributors to all of Congress include the National Association of Realtors, the Mortgage Bankers Association, the American Bankers Association, Fannie Mae and Freddie Mac, the investment banks and the hedge funds on Wall Street. It certainly sounds like every player in the current housing, mortgage, and banking crisis. In 2007 alone the securities and investment industry spent more than $86 million on lobbying and the real estate lobby spent $78 million. Tell me when the evidence becomes more than just simple coincidence.

Do you want further evidence? Name another problem facing America today and I can tell you the lobbying force that is preventing a commonsense solution that would benefit all Americans. Global warming? The coal lobby and the electric utility lobby. Gas prices? The oil and gas lobby. Pharmaceutical prices too high? The pharmaceutical industry lobby. Health care costs and coverage? The hospital corporation lobby and the HMO industry. War and defense spending? The defense industry lobby. Social Security and Medicare reform? The AARP. Education reform? The teachers union lobby.

Coincidence? I don't think so. Look at the facts of the current crisis. Banks and nonbanks were completely unregulated and were allowed to leverage themselves up and extend mortgage financing in the craziest amounts on the craziest terms to home buyers. There was no supervision of real estate agents and appraisers or mortgage brokers. Fannie Mae and Freddie Mac's supervision was so lax that they both utilized 120 to one debt to equity leverage to buy or guarantee half of all mortgages in the country, approximately $5.2 trillion worth. Is it a coincidence that Fannie Mae and Freddie Mac also spent hundreds of millions of dollars on lobbying and campaign donations to your Congress? Rating agencies' and investment banks' activities went completely unregulated as they packaged these mortgage securities and sold them worldwide. Hedge funds, some of the biggest contributors to your Congress and President, had no reporting requirements, no transparency, and no supervision as they helped grow the credit default swap market from a $140 billion market 10 years ago to a $65 trillion completely unregulated market today. AIG, a supposed insurance company, had $420 billion of exposure in the credit default swaps market, an exposure that ultimately was their undoing.

As certain as the sun rises, as sure as the rain falls, as predictable as the tide, this financial crisis was guaranteed to happen. Not only has the U.S. government allowed deregulation at home, it has exported the idea worldwide as a solution to the world's economic problems. There is good regulation and bad regulation. In Peru and India, it can take six months and 850 bureaucratic steps for an entrepreneur to acquire a government license to start a new small business. Certainly this type of over-regulation is bad for an economy.

But what American advocates of deregulation failed to realize in promoting unregulated capitalism around the world is that you cannot have a free market without proper regulation. There can be no market without the rule of law. The reason capitalist free markets were slow to catch on in Africa and much of the rest of the developing world was not a problem of business, but one of government. The governments did not provide the essential rules and regulations and the rule of law necessary to conduct business effectively. Without the rule of law, contracts are not honored, fraudulent activity is not punished, and property rights are not protected. If you look at a map of the world, of the 160 countries on the planet with more than a million population, all are doing quite well economically, growing fairly well, with the exception of approximately 50 countries. All 50 of these countries share one attribute—bad government. The corruption endemic in many Third World countries' governments means that individuals forming new businesses and building factories will face the constant fear that government representatives will someday steal their profits.

In one of the great ironies, rather than America exporting our model of good government to the world, it appears that America has imported some of the government corruption endemic to the Third World. As our government became more corrupt and more co-opted by corporate donations and lobbying, they regulated business less and business itself became threatened. Karl Marx said that the capitalists will manufacture the rope that hangs them. As Raghuram G. Rajan and Luigi Zingales said in their book of the same title (Rajan 2003), it's a matter of "Saving Capitalism from the Capitalists." It would be ideal if businesses operating in their own individual self-interest and profit-maximization does nothing but good for the planet. But this is not the case. Businesses pollute, cause global warming, cause conflicts over access to raw materials, rip off consumers, make false advertising claims, and put their workers in competition with the lowest wage workers around the world. Anyone who believes that corporations acting solely in their own self-interest to maximize profits in a world of no regulation will ensure a prosperous global economy, a healthy environment, and a stable world needs to go back to school and study externalities and collective action problems. Although governments should not do anything that the free market can do, there are enormous problems that cannot be solved by self-interested corporations in the free market and need government involvement. Perhaps one of the most important of these problems is the regulation of the market itself. Be wary every time a government official tells you that an industry has agreed to be regulated and that they have decided to regulate it themselves.

In this book I examine the evidence and try to gain a better understanding of how the United States got into this mess. I examine the housing price boom and collapse in detail because it was the primary

> *Although governments should not do anything that the free market can do, there are enormous problems that cannot be solved by self-interested corporations in the free market and need government involvement.*

cause of all of our current financial problems. But the primary focus of the book will be a look forward to try to describe how far-reaching this contagion might spread. The word contagion entered the lexicon of regulators of financial markets during the Asian meltdown in 1998, also known as the Asian flu in finance circles, and came to be popular in describing a crisis in one market that has the ability to mutate into others. I use a much broader definition of the term to not only include financial matters, but also government concerns such as corruption and societal problems such as greed. Although I will not be accurate in all of my predictions, it is helpful to investors and businesspeople and concerned citizens to take this look forward as they are much more interested in what might occur in the future than what has happened in the past.

A question facing many homeowners today is: When will the current housing price decline cease? Unfortunately, I show that the country as of the end of 2008 is only approximately halfway into what is already a record housing price correction. A recession is spreading now in the United States, but I argue that it will become one of the deepest and longest in our nation's history. Already many European countries have entered recession and it will be some time yet until they return to positive economic growth. The United States and Europe drive global consumer demand for goods and products and so the other economies of the world, especially the emerging growth economies that specialize in manufacturing products for these markets and providing raw materials and commodities to them, will suffer. I cannot think of a single country on Earth that will be exempt from this economic downturn.

I describe what is happening on Wall Street and spend some time talking about the credit default swap market, that $65 trillion completely unregulated market in which people can make bets on which company bankrupts next. I then turn around and demonstrate how problems on Wall Street and the freezing of credit worldwide can lead to serious problems on Main Street, in our own communities and in our own state and local governments.

An important question for investors is whether this is a temporary problem for the United States and the world or whether this is more permanent. The losses that have occurred in the housing market are permanent because no bank in the foreseeable future will be lending home buyers 10 times their annual income to buy a house as they have done in the past. If bank lending declines, the home prices have to follow. But it is also true that the problem extends further than just the housing price crash. The demographics of the United States are such that the baby boomers are just now starting to retire and this will represent a significant hit to our productive capacity and to our economic output. Just when the country starts to get over the housing collapse and the ensuing recession, demographically speaking, Americans will run into the baby boomer retirement, which will harm economic growth in the United States for decades.

In such a difficult crisis and terrible economic environment you can quickly see why cash is king. It is hard to come up with a list of good investment alternatives, but I do find a couple of interesting candidates. Similarly, there is not a long list of countries that I would recommend investing in, but there is at least one large one.

This analysis would not be complete without an understanding of the administration's plans to solve this crisis and a critique of their approach. Even after you stop the immediate bleeding of the financial institutions, you have to ask the question: What required reforms are necessary to the banking industry in general and to our government specifically? It makes no sense to talk about health care reform or global warming or high pharmaceutical prices until big business is thrown out of our government. Until effective lobbying reform is enacted, this country is not going to be able to address any of the problems that Americans face. Remember, when these corrupt politicians were asked to come up with a plan to help the economy, they wanted to give $700 billion of your money to the guys on Wall Street who caused the mess to begin with. The fact that many congresspeople and senators voted for this proposal even though their constituency e-mails and phone calls were 95 percent against the proposal makes you realize who they are really working for. I have some bad news for you, it isn't the American worker.

I conclude the book with a philosophical note as to what people in this country may have learned from this crisis. If the citizens survive it, it will make them stronger because everyone needs to do some serious introspection to determine if this country and this government and the their own lives are headed in the right direction. In a strange sense, it is good this crisis has happened. Americans never would have seen the error in their ways unless they were subjected to great pain and inconvenience. Now that they are feeling real pain with their jobs and homes threatened, only one final question remains:

Will they change?

Chapter 2

What Didn't Cause the U.S. Housing Boom and Bust

To understand the future, it is sometimes helpful to gain a firm understanding of the past. You cannot make predictions about what is possible in our economic future until you understand exactly how the United States got here. Many years from now, when people reflect back on the global financial troubles of the early 21st century, it is important that they remember that it all started with the housing crash in the United States.

Even this analysis is not completely accurate, because you can't have a good crash without a preceding boom. For home prices to have declined dramatically over a period of years there had to have been a necessary boom preceding it, during which home prices grew beyond reason, and in the United States this is exactly what happened. To understand why a housing crash in the United States was inevitable and to have an idea of how much more pain there might be on the housing front, it is important to look back and determine exactly how housing had become so overpriced over the past 30 to 40 years.

As Americans are well aware, nominal housing prices increased in the United States for nearly 50 years, from 1955 to 2005. In 1968 a typical home in the United States could be purchased for $20,000 and by 2006, that average median home sold for close to $220,000. This appreciation was not limited to any one geographic area of the country as all four regions—Northeast, Midwest, South and West—all showed remarkable appreciation during the period.

But it is not enough to say that nominal home prices increased every year over the past 50 years. Inflation also increased every year during the period, but rather how much did home prices appreciate more than general inflation. In other words, after accounting for the lower purchasing power of the dollar, did the average home in the United States still show significant real price appreciation?

The answer, of course, is yes, after accounting for general inflation, the real price of a typical home in the United States doubled from 1968 until 2005. And this is a median price of the average home for all the United States. There are a few cities in the United States, such as Phoenix, San Francisco, Las Vegas, New York, Boston, and Miami, that showed real appreciation in their homes of more than 500 percent during the period. In general the areas of highest appreciation were on both coasts and in Las Vegas and Arizona.

It is not enough to say that because housing prices went up during that period that they were overpriced. The reasonableness of prices, by definition, is always relative. With regard to houses, the appropriate relative measures seem to be how the market price of the home compares relative to its replacement value if you had to rebuild it; what is the home's value relative to its affordability, that is relative to one's income; and finally, what is the house's value relative to alternative living arrangements, namely renting.

By 2006 it should have been apparent to homeowners that the prices of homes in many American cities had become out of whack relative to their replacement values; that is, the cost of buying a piece of property, acquiring a building permit, and constructing a home. Homes in California by 2006 were selling at three to five times what it would cost to build a similar home from scratch. Even if you included the high cost for the underlying land, it is difficult to justify the high prices paid for homes in many cities across America relative to the cost of new construction.

This inequality can be seen most readily by looking at the profits of American homebuilders during the housing boom. In effect, homebuilders are sellers of homes. They do best when homes are overvalued because they step in and act as arbitrageurs, taking raw materials like nails and wood and dirt and turning them into homes for sale. Their profits increase if homes are overvalued. And boy did their profits increase. The homebuilders in America saw their profits increase more than 20 percent per year every year for 10 years running. In the Midwest, it is common for the cost of building a new home to run from $70 to $120 per square foot. In California and New York, this cost of construction can approach $200 to $300 per square foot because labor prices are higher, materials prices can be higher, the work area can be more congested, and the quality of the final house can be higher with more amenities (such as nicer cabinets or fancier kitchens). But, even these high costs of construction cannot justify homes in California and New York and elsewhere that sold at their peak price of more than $1,000 to $2,000 per square foot. There are many condominium apartments in New York City that sell between $1,000 and $3,000 per square foot, and yet the cost of new construction in New York, even in the most congested areas, is less than $500 per square foot at most, especially if all you are doing is adding an extra floor to an already planned new high-rise.

To determine whether houses are overpriced on an affordability measure, it is best to look at housing prices relative to income. What first alerted me to the unsustainable nature of the increase in U.S. house prices was that most wages in America have been stagnant for 30 years. There are disagreements as to why workers wages have not increased as U.S. productivity has expanded, but it is probably some combination of increased globalization in which American workers are forced to compete with low-wage countries such as Mexico, China, India, and Vietnam, and increased technology. Increased technology has dumbed down many jobs in America so that these jobs now require few skills. I met a woman in Kentucky who surprised me by telling me that she got a job as a welder at a car assembly plant. I was surprised because I knew she had no welding experience and no welding training. It turns out, as she proudly told me, that she was able to accomplish 140 complex welds per hour. The total effort required on her part was pushing a red button on the wall 140 times each hour. Technology did the rest. In a world where employees only require the skill necessary to push a red button on the wall, it is hard to argue that they deserve a premium wage.

Finally, there is a growing school of thought that what really happened to the American worker was a great power shift from workers rights to management and shareholders. Because of the Reagan revolution, and because of globalization and technology, it has been more difficult to organize workers, and unions have seen a dramatic decline in their membership. In the private sector, union membership peaked in the 1950s at 35 percent, but have declined to just over 9 percent today. Regardless of what you think about unions, it is rather apparent from their demise that workers do less well relative to shareholders and management in their absence. According to the Institute for Policy Studies (2008), because of the weakening role of unions and the increased difficulty of workers to organize, management at our biggest companies has been able to pay themselves 334 times what the typical worker makes. If workers make $2 an hour less today than they otherwise would have, this translates into a $4 trillion wealth shift from workers to shareholders, just about exactly what the stock market has increased over the period in real terms. By this argument, there has been little real growth in business profitability over the recent past, just a shift in wealth from workers to owners and management.

So regardless of the exact reason for wage stagnation, the flat wages mean that any real increase in home prices make them less affordable to the typical American. Home prices have doubled from 1968 to 2006 with little increase in real wages, which means it is twice as hard for the typical American to afford a home. There was a commensurate nominal interest rate decline from 1981 on, and it is important to this analysis, but I will hold that discussion for later in this chapter.

When you think about it, it's almost impossible for housing prices to double in real terms because wages never move that rapidly. If housing prices from an affordability standpoint stay constant relative to wages, then housing prices shouldn't be able to increase each year more than wages, and real wages typically increase less than 1 percent or 2 percent per year, if at all.

The data is quite conclusive. In 1968, the typical house in America sold for approximately 2.6 times household incomes and by 2006 this ratio was approaching five times, almost double. This is important because housing costs dominate the average household's annual expenses. For example, in 2000, according to the U.S. Bureau of Labor Statistics, housing costs were $12,000 per year for the typical American, and this dominated other annual household costs such as transportation costs of $6,700, taxes of $6,200, food at $4,600, and health care costs at $2,100.

Since 1960, the percentage of women working in America has dramatically increased from approximately 32 percent to more than 62 percent. So the price of a home relative to a household income doubled since, and this was during a period in which many married American women went to work. Given that 50 percent of American marriages end in divorce, it may be helpful to express these house price ratios as a multiple of the average worker's income rather than a two-wage household income. Here again, the increase during the period has been dramatic, with housing prices as a multiple of the average worker's income increasing from 5.3 times to more than 9.0 times annual income.

Even this large number does not tell the full story because this average worker has a number of nondiscretionary expenses he must make each year. In other words, it is more accurate to examine housing prices as a multiple of the average worker's free cash flow after his nondiscretionary expenses such as taxes, food, and utilities. This final calculation shows that home prices had increased dramatically over the period, increasing from 10.7 times the typical worker's free cash flow to more than 19 times by 2006.

Most homes during the housing boom were financed primarily with mortgage debt, so it is safe to say that these multiples of free cash flow are extraordinary. People familiar with the leveraged buyout industry, in which debt is employed to finance the purchase of entire companies, will quickly realize that healthy, conservatively financed leveraged buyouts involve debt structures with five to seven times free cash flow of the business, while the leveraged buyout industry gets into enormous trouble when it tries to finance deals north of 10 times cash flow. The reason is simple. There just isn't enough cash flow at these price levels to pay off the interest on the loan. Similarly, when you buy a house at 19 times a person's free cash flow it makes it all but impossible for the loan to be repaid. I will speak in depth why the banks were willing to extend such large amounts of money to homeowners during the boom, but obviously part of the problem was qualifying potential buyers for an adjustable-rate mortgage at an initial teaser rate of 3 percent, knowing full well but ignoring that the rate would double or triple in three to five years.

From an economic perspective, the most pure form of determining the reasonableness of housing prices is to compare it to an alternative means of achieving a similar mode of shelter. Although certainly not a perfect comparison, the alternative to owning a house is to rent a similar house in the same neighborhood. The cost of renting a similar home in 2006 in Las Vegas, Phoenix, Los Angeles, or New York was from 20 percent to 50 percent of the total cost of owning a home. This fact alone should have set off warning bells to potential buyers in these markets. The first rule of economics and pricing is that similar assets in similar locations that serve similar functions should have similar prices. Buyers, trying to justify the higher costs of ownership, did so by arguing that they were capturing the potential price appreciation through ownership that the renter never would enjoy. But, as any economist should have told them, when you buy an asset it is just as likely to go down in price as go up.

When you look at the increase in house prices over time, what is most striking is that it is a relatively new phenomenon. Robert Shiller in his book, *Irrational Exuberance, Second Edition* (2005), plots real home prices over time, over a very long period of time. His data starts in 1890 and shows that until the mid-1990s, home prices really showed no meaningful appreciation. In essence, real home prices in America were relatively flat for more than a hundred years. Shiller then shows real home prices more than doubling by 2006, but this is not a complete analysis.

Although certainly not a perfect comparison, the alternative to owning a house is to rent a similar house in the same neighborhood.

When you purchase a home you are really purchasing two distinct assets, the physical house and a fairly significant tax shield, the deductibility of mortgage interest for tax purposes. It turns out that the second asset, the value of the tax shield you are buying, has declined since

1981, because inflation has eased in the economy. In effect, the mortgage interest deduction is more valuable to a homeowner during periods of high inflation, the homeowner gets to deduct for tax purposes the nominal levels of interest that don't turn out to be real. So, what this means, is that since 1981 the second asset, the tax shield you purchase, has been declining in value, which means the primary asset, the physical house you purchased has been increasing in value even faster than you thought. Although this is a complicated point, the essential takeaway from this analysis is that the dramatic increase in home prices did not begin in the mid-1990s as posited by Shiller but rather in 1981, if you ignore the decline in value in the associated tax shield.

So if figuring out what was unique about the year 1981, what changed dramatically in 1981, then what caused housing prices to begin their rapid and unsustainable growth might be revealed.

As Americans well remember, 1981 was the first year of the Ronald Reagan presidency. Ronald Reagan came into office with the prime rate at 21½ percent and some tax-free municipal bonds yielding were more than 16 percent. He ignored conventional economic wisdom in his attempts to control inflation by slowing dramatically the fed's printing of new money and instead borrowed the government's deficits in the debt capital markets. Economists argued that such government borrowing would crowd out private companies from the debt markets and cause interest rates to increase. Economist Milton Friedman and other monetarists proved correct, that inflation was primarily caused by the printing of money by the Federal Reserve and that if this new printing of money could be ceased, inflation would come down and so would interest rates. Stated in its most simple form, you cannot have price inflation of all goods unless there is more money chasing the same goods, unless somebody is printing more money each night. President Reagan realized this, slowed the printing of money dramatically, and inflation and interest rates came down every year for the next 20 years.

Thirty-year fixed-rate mortgage interest rates declined from a high of 16.5 percent in 1981 to just more than 5 percent by 2006. At first blush, this appears to be the explanation for the run-up in housing prices since 1981. If interest rates declined by more than 70 percent, then it would be natural to think that housing prices should more than double because housing is primarily financed mostly with debt. All other things being equal, such a large decline in interest rates would mean that the first-year payment for the home buyer on a fixed-rate 30-year mortgage would be dramatically lower and the potential home buyer could afford to pay much more for his house.

But looks can be deceiving. Remember, these rates are nominal interest rates. Previously I said that inflation was declining dramatically during this period. As a matter of fact, real interest rates during this period hardly changed at all. Real interest rates have always been constant in the 2 percent to 3 percent range for decades in the past. And if real interest rates don't change, there is no reason why an asset value like a house or a home should change. Nominal interest rates at 10 percent are what you see in the paper. These rates include expected inflation, say 7 percent, and the underlying real rate of, say 3 percent. The nominal rate is not the real rate because an investor is losing the rate of inflation each year in his purchasing power. The investor's real return, after accounting for inflation, is only 3 percent in this example. Much more on this later in the chapter.

So from 1981 to 2006 home prices in the United States more than doubled and specific cities in the United States, primarily on the coasts, saw home-price appreciation of more than 400 percent to 500 percent. This appreciation could not be explained by increasing incomes, increasing rents, or increasing construction costs. Similarly, just because nominal interest rates came down, real interest rates changed little during the period so interest rates alone cannot justify the boom in housing prices. Before I describe the real reasons behind the housing boom in prices let's take a few minutes and debunk some popular theories about what supposedly caused the boom. There were many theories expounded during the boom that were utilized to try to justify the high prices of homes. The chief economist of the National Association of Realtors never saw a house that he thought was overpriced and was proficient at coming up with reasons why the housing boom would continue ad infinitum into the future.

One often-repeated argument as to why high home prices were justified, especially on our coasts, was that there was a scarcity of land in United States. Anybody who has flown in an airplane over the United States would have to laugh at such a proposition. The country is enormous and the great majority of its population lives in metropolitan areas that represent less than 10 percent of the total land mass of America. Experts tried to justify the high prices paid for homes during the boom, so they made two distinct arguments. One argument is that America's premier cities are unique and cannot be duplicated elsewhere and the second argument says that waterfront properties are unique and scarce and, by definition, cannot be duplicated inland.

There is something certainly unique about living in San Francisco or New York City, but when the housing prices in those cities become tremendously high relative to the national average, people will live elsewhere. And great new cities will grow, sometimes even from the desert. Las Vegas, Miami, Phoenix, and Seattle are all examples of wonderful cities that have grown up almost from nothing in the past 20 years and now rival New York and San Francisco and all the great cities of the world as far as the lifestyle desirability and quality. Although New York is unique, there is no reason the amenities available there cannot be duplicated in other newly formed and rapidly growing metropolises.

The argument that waterfront properties, especially on our coasts, are unique and not reproducible can be summarized in the argument that a coastline is only so long, it cannot be lengthened and once filled with homes, the number of oceanfront properties cannot increase. At first blush, it appears to be a solid argument. But there are two countervailing arguments against it.

First, if the number of homes on the coastline is fixed, how could there be significant price appreciation of those homes over the past 10 years? Didn't homeowners on the coast 10 years ago know that the coastline was fixed in length? Because the coastline didn't grow, and the number of properties on the coast didn't grow, either the price for the homes on that coast were properly fixed 10 years ago by their homeowners or are properly fixed today at a significantly higher level. Both prices can't be right.

And a stronger argument against the fixed coastline debate can be found in San Diego. In San Diego people realize that development on the coast had reached its maximum, and rather than stopping development, builders decided to build up, rather than out. By building literally hundreds of multistory condominium buildings in and around San Diego, developers demonstrated that there was little difference in value between a 30th-floor condominium overlooking the ocean and a prime property sitting on the beachfront. In San Diego, at the height of the boom, it was typical for a penthouse in some of these multistory condominium buildings to sell for more than $3 to $4 million each—about the same cost to live on the beach in a stand-alone house. It turns out that a good view of the ocean is not restricted to people who happen to have a home directly on the beach.

Another common argument made to justify the boom in home prices in the United States was the dramatic increase in legal and illegal immigration. Completely ignoring economic reality, proponents of this theory argued that new immigrants needed houses to live in and that their arrival caused a housing shortage, which drove up housing prices to a level that was sustainable because it reflected this new demand of immigrants. Unfortunately, the facts just don't fit this story. The majority of immigrants to the United States over the past 20 years have been illegal immigrants, almost all of them from Mexico. They did not come to America to buy million-dollar homes. These immigrants were very poor, in search of jobs, and the majority did not buy homes but rented. Over time, the lucky ones settled in America and did buy homes, but they were of more modest price in even more modest neighborhoods. Most dramatic price appreciation in homes in America occurred in our wealthiest and most prestigious cities, like New York, San Francisco, Beverly Hills, and Palm Springs, and this fact makes it impossible to believe that Mexican immigrants could have been the cause of such dramatic appreciation in these wealthy enclaves across the country.

Similarly, there were people who argued that rising construction costs and rising incomes in America justified higher home prices, but this just wasn't true. Construction costs were not increasing during most of the boom until the last couple of years, and incomes have been relatively flat in real terms for 30 years or more.

Proponents of increased home prices who argued against the potential for a housing price correction said that there had never been a national price decline in housing and that housing was not a national issue but a local issue. Just as commercial real estate's first rule is location, location, location, so realtors and mortgage investors had convinced themselves that real estate downturns in the housing industry were always local, local, local. But this was a different type of real estate boom. It was truly national. The entire country had seen housing prices increase dramatically. Although the coasts experienced even greater price appreciation of homes, the middle of the country saw unsustainable increases of 35 percent to 70 percent in real terms during the boom. And when the real causes of the housing boom and its eventual crash are examined, these real causes were not local in nature but were truly national and international. No region of the country had a monopoly on loose lending from the banks or how they misinterpreted the decline in nominal interest rates as a real effect.

Some people argued that housing couldn't crash because the economy was strong and doing well. I will examine just how strong the economy was doing in a later chapter, but for now let us look at the theory that housing cannot go down in an up economy. Typically home prices decline and foreclosures increase in weak economies because weak economies accentuate the number of foreclosures because of job loss. When a local economy suffers, such as semiconductors in Silicon Valley or the oil and gas sector in Houston, job losses increase in the region, foreclosures increase, and house prices come down.

But this was not going to be your typical housing cycle. This time, housing prices came down first, and the housing downturn then caused a subsequent economic slowdown and recession. This is just the opposite of the traditional housing cycle. The reason housing prices started heading down in this cycle is not because of the weak economy and job losses, but because home prices had risen to unsustainably high levels and eventually needed to adjust downward. Then, declining house prices caused increased foreclosures, less economic activity in the real estate, mortgage, and banking sector, and slower economic growth in the country. So, this time, Americans didn't need a weak economy to see home prices began to decline nationally.

Now that the United States is three years into this housing price decline, some experts are coming up with all new kinds of explanations for what caused the real estate bubble and its eventual burst. These experts are not completely disinterested or unbiased. Many experts are strong proponents of less regulation and think that free markets can be a panacea. No matter what the problem, these experts argue that less regulation and more free markets will solve the problem. In this current downturn, they have tried to argue that there was not too little regulation but too much regulation that caused the real estate boom and bust.

In a frequently cited academic paper that appeared in the *Economic Policy Review* in 2003, Edward Glaeser and Joseph Gyourko try to uncover statistical evidence that too much government regulation is causing the boom in housing prices in many cities in the United States. Their thesis, simply stated, is that when you purchase a home you are really buying three separate assets, the physical house and its cost of construction, the underlying land, and the legal right to develop and build on that property. Homes in residential neighborhoods lie on property that has been zoned residential and the appropriate building permits have been secured prior to construction. The authors found statistically that there was a significant difference in the value of land beneath your house as opposed to excess additional land alongside your house.

The authors conclude that it must be restrictive regulations and tough zoning boards that prohibited you from developing the land adjacent to your home and thus caused a diminution of its value. What the authors failed to realize is that in their own study the average size of the adjacent, lower valued property was less than a one-tenth of one acre, hardly large enough to build a home on. In essence, what the authors had found in aggregate was a large amount of land that remained undeveloped, but that turned out to be in such small parcels that it made no sense to build on. The authors incorrectly concluded that it was government regulation that prevented development on these adjacent properties and that government regulation was responsible for people not increasing the supply of new homes and therefore causing the housing bubble to continue. Unfortunately, the author's own statistics show that these parcels of land were too small for development and that government regulation had nothing to do with why they were not being built on. For the authors to be right that this was the reason for owners not to be increasing the supply of new homes, homeowners in Beverly Hills would have to allow small half-size homes to be built and squeezed onto their front lawns.

Defenders of the big banks and the theory of the infallibility of completely free markets have come up with two additional innovative arguments as to why banks are not the cause of the housing boom and ensuing crash. These defenders point to a specific government regulation as the cause of the housing boom and bust, namely the

Community Reinvestment Act (CRA). The Community Reinvestment Act is a law that Congress passed to ensure that banks that took deposits in poor neighborhoods and communities also loaned money into those communities. The CRA was very effective in getting large commercial banks to lend to poor neighborhoods, especially to extend mortgage financing to first-time homebuyers and to stimulate greater home ownership in these poor neighborhoods. Homeownership in poor neighborhoods has been found to be a great stabilizing influence on the community.

Critics of the CRA, who tried to blame it for the housing boom and bust argue that many of these poor and middle-class working Americans never should have been offered homeownership as they never had the financial resources to be able to afford it. Their argument is that these people eventually defaulted on their mortgages.

Unfortunately the facts just don't fit this explanation. It is true that poor and more middle-class homeowners were the first to default to the current housing downturn. But this is always the case. Middle-class and poor homeowners always have less cushion, financially speaking, to pay their mortgage, and if they get in trouble have less alternative financial sources to tap to stay current on their mortgage. A wealthy person who suffers a job loss typically has substantial savings to tap to stay current on her mortgage or can make phone calls to friends and parents and secure the necessary monies. A poor person is much less likely to be able to do that. So, regardless of whether the CRA was passed, it is typical in housing downturns that those people with lower incomes typically default first, and that is what people are seeing in this housing cycle.

But, more importantly, the greatest home price appreciation in this country was not in the poorer neighborhoods where the CRA was utilized. The tremendous home price appreciations that occurred in the United States were in our wealthiest cities—San Francisco, New York, Miami, Palm Springs, Palm Beach—not typically areas in which you'd expect to find poorer neighborhoods. It is a statistical fact that those cities with the highest priced homes in 1997 also had the fastest growth rate in the price of homes over the next five years. Cities that had average house prices of $100,000 in 1997 saw 20 percent to 25 percent growth in total during the next five years of the boom, but this paled in comparison to wealthier cities where the average home price was $250,000 in 1997 where they enjoyed 65 percent cumulative appreciation over the next five years. Recognize how counterintuitive these statistics are. They say that the highest price cities in 1997, instead of reverting to the mean and declining in value, accelerated their growth and grew at a faster rate than those cities with more modestly priced homes. Certainly, the CRA cannot explain this phenomenon. It turns out that home ownership increased some 3 percent over the past 15 years, and about 1 percent of that 3 percent is at risk of defaulting. But, nationwide the delinquency rate is nearing 20 percent for subprime loans and pushing 9 percent for all mortgages. This slightly higher default rate for new homeowners explains approximately 1 million defaults, but more than 6 million defaults are expected in the next two years and most of these defaults are in nicer neighborhoods because of adjustable-rate mortgages (ARMS) and option-pay mortgages resetting.

Possibly the biggest argument the pro-business crowd uses to argue that too much government and too much regulation caused this housing boom and bust is based on what happened to Fannie Mae and Freddie Mac. Fannie Mae and Freddie Mac were private companies that enjoyed an implied guarantee of their debt and contractual obligations from the federal government. This guarantee, even though it was not explicit, gave Fannie Mae and Freddie Mac an enormous competitive advantage in the business of buying and packaging mortgages in the capital markets relative to

The greatest home price appreciation in this country was not in the poorer neighborhoods where the CRA was utilized.

their completely private competitors. There is no question that over the long term, the involvement of Fannie Mae and Freddie Mac was a great destabilizing influence to the growth of a healthy and vibrant mortgage resale market. But, to say that their implied government guarantee caused the housing bust overstates the case.

The reason is that Fannie Mae and Freddie Mac had to sit out the biggest boom years of the housing growth. In April 2003, my first book on housing was released entitled *The Coming Crash in the Housing Market*. During the first week after publication, the *Wall Street Journal* dedicated its back page to a detailed review of my new book and its emphasis was to talk about my fear that Fannie Mae and Freddie Mac were over-leveraged with debt and were mismanaged. I'm not certain who may have seen this review or read my book, although it did have some critical success becoming the number three bestseller in the country, but within three months government regulators, including the Federal Reserve began to crack down on Fannie Mae and Freddie Mac, and within the year Fannie Mae and Freddie Mac had announced accounting irregularities in the billions of dollars with the result that both replaced their chief financial officers and their chief executive officers. As a result of the government's investigation, Fannie Mae and Freddie Mac's asset growth was frozen and each had to dispose of approximately $200 billion of mortgage assets on their balance sheet. This meant that from 2003 until approximately 2007, Fannie Mae and Freddie Mac were pretty much out of the business of buying mortgages and putting them on their balance sheet. It turns out that this was the period of the most rapid appreciation in home prices over the last 30 years and it is also the period during which the commercial banks became the most aggressive in offering lending terms to homebuyers. So although Fannie Mae and Freddie Mac share some of the blame for getting the boom started, the boom certainly continued without their participation.

Now that I have explained what didn't cause the boom and bust in housing prices, I will explain what the real causes were.

Chapter 3

What Did Cause the U.S. Housing Boom and Bust

The real cause of the housing boom and subsequent crash was not any one entity, but an entire system that had grown corrupt over the past 30 years. Detailed here is a story of mortgage lending excess and banking aggressiveness that is the primary cause of this bust, a crash that could not have happened without a government that was paid to look the other way and a population that had been trained to grab profits at all costs, including risking their accumulated wealth, status, and the very foundation of their personal ethics.

Typically when someone pays too much for an asset the obvious blame goes to the buyer, here the home buyer. But it turns out in this case that many home buyers were not spending their money, but other people's money. Many academics and economists have accused American home buyers of acting irrationally during the housing boom, bidding house prices to higher and higher levels. But on closer examination, it's hard to see how the individual home buyer was acting irrationally.

Suppose for a minute that I set you loose in a Las Vegas casino at a roulette wheel. For unexplained reasons, the roulette spin had landed the roulette ball on black 50 times in a row, similar to the fact that housing prices have increased 50 years in a row through 2005. Now, suppose that I ask you if you would like to wager on the next spin of the roulette wheel. I assume that you might want to and that you would be willing to make a reasonably large-size bet on black, understanding by now that there must be something physically wrong with this roulette wheel that only seems to return black playoffs. Now what if I told you as the owner of the casino that you could play with the house money, that you wouldn't have to put up any up-front money, that you could sign a note for any amount you wish to play with, and I told you in advance that because of bankruptcy laws it would be very difficult for the casino to ever collect on such an agreement. I would argue that not only would you be motivated to play with the house's money, but that you would be smart to make a large bet with the house's money. In effect, the casino is giving you a pure upside option in which if black comes up on the roulette wheel you win big and if red comes up you walk away from your note. Under such a one-sided option game, it is always rational to put as big a bet down as possible, sometimes equal to even more than your total assets.

And this is exactly what homeowners did. They saw home prices increase for 50 years in a row, possibly they believed that there was some small probability that they wouldn't increase for the 51st year, but they really didn't care. They were playing with other people's money. Many were playing with 100 percent financing deals offered by their mortgage broker. In these deals buyers put up no new equity and some were playing with highly leveraged deals of 90 percent to 95 percent in which their equity had been secured by a previous sale of other houses during the boom. These buyers were all playing with the house's money. And they knew that if things turned against them they could always walk away. In the modern world, there is much less stigma attached to not repaying such a loan and the only fear of someone defaulting on a large mortgage was how long it would damage their credit and prevent them from borrowing again to buy another house.

Just showing that homeowners were acting rationally during the housing boom is not enough to explain why housing prices reached such stratospheric levels. It just pushes the question one further step up the food chain. If the homeowners' money wasn't at risk, then what was the bank thinking by extending such large amounts of money to purchase what seemed to be very high-priced homes?

The failure of banks and mortgage lenders to properly constrain home buyers and the amount of money they were able to borrow for overpriced homes was the primary cause of the housing bubble and eventual crash. There are numerous reasons why the banks lent such large sums of money to buy what appeared to be fairly highly priced assets. The most obvious reason is that the banking industry had changed over the previous 30 years. Banks no longer make credit decisions, create mortgage assets and hold them to maturity on their balance sheets. Since 1984 Wall Street had developed the mortgage pass-through market in which banks and other mortgage lenders were able to negotiate the terms of a mortgage and decide the price a buyer could pay for a home, but then sold the mortgage upstream to a Wall Street investor. Traditionally, banks have been conservative in their lending practices because the mortgage asset they create when you buy a home ends up on their balance sheet for 30 years. Today, it would be unusual if your mortgage resided on the bank's balance sheet for 30 days.

Just because mortgages could be sold by the bank does not mean that all concerns over the creditworthiness of the mortgage should be eliminated. The new investor, knowing that he will hold the mortgage for the ensuing years should be very concerned about its creditworthiness. But, it turns out these buyers, sovereign governments and pension funds to name two, were much less sophisticated than people realize when it came to buying mortgage assets. They did not have the statisticians and in-house experts to analyze the complex mortgage arithmetic that results from bundling various types of mortgages into a single pool. These experts would have analyzed what interest rate was appropriate and determined what percentage of their mortgage portfolio might be called early or could default. They relied to a great extent on their relationship with the investment bank that sold them the product, and as a secondary source of comfort they relied heavily on the rating agencies. It turns out that this reliance on the investment bank and commercial banks who sold them the mortgages and the rating agencies was misplaced. The investment banks and the commercial banks were making hundreds of billions of dollars selling this product upstream and they were directly paying the rating agencies to call AAA whatever security they created.

Banks and mortgage lenders ever since approximately 1997 have found themselves in a competitive race to offer ever more lenient terms and ever more generous amounts to homeowners seeking mortgages. You might ask why a well-managed bank would decide to compete on these terms knowing full well that if banks became too aggressive it would be reflected in future losses. But this is the nature of a number of industries in America today and around the world. Certain industries such as banking, insurance, and the airlines have long-lived assets and liabilities, sometimes as long as 30 to 50 years. The assets and the liabilities of the business often outlive the current management's tenure there.

Capitalism typically rewards good management and punishes bad management. A management that figures out how to market its products at lower cost typically wins greater market share and increases profits, while poorly managed businesses typically face losses and possible bankruptcy. But in certain long-lived asset industries that theory is not necessarily the case. The time frames are so lengthy for the assets and liabilities being managed that bad decisions can be made today and not be reflected in cash flow and earnings of the company for decades. Often, the management teams themselves that made the bad decisions have packed up and moved on before the repercussions hit the company's earnings statements and balance sheets. As an example, think of the American automobile company managements that decades ago agreed to union demands for increased wages and benefits. Those management teams and their stock option plans cashed out long before the true costs of such expensive retirement and medical plans actually hit home.

In a typical industry, with more normal length life assets, if a competitor does something stupid and starts selling its product down the street for less than it costs to manufacture, few would feel compelled to emulate this approach. The good news for the industry is that the overly aggressive competitor would quickly go bankrupt because his annual revenues from underselling his product do not cover his annual expenses. But in a long-lived asset industry such as banking, your competitor across the street might start offering outrageous and overly aggressive and attractive terms for new mortgages such as no money down, or interest only, or negative amortization mortgages. You may indeed see the risk in offering such products to your eventual bottom line, but if you don't match their offer it will be you who are threatened with bankruptcy, not them. No one will go bankrupt immediately from offering overly aggressive terms on mortgages. As a matter of fact, the aggressive, and fairly stupid competitor, will attract more customers and do more business and his market share will improve. It is only in the long run, when the true economic cost of his aggressiveness is reflected in the company's profits that his firm will come under pressure. But by then, it would be natural to assume that all the other competitors for years would have matched his aggressive terms and they would suffer equally.

Free markets are not well structured to deal with such long-lived asset industries. It is not just mortgage banking that suffers from having to deal with such long-lived assets; insurance companies face this dilemma every day as do airlines. Established airlines often face the prospect of having to match low fares with a new startup airline, even when the startup has not properly factored in the true long-term costs of its airplane fleet including real depreciation and maintenance costs. You can run an airline for a while and cover your fuel costs through low fares, but it is quite another challenge to constantly have to be the low-fare provider and allow sufficient capital funds in the future for fleet maintenance and replacement.

There is one further fundamental mistake that the banks and mortgage lenders made when they over-financed the housing sector during the boom. While the bank looks at a number of factors to determine credit quality, the overriding factor is the use of a qualifying formula that is solely based on the applicant's first-year earnings. No attempt is made to model the cost of the mortgage over a 10-year or 30-year horizon and compare it to the applicants' incomes in those years. Rather, the entire process is simplified by developing common rules about the amount of mortgage money that a bank will extend to an applicant based on his first-year reported income. Historically, banks lend approximately 2.3 times an applicant's first-year income, and anything over 3.0 was considered high. By 2006, the nation's typical new home purchase was financed with more than 5.0 times debt to household income and in that year, the entire city of San Diego had an average home price equal to 11 times their average household income. Not all of this was financed with bank debt, but many deals were 100 percent mortgage financed.

A banker would quickly justify the increase in lending multiples relative to applicants' first-year incomes over time to be a direct result of a dramatic decrease in nominal interest rates over the past 27 years. But as I said previously, this dramatic decline in mortgage interest rates from 16½ percent in 1981 to 5 percent in 2006 was totally nominal in nature. The real interest rate during the period did not change material and remained constant in the 2½ percent to 3 percent range. The only reason interest rates came down was that general inflation came down an equal amount. In effect, from a real cash flow perspective, nothing changed. If this is so, the bank or the wise banker should not have loaned more money to applicants relative to their first-year income.

In 1981, it was much easier to repay a mortgage equal to three times your income because general inflation at the time was running close to 13 percent per year. This meant that solely because of general price inflation of all goods, you could expect an inflationary adjustment to your salary each year of 13 percent and your home should appreciate 13 percent just to maintain the same purchasing power. This dramatic increase in nominal salary, combined with the dramatic increase in the nominal value of the asset collateral, assured that these loans would most certainly be paid off. If there were ever a problem, the collateral would ensure that no one would default to the bank, but rather the asset would be sold and the loan would be repaid in full.

By 2006, with inflation in the 2 percent range and the bank lending you 5 to 11 times your first-year income, there is a much greater chance of foreclosure to the bank. First of all, there is little general inflation in the economy so any salary increases that you earn will have to be real, there will be no general inflation to increase your salary over time and help pay off the mortgage. Secondly, the house itself, the collateral, will not be increasing dramatically in price due to general inflation and, again, if there is going to be any increase in value of the collateral, it will have to be a real increase. Under such a scenario, you can see that it is much more likely that the loans will not only get into trouble if for some reason your earnings decline, but if they do, there will be a much higher probability that the homeowner will default to the bank because his collateral may not be substantially worth more than the mortgage loan he took out.

This is a complicated concept, and one that I'm just not sure many banks have completely learned today. But it is the essence of the entire housing boom and housing crash fiasco. Banks during periods of high inflation like 1981 were not lending as much as they should have to homeowners and so they created a track record of mortgages almost always being repaid with very little default or foreclosure experience. As inflation and interest rates came down, banks over-lent to the same homebuyers by 2006, giving them so much money to buy a home that without inflation to help them, the homeowners had great difficulty growing their salary quickly enough to repay the loan.

And this gets at one final problem bankers and the investment community made in the mortgage markets: They relied on historically low numbers of foreclosures in the United States residential real estate market to convince themselves that the foreclosure rate would never be materially significant in the future. When they ran *what-if* scenarios as to how badly things might get, they supposed that possibly the foreclosure rates might increase 5 percent to 10 percent or as much as 15 percent. They never understood that the future quite possibly might not look like the past in one very important regard. They should have asked themselves what would happen theoretically to the foreclosure rate if housing prices declined significantly. Their historical record of low defaults was based on a 50-year, constantly increasing home price appreciation market. Of course in such an ever-increasing market no one would ever default to the bank and allow foreclosure of their home. The reason is obvious. If the home has been worth more each year since you initially took out the mortgage, then it would make sense that if you got into trouble financing the mortgage, to sell the home in the open market and pay off the mortgage and keep any remaining equity for yourself.

But consider this same set of facts in a declining price environment for homes. If home prices are declining, that means there is a significant likelihood, especially for recently signed mortgages, that the value of the house will be less than the value of the mortgage outstanding, commonly known as an underwater mortgage. The homeowner is then more likely to default and allow foreclosure and the bank to take his home rather than selling the home and taking a loss in the market. What this means is that during the inflection point like 2006 and 2007, when the market goes from one that constantly increases in price market to one that turns downward, you would expect the foreclosure rate not to increase 5 percent or 10 percent, but to explode. And this is what occurred. Foreclosure and delinquency rates went from 0.2 percent default and 2 percent delinquent rates during the boom to today where more than 9 percent of all mortgages are in default or delinquent and 19 percent of subprime loans are in default or delinquent. This is not a 5 percent or 10 percent increase in the default rate; this is a 500 percent rise in the delinquency and default rates. I can assure you, few banks ran worst-case scenarios that included this level of defaults in their analysis.

I don't want to leave the impression that the homeowner was completely without blame during this boom-and-bust cycle. Although some might applaud homeowners that maximized their financial leverage and took advantage of upside options by placing the maximum bet in an up housing market knowing that they could simply walk away on the downturn, there are still others who see a collapse of ethics in such a situation. There are many stories from your parents' generation of people who fell on hard times, borrowed money to get

It is a function of what has happened to ethics in America, but many homeowners forgot that it was their family's name, their father's and mother's name, that they signed on to that mortgage agreement.

by, and then spent decades repaying the monies to protect their honor and morals. I think they would frown on many of today's homeowners whose only calculation when deciding to walk away from a mortgage responsibility was whether they would suffer a smaller loss and how it would impact their credit report going forward. It is a function of what has happened to ethics in America, but many homeowners forgot that it was their family's name, their father's and mother's name, that they signed on to that mortgage agreement. You have to wonder what these home-owners' parents and grandparents would have thought of their offspring's decision to violate a legal contract and stick a business partner like a bank with their own losses.

Many experts have also argued that homeowners were caught in a sort of Ponzi scheme that prevented them from acting rationally. It was the nature of the boom that those people who decided to play the game and leverage up and buy homes and flip them every couple of years were generating enormous profits. They were not just paper profits. There was real cash flow being generated and if you decided not to participate in this Ponzi scheme you were punished by having to watch active buy-ers and sellers of homes during the period generate enormous profits and end up living in very large homes and buying numerous automo-biles, boats, and vacations. This is the temptation of Ponzi schemes. The evidence of profits in a Ponzi scheme while it is still working are real, not imaginary. It looks like hard evidence that the Ponzi scheme works because so many people are taking out so much cash flow. But like any good Ponzi scheme, all good things must come to an end. To buy an overpriced home and expect to make a profit requires a greater fool who will pay an even higher price to take you out. At some point that greater fool does not appear at your open house and you are left hold-ing the bag. And when it turns, it turns rapidly. The reason more people didn't sell and get out even though they thought home prices were quite frothy was that they all believed they would get out at the top. They didn't realize that once the top is reached, the window to sell shuts very quickly. In other words, there is a day on which home prices reach their all-time high, but it turns out it is almost impossible to sell on that date because liquidity disappears. In other words, there are no buyers. That is why prices are coming down. Everybody waited until the last minute to sell, not realizing that in the last minute there are no buyers.

Another driving force that pushed homeowners into ever more expensive and larger homes was a constant drive for status. Seeking status is a strong genetic urge, not limited solely to humans. Many species fight over status as it appears to be rewarded, evolutionarily speaking, by greater chances to mate. Human beings, and particularly Americans, have excelled at taking a role at an old genetic game and expanding on it. It is hard to see the rationality of an American couple with fully grown children who had left home wanting to live in 12,000 square foot monster homes or own four and five cars. If not for status, that is. It turns out that homes were not the only asset that appreciated wildly because of the demand pressure of status seekers. From 1976 to 2004 the overall CPI index increased 3.3 times. During this period home prices increased 5.5 times. But other luxury goods favored by status seekers did even better. A 75-foot Hatteras motor yacht increased 21 times in price from $214,000 in 1976 to $4.5 million in 2004. A Sikorsky helicopter during the same period increased 6.9 times and the price of a new Rolls-Royce automobile increased 8.7 times. Two season tickets to the Metropolitan Opera increased 9.8 times during the period and one-year tuition to Harvard University increased 6.8 times. It appears status seeking was not limited just to the size of one's home.

Status seeking is one explanation why the most exclusive and priciest neighborhoods and cities in America show the greatest price appreciation during this period. People were paying up to join exclusive communities, not for the school system or the view, but rather just to belong to a higher status group that few could afford. You could not rent in these neighborhoods and be accepted as a member of the high status group. You had to be an owner. And what better way to maintain exclusivity in these wealthy enclaves than to drive home prices up to nearly unattainable levels.

There is one more group that fundamentally I believe was a big-ger cause of the housing boom and bust than even the banks and mort-gage lenders. Their involvement was fundamental in allowing the banks and lenders to do whatever they wanted to do to attract business. Here I speak of the federal government. Since President Ronald Reagan's rev-olution in 1981, the free markets have been held up as being able to solve any problem on their own and anything that got in the way of com-pletely free markets such as regulation was anathema. Vice-President Dick Cheney and President George W. Bush profess this new free-market reli-gion and their Federal Reserve Chairman Alan Greenspan was its biggest proponent, even studying the gospel under its prime architect, Ayn Rand.

There is no question that in countries like Peru and Egypt, where it takes six months to get a government license to start a new busi-ness, that government regulation can be harmful to entrepreneurship and to a healthy economy. But that does not mean that all regulation is bad. These anti-regulation folks forget that the basis of any healthy growing free-market economy is the rules and regulations that underlie it. Without regulation there would be no free market. Capitalist free-market societies are built on the rule of law, a court system, the pro-tection of property rights, and the prevention of fraud in contracts and business dealings. To remove all regulation from a market encourages theft because there will be no police officer to prevent fraud and stealing. When deregulation of this country's finance industry was emphasized, banks were in fact opening their vault doors and telling the security guards in the bank that all the money would be safe on its own. It made absolutely no sense. As I note in Chapter 2, especially in long-lived asset industries, pure competition does not encourage thoughtful and proper pricing and marketing, but rather rewards irrational and crazy pricing. Without oversight and regulation, anything goes.

And that pricing is what occurred during the real estate boom. Potential home buyers hired real estate agents to represent their interests in the purchase of a home, only to find out that the real estate agent was more interested in getting paid his commission than securing a house at a reasonable price. And because the fees were so big, and so many real estate agents were in competition with each other, and because only the winning bidder paid his realtor's fees, it led to the upside-down world where your agent as a potential buyer of a home was encouraging you to spend more money and offered a higher price than was necessary to acquire the home. It lowered your returns, but assured that your real estate agent would be paid.

If that process weren't enough, the real estate agent contacted a supposedly independent appraiser to convince you and the banks that the price you were paying was a good deal relative to the underlying inherent value in the property. But the relationship was not completely independent. Typically, a real estate agent would call an appraiser and tell her the number the appraiser had to achieve for you to receive the bank financing. In essence, at the end of the first phone call, the appraisers had given a wink and a nod to the real estate agents saying in effect that they could achieve the required valuation in their appraisal. Putting this cart before the horse, and given that the appraisers relied solely on other recently overpriced sales in the market, ignoring replacement, multiples of rent, and multiples of income paid in their analysis, the appraiser magically came up with the right number to get the deal done.

Applications were made to mortgage brokers to solicit bank financing for the home purchase. But many mortgage brokers realized that the income you reported on your application was not going to be sufficient for the bank to be willing to approve your loan. No problem. The mortgage broker just erased the figure on your application and typed in a new income, sometimes as much as double what you had reported. Although completely fraudulent, the income was not investigated, and since most of these mortgage brokers are now bankrupt, this fraud probably never will be investigated.

The story doesn't end there. The bank indeed ends up financing your mortgage, and thanks to the repeal of the Glass-Steagall Act in

1999, the commercial bank is free to process investment banking type transactions in which the bank packages your mortgage with other mortgages and finds a buyer for this pooled security around the world. Although supposedly having the best and the brightest analysts that can be found, the bank makes presentations to big institutional investors around the world and yet fails to tell them the increased default risk inherent in these mortgages if housing prices decline. These analysts simply tell the potential buyers that, historically, foreclosure rates have been extremely low, conveniently forgetting to tell them that foreclosure rates have the potential to explode if housing prices begin to decline.

Sophisticated institutional investors don't believe everything their bank tells them, so they brought in what they thought was an independent adviser to speak about the quality and creditworthiness of the mortgage securities they were considering purchasing. There are only three companies in the rating agency business, Standard & Poor's, Moody's, and Fitch. Again, in a move that makes no sense whatsoever, each of these rating agencies was paid by the issuer, not the investor, to double check the quality of the issuer's paper. And paid they were— sometimes as much as $50 million in fees for one issue of mortgage-backed securities. The only analogy I can think of to show you the ridiculousness of this situation is to suppose I were trying to sell you a car and you told me you wanted to independently check the running condition and mechanics of the car so I convinced you rather than hiring a mechanic of your own to go see my brother-in-law who I told you was a mechanic. Not only was it suspicious, but the large fees in the hundreds of millions of dollars paid to the rating agencies and their involvement in the structuring of complex mortgage products assured that the system would get out of control and that it did. Eventually, triple BBB, low-rated subprime loans, whose applicants had no income and no job and had not demonstrated any record of taxable earnings, could be packaged together and even though each mortgage individually was rated triple BBB, 65 percent to 70 percent of the entire package was rated AAA. A AAA-rated security, by nature, rarely defaults and even in default usually recoups a high percentage of its value, say 95 percent. These AAA mortgage securities that were sold worldwide unfortunately experienced a high default rate and ended up reselling, sometimes at less than 60 percent of their face amount, as was the case of the supposedly senior tranches of many collateralized debt obligations.

And this then gets to the key point to be made. How is it that real estate agents could collude with independent appraisers; how is it that mortgage brokers could fraudulently doctor mortgage applications; how is it that commercial banks could lie about the quality of the products they were selling; how is it that rating agencies could reinforce these lies with phony and inflated ratings; and how is it that all of this occurred without some government intervention and supervision? The answer, and what I think is the real underlying cause of not only this boom and bust, but also the answer to many of the major problems facing America today, is that these organizations, the National Association of Realtors, the Mortgage Bankers Association, the American Bankers Association, the major investment banks, the biggest hedge funds and private equity players, and Fannie Mae and Freddie Mac were all some of the very, very biggest lobbyists and campaign contributors to your federal government. These organizations spent hundreds of millions of dollars each year to encourage deregulation and nonsupervision by the government of their illegal and immoral activities. They contributed hundreds of millions of dollars each year to the campaigns of your elected congresspeople and senators, and, yes, to your president, to ensure that no one would interfere with the enormous and very profitable Ponzi scheme they had set up across this country.

I believe America today is about equally split, 50 percent of Americans haven't realized yet the damage that lobbyists are doing to the U.S. economy and to the country and 50 percent realize it, but are resigned to believing that nothing can be done to control it. It is not just a housing boom and bust that was ultimately caused by corporate lobbying power. Look at any major problem facing America today and there is a lobbying power quietly working in Washington to prevent a solution from being found. For health care and artificially high pharmaceutical prices, look no further than the American Medical Association and the Pharmaceutical Research and Manufacturers of America lobby as well as the HMO and hospital corporation lobby. Concerned about high gas prices? Some of the biggest lobbyists in Washington are the oil and gas lobby and the automakers' lobby. Are you concerned about global warming? The utility lobby, including Edison Electric Institute and the coal lobby, are extremely deep-pocketed lobbyists. Frustrated with how slow reform is happening to Social Security and Medicare? Witness the AARP lobby at work. Wondering why it takes seven years to defeat a Third World country like Iraq and find Osama bin Laden? Realize that the defense industry has taken hundreds of billions of dollars from the military budget, often meaning that the fighting men and women, the veterans and their families are poorly paid, and poorly taken care of once they come home. Total lobbying expense in the United States totaled $2.8 billion in 2007 alone (Talbott 2008).

The problem of lobbying is addressed at the end of this book where I try to figure out what reforms are needed to fix this problem. And fix it we must. The housing crisis alone has taken America and the world close to a complete global banking system meltdown. The crisis will cause a global recession with enormous suffering from job losses and economic contraction. But no book can describe to you the personal suffering of the many families that have lost homes and livelihoods and relationships because of this terrible and preventable event. I do not wish to live in a country that, having seen how terrible this crash is in the suffering it has caused, would not want to reform to prevent this problem from ever happening again.

Chapter 4

The Contagion Spreads from Subprime to Prime

S o, the question on everyone's mind is when will the housing slump in the United States end and how bad can it get? To date, it has already been devastating and so it's reasonable to ask is the worst over, are the bad times behind us?

Let's summarize just how bad it has been to date. In the 1929 stock market crash, all publicly traded companies listed in the United States lost approximately $30 billion in value. So far, since the beginning of the housing crash in early 2006, the U.S. stock market has lost some $6 trillion in value, or nearly 40 percent of its aggregate value. Even after adjusting for general inflation this loss is much greater than anything that happened during the Great Depression.

When I describe the carnage that has occurred just since the beginning of the housing market collapse, and keep the description in fairly general terms, it is easy to think that I am talking about the Great Depression. It has been that bad. Remember:

- Two of the world's largest corporations with combined $5.3 trillion in assets were nationalized by the U.S. government.
- Three of the five largest investment banks in the United States have gone out of business.
- The vast majority of the mortgage brokerage companies in the United States have shut down.
- The eighth largest bank in Britain has collapsed and been nationalized.
- The largest S&L in the United States has gone bankrupt.
- The world's central banks, including the Federal Reserve and the federal home loan banks in the United States have committed more than $4.0 trillion in new money to try to save the commercial and investment banks.
- The U.S. dollar has declined by some 40 percent relative to European currencies.
- Gold has appreciated by some 200 percent.
- The most populous country in the world, China, temporarily suspends all bank lending.
- Iceland and Ukraine need emergency IMF loans to avoid bankruptcy.

Certainly you would have to conclude that these are scary times.

From the beginning, this housing crisis has been called a subprime mortgage problem. Subprime mortgages are those loans extended to people with less than stellar credit. Poor and middle-class borrowers are the first to default in a housing downturn, simply because they have fewer assets to fall back on if they get in trouble with their mortgage. It may be helpful to the banks from a public relations perspective to try to blame this crisis on poor Americans with bad credit histories, but that is not the real cause of the housing crisis. The greatest home price appreciation and the homes most subject to price readjustment are in America's wealthiest cities and its glitziest neighborhoods. The vast majority of defaults to date have been subprime, but this is just one indication that this housing downturn is nowhere near the end. Subprime delinquency rates have approached 19 percent at this stage in the cycle, but now prime mortgages are beginning to default and total mortgages have a delinquency rate nationwide approaching 9 percent.

There are approximately $1.3 trillion of subprime mortgages in the United States. This is a small fraction of the total of $12 trillion of mortgages outstanding.

Above-subprime mortgages in credit quality are what is known as Alt A mortgages, primarily NINJA loans, which total $500 billion. NINJA stands for no income, no job, and no application loans. In essence, more creditworthy customers were given the opportunity to quickly secure bank financing for a home purchase without demonstrating any proof that they had a job or income; basically there was no application. These loans are just now beginning to default in sizable magnitudes. Mortgage brokers were fraudulently reporting false incomes for these no application loans in order to make it easier to qualify.

In addition, there are approximately $1.5 trillion of adjustable-rate mortgages (ARMs) outstanding. These are prime candidates for default because they were issued initially with a small teaser rate, sometimes as low as 2 percent per year. After two to three years the rate adjusts up to a more market-determined rate, today something closer to 7 percent or 8 percent per year. Adjustable-rate mortgages issued in 2004 and 2005 are just now resetting for the first time and causing enormous defaults. Banks continued to make adjustable-rate mortgages available in 2006, 2007, and 2008 so the problem is not going to go away anytime soon.

There is also another $500 million of what are typically called exotic mortgages outstanding. These mortgages include interest-only mortgages, option-paying mortgages, and reverse-amortization mortgages. They remain a significant risk to default because these mortgages also had additional teaser rates that were low, but unlike adjustable-rate mortgages, they are reset periods that were typically longer, say four or five years rather than two to three years. They have just begun their initial resets and this will lead to significant defaults in 2009 and 2010.

Unfortunately, the numbers only get bigger. Small monoline private mortgage insurance companies—such as MGIC, the PMI Group, and the Radian Group—have guaranteed approximately $1.2 trillion in mortgages. Many of these are second mortgages that are at a high risk of default because they were taken out to cover equity down payments and to further leverage the home purchase beyond the first mortgage. If you bought a million-dollar house financed with an $800,000 first mortgage and a $200,000 second mortgage and the home value declines to $700,000 and you default, the second mortgage holder and the private mortgage insurance company who guarantees it will probably lose everything.

It begins to get a little complicated, but there are more than $4 trillion of Collateralized Debt Obligations (CDOs) outstanding, many of these backed by U.S. mortgages. More than $420 billion of the CDOs are held by U.S. commercial banks and investment banks, but off their balance sheets in Special Investment Vehicles (SIVs).

What exactly is a CDO? It is a pool of mortgages that secure a series of bonds that are divided into tranches so that the higher tranches get paid first and the lower tranches are subordinated and have to wait to get paid after any defaults in the pool. Basically, a large number of poorly rated mortgages such as BBB-rated bonds are pooled into one security. The cash flow that is generated by these mortgages is used to first pay back the senior tranche of the CDL and any remaining cash flow is used to pay back the subordinated tranches. Through this tier process, the commercial and investment banks were able to turn BBB-rated bonds into AAA-rated bonds. The senior tranche, which might represent 75 percent of the total pool, is now rated AAA even though the mortgages underlying it are all BBB.

Because of the leverage involved, and because of their complicated structuring, and because the underlying mortgages were really BBB securities, not AAA rated, many of these CDOs were some of the first mortgage securities to give the big banks trouble. The losses due to CDOs by the commercial banks and investment banks are really the tip of the iceberg because these banks are the issuers of the securities, not the buyers. These banks had some unsold CDO securities on their books when the housing market began to collapse, but most of the securities they held were the senior-most rated tranche and were rated AAA. Although these AAA tranches declined in value as much as 30 percent to 40 percent, that was nothing compared to the lower tranches, which saw 90 percent to 99 percent losses. The bank's clients ended up holding the bag on these lower rated tranches and the total losses have still not been disclosed. Commercial banks and investment banks are typically publicly traded companies and have to mark their assets to market and report their losses quarterly and so have disclosed much of their losses to date. Their investors, sovereign wealth funds of foreign countries and pension funds and municipal and state agencies, do not have such rigid reporting requirements and to date have not admitted to their substantial losses in mortgages in general and CDOs specifically.

The biggest holder and guarantor of U.S. mortgages in the world, Fannie Mae and Freddie Mac hold or guarantee approximately $5.3 trillion in U.S. mortgages. They have been put into conservatorship by the U.S. government because the stock prices of each company declined by more than 95 percent. The question on everyone's mind is how much this government bailout is going to cost the U.S. taxpayer. The Congressional Budget Office, at the time the Congress voted to give the U.S. Treasury authority to take over Fannie Mae and Freddie Mac, estimated that the potential loss was between zero and $25 billion. At the time of the bailout, Morgan Stanley, whose experts are advising the U.S. treasury, suggested the number might be as large as $50 billion. The preferred stock issues that were created to bail out Fannie Mae and Freddie Mac were each initially capitalized at $1 billion but their charters allow them to be as large as $100 billion for each of the two companies.

Sadly, even this $200 billion number greatly underestimates the losses that Fannie Mae and Freddie Mac will experience in the U.S. mortgage markets and the amount of money the U.S. taxpayer will have to contribute as a result. With $1.6 trillion of mortgages on their books and an additional $3.7 trillion of mortgage guarantees, the total losses that these two enterprises will experience will be enormous; $600 billion is a conservative estimate and the loss could grow to $1 trillion.

You would expect Fannie Mae and Freddie Mac to have a lower rate of default in their mortgage portfolio than some of the large commercial banks because Fannie Mae and Freddie Mac can only invest in qualifying mortgages. This meant that you could not attain a Fannie Mae or Freddie Mac mortgage if the total mortgage amount was greater than the qualifying amount, which recently was $417,000. So, by definition, Fannie Mae and Freddie Mac were precluded from investing in high-priced homes in expensive neighborhoods, those assets that have the greatest risk of declining in value.

Second, Fannie Mae and Freddie Mac have already gotten in trouble before. In 2003 there were accounting irregularities found at each firm, the CEOs and CFOs were fired, and the regulator that oversees them not only insisted they freeze their balance sheets and stop acquiring new assets, each company was required to divest approximately $200 billion in mortgages. The result of this intervention is that Fannie Mae and Freddie Mac were pretty much sitting on the sidelines and not participating in acquiring mortgages for their own account during the craziest days of the housing boom from 2003 to 2006. In effect, Fannie Mae and Freddie Mac each missed out on many adjustable-rate mortgages, option-pay mortgages, and reverse-amortization mortgages issued in this period. Because they were divesting assets during this period, they didn't acquire many mortgages from 2003 to 2006 that were based on the craziest and highest home price valuations.

Having said that, Fannie Mae and Freddie Mac are not without risk. They have not yet disclosed their total exposure to the more exotic mortgages, and they went so far as to claim there were no lawsuits in this portfolio because rather than marking them to market they claimed to their accountants that they were going to hold them to maturity. This allowed them to avoid taking any quarterly losses on their exotic mortgage portfolio. But rumors are that they combined to hold something like $700 billion in exotic mortgages, of which they have taken few losses to date and which you would expect, based on the banks experience, to have significant losses going forward.

It is not all good news that Fannie Mae and Freddie Mac were constrained to making smaller mortgages. Although this meant that their exposure to expensive, overpriced neighborhoods like Beverly Hills and Palm Springs were probably limited, it meant that their primary customers were middle class. The houses in middle-class neighborhoods did not appreciate as much in the wealthier coastal U.S. cities, so default rates are much higher among moderate-income borrowers, simply because they do not have the alternative resources to fund a mortgage if they lose their job. And, it is the nature of America that when job losses occur, the middle class suffers first.

Fannie Mae and Freddie Mac have not reported substantial losses to date, but that will change. They have been prevented from recognizing losses because their book equity was barely above regulatory minimums and even this was done with some creative accounting. When their assets were marked to market their book equity went to zero. Included in their regulatory capital where such phony assets as tens of

Fannie Mae and Freddie Mac have not reported substantial losses to date, but that will change.

billions of tax carry loss forwards that are not true assets for companies losing money like Fannie Mae and Freddie Mac because you have to have positive profits before you can utilize a tax shield.

Now that the U.S. government has effectively nationalized Fannie Mae and Freddie Mac, the losses could increase even more rapidly. The reason for the increase is that the government wants to utilize them to solve the mortgage credit crisis. The government is going to be much more lax in the amount of money they extend to new homeowners in an attempt to stimulate new home buying, and you must believe they will be more lax on the terms. This has to create greater losses going forward. In addition, similar to what the FDIC is doing at IndyMac, a recent bankruptcy, the government most likely will be generous in restructuring existing mortgages that get into trouble. Swapping an adjustable-rate mortgage borrower from a floating-rate 3 percent initial teaser loan into a fixed-rate 30-year 4 percent loan may not make good business sense, but it will hide the loss from the books of Fannie Mae and the eyes of the U.S. taxpayer. It is not right to call a 30-year 4 percent loan par value when comparable loans in the private marketplace are yielding 7 percent, but that is the advantage of being the government and making the rules.

Given a total mortgage exposure of $5.3 trillion, it is easy to see how total losses at Fannie Mae and Freddie Mac might exceed $600 billion. Total asset values of the homes behind these mortgages are close to $9 trillion; or *were* close to $9 trillion. Today, more like $7 trillion, probably on their way to $6 trillion. But not all of Fannie and Freddie's homes are fully leveraged, so the actual loss to them will be much less than to the underlying homeowners. If a true economic calculation were made as to the total cost of this bailout to the U.S. taxpayer, including the foregone revenue and bargain interest rates extended by the government, the cost to the U.S. taxpayer of the Fannie and Freddie bailout will probably exceed $1 trillion.

Total losses from the entire U.S. housing and mortgage collapse are going to be huge. Something like $500 billion in losses have already been claimed worldwide by global financial institutions. The total U.S. mortgage market is greater than $12 trillion. Total residential real estate in the United States at its peak in 2005 was valued at $24 trillion. These are huge incomprehensible numbers. One trillion is a million bags of $1 million each, still somewhat incomprehensible.

Nationally, residential real estate to date has declined approximately 20 percent in value with some cities seeing average declines exceeding 35 percent already. This decline represents a loss to homeowners of almost $5 trillion. I estimate that the total loss to homeowners by the time this crash concludes will be more than $8 to $10 trillion. You would not expect that the percentage loss on U.S. mortgages can be as high as a percentage because some people in America are not highly leveraged and others own their homes outright with no mortgage. Having said that, many Americans bought new homes or refinanced their existing homes at least once during the past 10 years, and many utilized a great deal of mortgage leverage. I believe by the time this cycle is over, investors and banks worldwide will lose close to $2 trillion from the collapse in value of U.S. mortgages. If corporations have only admitted to $500 billion of this eventual $2 trillion loss, you can conclude that there are still very hard times ahead of us.

So from a macro perspective it appears that the housing price decline is far from over in the United States. This simple examination of the sheer volume of mortgages outstanding and understanding the different types of mortgages leads us to conclude that regardless of how shocking it may be, the worst is still probably ahead of us.

Chapter 5

How Low Will Housing Prices Go in the U.S.?

H ome prices in the United States at the end of 2008 represented about half of the total potential decline that will occur by the time this housing price crash is completed. Let's now examine the reasons why this might be true.

Typical housing price declines last anywhere from five to seven years. In the United States there has never really been a national housing crash so the evidence is based on regional price declines that have occurred in various cities in the United States over time. But there are lots of examples. San Francisco, Silicon Valley, and Boston have all had significant housing price declines as the semiconductor and high-tech business market cooled. Houston had a similar price decline in its residential real estate but it was because of softness in the oil and gas industry. Even New York and Los Angeles have seen real estate declines as the general economy slowed and the investment banking and commercial banking business suffered. In each case, real prices of residential real estate did not recover for five to seven years. I say real prices, because if inflation is 5 percent per year and your home does not appreciate in value at all but remains flat in price that is a real price decline of 5 percent because at the end of the year you have lost 5 percent of your purchasing power. This is important because often inflation masks real losses in assets. Nominal prices are declining rapidly across the country now. In one or two years the stated price declines tend to level out and then have two to three more years of flat nominal prices where the real loss is hidden in the inflation rate. In other words, home prices nationally that have declined some 20 percent to date may decline an additional 6 percent to 8 percent over the next one to two years and then level off and not keep up with inflation for two to three more years.

It shouldn't surprise you that residential real estate downturns take five to seven years to resolve. Why does it take five to seven years for people to readjust their value thinking on residential real estate? There have been academic studies done that show that when new information like a takeover bid is received publicly in the stock market it takes traders less than two minutes to accurately reflect the higher valuation in a company's stock price. Homeowners and real estate agents aren't stupid. Certainly they are capable of doing something that professional stock traders do in two minutes faster than five to seven years.

The answer to this dilemma is apparent to many today. The answer is that no one during a real estate decline really knows how bad it will get and when the bottom will come. If everybody thought that home prices were certain to decline 30 percent, then the decline would have to be immediate in the first year. The fact that home prices only declined some 8 percent in the first year of this downturn and that there were buyers still actively buying in the market that year tells you that not everyone believed that the downturn would be severe and last for five

to seven years. What happens during a long five- to seven-year housing decline is that new buyers each year must believe the worst is over
and the decline has ended. To date these buyers have all been wrong.
After purchasing their new homes sometime over the past three years,
each of these new homeowners has experienced immediate losses as
home prices continue to deteriorate across the country. At some point,
the new buyer will be right and housing prices will turn and they will
have accomplished what everyone hopes to accomplish, to have bought
a house at the bottom. Here are some more statistics that might help to
determine when that bottom might occur in U.S. residential real estate.

Another indicator that housing prices still have some further
downward adjustment in them and have not reached bottom is that
even after their 20 percent decline nationwide and their near 30 percent decline in some cities like San Francisco, Phoenix, and Las Vegas,
the current housing prices as of the end of 2008 are still just about
equal to where housing prices were during the boom in the beginning
of 2004. In other words, about two to three years of the appreciation
seen in 2004 and 2005 have been given back. To argue that real estate
has reached bottom, you must be convinced that current prices that
reflect housing prices in 2004 were indeed reasonable.

But were 2004 prices reasonable? As previously noted, the run-up
in real prices of homes in America began in 1981 and the exponential
increase in prices began in 1997. Also, the primary reason for the unsustainable increase in prices was crazy bank lending and the outlandish
mortgage terms these banks extended. Most of these exotic mortgage
products were created and marketed since 1997. By 2004 banks were
lending huge amounts of money under fairly crazy terms, so to conclude that 2004 prices were reasonable seems excessive. It's hard to
imagine banks willing to be as aggressive today as they were in 2004.

Bank-lending terms today really are the key to understanding when
the bottom in real estate prices will be reached. The reason is quite obvious. If you want to sell your home, somebody has to be able to afford it.

Most homes are purchased with funds secured from the bank by a mortgage. If the bank is not going to give money to your potential buyer, it is unlikely the buyer will be able to afford the house. If during the height of the boom, banks were willing to lend 6 to 11 times household income to buy a house, and banks in the future will only lend four to five times your household income, then simple math says many homes have to decline in value by as much as 50 percent to attract new buyers. In other words, unless the buyers are willing to put up substantially larger equity down payments, you probably shouldn't bet on the sale.

Since I wrote my first book on the housing and mortgage markets (*The Coming Crash in the Housing Market,* 2003), there has been much greater attention paid to the reasonableness of home prices. Experts today run sophisticated models to try to determine how expensive prices are today relative to other measures. At today's price levels, across the country prices are still quite high relative to replacement value. Homes in central California that could be built for less than $200,000 were selling in 2006 at the market's peak for more than $700,000. Some areas have seen dramatic price declines of 40 percent to 50 percent in auctions and these homes now sell for $320,000. But, even at $320,000 these homes exceed their replacement value. It is more difficult to assign a fair value to the underlying property, especially in a popular state like California, but no one should conclude that just because a home value has come down 40 percent that it cannot come down further in price.

Similarly, when experts today look at home prices across the country and compare them to relative measures like similar rental values and household incomes, many experts conclude that housing today is still overvalued by some 20 percent or so. There is no reason to think that home purchases have to come down completely in line with home rentals as there are added benefits to homeownership rather than renting. But these studies support the idea that we have not seen the bottom yet of this housing cycle and it is not unreasonable to think that we might just be approximately halfway through the decline as of the end of 2008.

Even if a home buyer were able to finance a new home at a large value, he still has to ask himself if he wants to. As indicated earlier, in a constantly increasing housing boom market it even made rational sense for buyers to own as large a home as they could so that they could grab the biggest price appreciation. In an always increasing home market it is simply logical if you are certain that prices are going to increase 20 percent each year that you would prefer to own a million-dollar house rather than a half-million house. The absolute dollar returns double.

But that world no longer exists. People now understand that housing markets, just like any other market, can go down as well as up. Families with little savings during the boom wanted to own a house that was worth 5 to 10 times their total household income because they assumed they would only go up in price. Now, with more realistic price expectations, there is no reason why a homeowner would want to be so heavily invested in residential real estate. Diversification theory would suggest that a family with $100,000 of household income and $100,000 of total savings should hold something like $20,000 to $30,000 in residential real estate to be properly diversified, not a half-million to $1 million that many families find invested in their homes. And here it is important to recognize that this refers to the total value of the home, not just the equity portion of the financing.

This is a dramatic change in people's allocation of their household resources. Of course people are not going to move into $30,000 homes, but they now realize to be properly diversified they should not maximize the amount of

Now that homeowners know that real estate can go down in value and is not a guaranteed ATM machine or a guaranteed retirement income account, they will be much more likely to live in smaller homes with lower purchase prices than enormous homes costing millions of dollars.

money they have at risk in the residential real estate market. Simply stated, now that homeowners know that real estate can go down in value and is not a guaranteed ATM machine or a guaranteed retirement income account, they will be much more likely to live in smaller homes with lower purchase prices than enormous homes costing millions of dollars.

For a long time, people believed residential real estate to be an investment. The reason for this, of course, is that for 50 straight years it kept going up in price and generated significant returns. But now, in a more normal world, the home is not guaranteed to go up in real price terms. I predict that home values will deteriorate over the next four to five years. If home prices are not guaranteed to go up in the future then the return from the home investment has to be the rent that you could earn by leasing the property out. If you are in the business of buying homes and leasing them out you can indeed think of this as an alternative investment.

But the homeowner who owns only one home and lives in it is forgoing rental income to live at the property. It is as if they are consuming the rental income by living there. There is no cash flow generated from rent on the property. There is no investment return. This is a surefire way to see that a primary residence in which you live full time is not an investment but is pure consumption. A simple example will convince you of this fact.

Suppose you lived in San Diego in a $5 million home near the beach. For whatever reason, you decide to scale down and buy a smaller home farther from the ocean that costs $1 million. You take the extra $4 million from the sale of your first home and put it in real investments. I would argue that your consumption has gone down from $5 million to $1 million and that your investments have increased by $4 million. In other words, primary residences are 100 percent consumption. Of course, the $5 million home has much nicer amenities than your new $1 million home, more bedrooms, more baths, bigger swimming pool, or closer to the beach. But, these amenities are pure consumption. Bigger swimming pools and larger bedrooms are not investments if you live in the home. By living there, you are consuming whatever additional value they exhibit each year.

So those people who were buying larger and more expensive homes as an investment alternative now will awaken to realize that primary residences aren't really investment alternatives at all, but merely 100 percent consumption. They will do much better, from an investment perspective, to minimize the dollars they utilize in their primary residence, to diversify away from additional residential real estate, and put their money in non–real estate investments. This realization has to have a real impact on housing prices. It is not only that constrained bank lending will prevent buyers from paying big prices for homes, home buyers themselves will want to invest less money in their primary residence going forward.

Chapter 16 explores whether there is an additional component to the reduced demand for larger and more expensive homes in America going forward. Namely, this entire housing crash, mortgage and banking crisis, and ensuing recession may convince many Americans that a lifestyle dedicated to maximum consumption is not very rewarding. I certainly don't believe Americans are convinced yet because Tiffany's and Mercedes-Benz continue to do quite well. As people realize that their lives may become more stable if they save more, invest more, and consume less, especially with borrowed monies, this also would place a dampening effect on primary resident purchases in the future because the purchase of a primary residence is indeed a form of consumption.

> *Those people who were buying larger and more expensive homes as an investment alternative now will awaken to realize that primary residences aren't really investment alternatives at all, but merely 100 percent consumption.*

Another indicator that the housing price decline in the United States is not over is to track exactly which mortgages enter foreclosure each year. At the end of 2008, the vast majority of mortgages that entered the foreclosure process are on mortgages from 2005, 2006, and 2007. Somewhat counterintuitively, those mortgages that were entered into most recently are the ones that are exploding first. I say counterintuitively because typically when you make an investment, there is some time in which you have a good handle on the credit and credit statistics from that investment and there is usually an aging process until an investment begins to go bad.

But this is not the case with mortgages in a declining housing market. The reason is straightforward. As housing prices decline, the most recent mortgages are the ones that are going to be underwater first. Let's look at some real numbers.

Home prices in Las Vegas have dropped from an average of $330,000 at their peak to just more than $220,000 at the end of 2008. But home prices in Las Vegas had increased dramatically recently going from $240,000 in 2004, $275,000 in 2005, $305,000 in 2006, and $330,000 in 2007. If the homes in Las Vegas, for simplicity purposes, are assumed to have been purchased with 100 percent mortgage money, in other words no money down, then it is logical that the most recent mortgages written in 2007 would be subject to default first. As home prices decline, the homes purchased in 2007 would be underwater first, the homes would be worth less at the market price today than the mortgage amount on the home. Next you would expect 2006 homes to default, then 2005, and so on. The exception to this rule is that people typically are paying down the principal balance on their mortgages and so older mortgages should have larger equity cushions in them. The reason this exception rarely applies today is that many homeowners were refinancing and taking the maximum amount of leverage and cash out of their homes as quickly as they could. They weren't building equity in their homes, they were taking the equity out and buying cars, boats, and vacations.

Again, if the majority of foreclosures to date are mortgages from 2005, 2006, and 2007, what about mortgages entered into before 2005. They do seem well poised to default once home prices continue their downward spiral. People are just not going to pay their mortgages off if their homes are underwater, if they owe more on the home than it's worth. So, as home prices continue down, mortgages written in 2004, 2003, 2002, and so on will turn out to be worth more than the home.

I said previously that wealthier homeowners were slower to default or enter foreclosure than middle-class Americans because they have access to more pools of capital and additional borrowing resources. If wealthier people lose a job or have a medical emergency, they usually don't have to default on their mortgage. Also, as previously stated, the majority of the real estate boom occurred in wealthier cities in America with higher priced homes. The areas of the country with the greatest home price appreciation, the two coasts and Arizona and Las Vegas, do not represent a large percentage of the total land mass of the United States. The high prices of this area's residential real estate represent more than 40 percent of the total aggregate market value of all residential real estate in America. Experts who believe that the current housing price decline will be limited to subprime borrowers do not believe that these wealthier homeowners will default on their home mortgages. But this is not necessarily the case.

The reason for this case is straightforward. Imagine owning a $1 million home in Santa Barbara; as a matter of fact, the average home price in Santa Barbara Peak was close to $700,000 in 2005. You may have an adjustable-rate mortgage on your home, or an option-pay mortgage, and you may be faced with a doubling of your monthly payments, one very good reason why you might default.

But even if you financed your million-dollar home in Santa Barbara with a 30-year fixed-rate mortgage at 6 percent, you still might be at risk of default. Imagine waking up in your Santa Barbara home and going out in the morning to pick up your newspaper on your front lawn. What do you see? For sale signs on 5 of the 10 houses on your street. To make matters worse, three of the five homes for sale had been foreclosed on and are being offered by the banks at fire-sale prices. To put an exclamation point on this analysis, assume that all the homes on the street are identical and one just sold in the past month for $500,000. You quickly come to realize that you have a million-dollar mortgage but no longer have a million-dollar home. Your home, by all market measures, appears to be worth $500,000 and is dramatically underwater relative to your million-dollar mortgage. Are you going to continue to make payments on your million-dollar mortgage to stay current? Are you going to repay the principal on a million-dollar mortgage note to own a house that is worth $500,000? I don't think so. Default in foreclosure is a more difficult task for a wealthy individual because they have other assets the banks can come after in states in which mortgage debt repayment is not limited just to the house, and typically wealthier people are much more concerned about preserving their good credit. Bankruptcy is not a real option to a wealthy person because they have so many additional assets and are of substantial value. But, in my heart, I don't believe a smart wealthy person is going to pay a bank $1 million plus interest for a $500,000 house.

If I'm right, then this housing decline has only just begun. The reason is that these higher priced homes in wealthier neighborhoods represent a large percentage of total mortgage assets held by the banks given their high average home price. Subprime defaults by middle-class Americans might average $100,000 to $150,000, but when you start getting into coastal real estate in California and New York City condominium apartments on the Upper East Side, the average mortgage size could easily exceed $1 million. Given the high credit quality of these borrowers and their vast wealth, the banks would probably be smart to figure out a way to restructure their mortgage loans so as to avoid claiming a loss that impairs the banks' equity capital. But, many restructurings of this type just postpone the problem and push the loss to a later date. If you give a million-dollar mortgage to someone at below market interest rates because you are afraid of a default, you have just created a new fixed-rate asset, which by definition is not worth its stated value. A million-dollar mortgage that yields 5 percent in a world of 7½ percent interest rates is worth more like $700,000 than $1 million. The bank may think they have avoided a $300,000 loss on a million-dollar mortgage, but all they have done is negatively impacted their earnings in the future, and the net present value of this future cash flow loss is exactly equal to $300,000.

In 2006 I wrote a second book on the housing bubble (*Sell Now! The End of the Housing Bubble,* 2006) in which I was so bold as to predict that national housing prices would decline some 25 percent to 30 percent, and that some coastal cities would see price declines of 45 percent to 50 percent. I even included a detailed five-page table in which I listed the largest cities in the country, their average home prices at the end of 2005, and the home price decline I projected for each of the cities. Given that home prices nationwide are already off some 20 percent and are already off 30 percent in some of the worst cities, and given that this decline is only three years into what I expect to be a five to seven year pricing decline, I think I will stick with my original forecast for these cities and the nation as a whole. Let me summarize some of the cities valuations and expected declines from that table and tell you how I arrived at my estimate of the total expected price decline, as that will help you decide how much further downside risk exposure you may have in your home and your home city.

Rather than re-create the entire table here, I will cite a few examples from the table and then tell you how to make this calculation for your own city. The city with the highest percentage expected decline from its peak year-end 2005 home price was Santa Barbara, California, which had a year-end 2005 average price of $671,000 for its typical home and a projected real price decline of 59.6 percent. San Diego was just behind at 58.7 percent expected declines. As a matter of fact 17 of the 20 largest projected percentage declines were all cities in California, including San Jose, Santa Cruz, Stockton, Los Angeles, San Francisco, and Riverside. Given the significant price declines in California today, some approaching 30 percent to 35 percent, this makes these extraordinary projected price declines of 45 percent to 59 percent seem more reasonable if that's possible and potentially achievable over the next three to five years.

The Florida cities, Sarasota, Miami, Melbourne, Fort Myers, Daytona Beach, Orlando, Jacksonville, were all projected in the table to decline from 35 percent to 45 percent; Boston has a 49 percent decline expected; New York and northern New Jersey, a 44 percent expected decline; and Tucson, Arizona, a 27 percent expected decline. Larger cities in the Midwest such as St. Louis, Madison, Wisconsin, and Kansas City are all projected to decline 22 percent to 23 percent from peak to trough. Although no city in the table is forecast to appreciate in value during the period, Provo, Utah, and Montgomery, Alabama, showed the smallest percentage declines at 3 percent. There are approximately 25 cities listed, from Cleveland to Scranton to Indianapolis to Buffalo to Dayton to Salt Lake City, that show price declines of less than 10 percent. These are those cities of the country that never showed any real price increase during the boom, in these cities home prices barely kept up with general inflation.

Just because a city did not have unusual price appreciation and did not go up in price during the boom doesn't mean that home prices cannot decline during the crash. You could argue that home prices were more properly valued in the cities during the boom, but the crash, foreclosure activity, and the ensuing national economic recession and associated job loss could cause home prices in these cities to decline even though they never saw dramatic appreciation during the boom.

These projected declines by city and this table were created with one major assumption, that real prices in the cities would return to their average price levels in 1997, but measured in today's dollars accounting for general inflation. To determine what this means for your hometown and how much total potential downside there is in your city's average home prices, you need only to try to remember what prices were like in 1997. You can do this on your own home, but it is more statistically accurate if you think about the average home in your city. For example, if you live in a $500,000 house today, or at least the home had a peak value of $500,000 in early 2006, and you wish to know what the potential downside is due to the housing crash, you need only go back and calculate how much the home was worth in 1997 and then adjust it forward for inflation from 1997 to the present. Let's assume your home sold for $250,000, or would sell for that amount, in 1997. To see what this amount is in current dollars you have to adjust for inflation, so multiply this amount by 1.3 times, which means $250,000 in 1997 is equal to $325,000 in 2008. What this calculation says, and assuming the downside of the entire housing price collapse in your city is a return to real 1997 prices, then your home, which at its peak was worth $500,000, may today be worth something like $400,000 to $425,000 but by the end of the housing price decline will return to 1997 prices and be worth something like $325,000. The $175,000 real price decline divided by the peak price of $500,000 yields a 35 percent total decline from the peak. This simple calculation can be done for any house in any city in the country.

What is magical about 1997? Why did I choose 1997 as the year to which home prices will return? I have said that 120-year historical graph of real home prices in America was relatively flat for a hundred years and then began to increase in real terms in 1981 and then grew exponentially from 1997 to 2006. Although a return to 1997 levels would not return all of the real price increase that has occurred since 1991, at least it would get us out of the heady crazy days from

1997 to 2006 in which banks were lending large amounts of money under poor supervision and aggressive terms. The year 1997 was mostly before the advent of adjustable-rate mortgages, option-pay mortgages, interest-only mortgages, and other exotic mortgage products.

If all cities returned to 1997 pricing, this does not mean that all homes will return to equal pricing across cities of the country. San Francisco has always been more expensive to live in per square foot than in Buffalo. There are many reasons for this: the weather, the rest-aurants, the views. It is almost impossible to determine all the factors that enter into house price differences across the cities of the country. Rather than trying to determine exact prices, simply utilize the market price of the homes as a good proxy for their true value, not any recent market price that was subject to the bubble, but rather a 1997 price for a more normal time.

Some experts try to predict home values across cities of the coun-try by comparing them to the average incomes of those cities. It is true that people earn more money in San Francisco than in Buffalo, New York, but that is not necessarily why homes are more expensive there. In the long run, home prices should have little to do with incomes. Just because you make more money does not mean you have to put it into your house. Before the housing boom, there were some reason-ably priced homes available in Arizona because it costs so little to build them. Land was abundant and inexpensive and labor was costs were low.

The year 1997 was also a good base to use because it was before the tremendous run up in Internet stock prices and high-tech stocks that created fabulous, but temporary wealth. It was also before 2001 when that tax cut's trillions of dollars went mostly to the wealthiest citizens in this country. Finally, 1997 was before the real housing boom took off, so there was no Ponzi-like atmosphere of ever-increasing profits and potential from buying houses.

In summary, if you are trying to determine whether there is addi-tional downside to the current market price of your home, ask yourself the following question: What would it cost to buy the land and rebuild a similar house today? If this number is substantially below your estimate of your homes current market value today, perhaps you need to rethink the potential future downward pressure that may come on the price of your home. Similarly, if you rented out your home rather than lived in it, is a reasonable economic return generated based on your idea of its market value. If you think you have a million-dollar home but can only rent it for $30,000 a year that's not much of a return and it suggests you might want to be more conservative in your estimate of the home's market value. See what similar homes are selling for in the neighborhood, not what they are listed for, but actual real sales. Perform the simple calculation above and see what the 1997 valuation of your house would be today if adjusted up by 30 percent to adjust for general inflation. Talk to some of your neighbors and see what their views are about foreclosure, see if there is any scenario or future price decline in which they might walk away from their house and leave you with foreclosed properties on your street being sold by commercial banks. Ask yourself if a reasonable person would want to invest the money necessary to own your home given its amenities, or do people have alternative investments they wish to make today, or do they wish to hold less of their total assets in residential real estate. Hopefully, by such a thorough and quantitative analysis you will achieve a better understanding of the potential risks and possible price declines in your neighborhood and the amount your home may suffer in the future and you can plan accordingly.

If you are trying to determine whether there is additional downside to the current market price of your home, ask yourself the following question: What would it cost to buy the land and rebuild a very similar house today?

I am often criticized for writing books about housing crashes, some saying that I'm overly pessimistic. Given what has happened today in the market, I think of myself more as a realist than a pessimist. And I think that books such as this can do a great service to homeowners and investors because it provides them the answer to their most critical question: Tell me how bad it might get and I will do my own financial planning. Not knowing what might happen is the worst of circumstances. No, worse is someone telling you that things will be fine because they will benefit professionally and financially if it turns out so.

Chapter 6

The U.S. Economy Was Not in Great Shape to Begin With

S ome people argue that the United States is the most powerful nation on earth and the world's strongest economy so what is happening in housing and mortgages and banking can easily be absorbed by its strong domestic economy. These people say that this is just another blip in the U.S. economy, and 10 years from now no one will remember that it occurred. They compare the current housing and banking crisis to others crises that the United States has weathered in the past and survived, namely the stock market crash in 1987, the LBO crisis in 1990, and the bursting of the Internet bubble in 2001.

These are the same experts who suggest that when it comes to stock investing in the United States the best approach is buy and hold. If they are right, and the U.S. stock market always comes back, then it makes little sense to sell every time there is a downturn and have to repurchase after the recoveries.

But, these experts are not necessarily right. Markets don't always recover from cyclical downturns in the long run. Sometimes, markets stay down for a very long time. Sometimes, in bankrupt countries, they never come back. Just because the United States has bounced back quickly in the past does not mean it necessarily will in the future. You don't have to conclude that the United States is at risk of bankruptcy to sell risky assets with large downside exposures and shift your assets into safer less volatile instruments and markets. For example, if housing is going to be flat to down for five to seven years, even if you think housing will eventually recover, it makes much more sense to sell investment properties and vacation homes at the beginning of the real estate downturn, and buy them back later at significantly lower prices. The cash you have tied up in residential real estate during the seven-year decline can always be much better utilized in other assets, assets that have less volatility and less downside and much better protection for your principal.

So it is important to understand the underlying health of the U.S. economy to see just how well positioned it is to take this housing hit. If the housing crisis causes the expected global recession, it might also further damage the U.S.'s financial position so that it makes the recovery more distant into the future.

The U.S. government is an important player in containing the housing crisis, preventing the contagion to other asset classes and other markets and, hopefully, ending this financial crisis. If the United States itself is in poor financial condition, it limits the actions that the government might take. No country is so big that it can easily weather an $8 trillion loss in residential real estate values: $1 to $2 trillion deterioration in commercial property values and $6 trillion reductions in the stock market. When you are talking about numbers this large, in the tens of trillions, to simply ask the U.S. government to step in and bail out companies and provide financial guarantees is not reasonable or achievable. The entire economy of the United States is only $14 trillion. At some point, the problem becomes even too big for the world's largest economy.

The United States has enjoyed close to 30 years of fairly robust growth, especially when compared to other advanced countries of the world. Not that there haven't been some minor recessions along the way, but the growth of the overall economy during the past three decades has been rather spectacular. It is the nature of any economy, or for that matter any company, that it makes good sense to make plans and reserves during good times so that you can weather any potential storms on the horizon. This was Joseph's good advice to the pharaohs of ancient Egypt, that they fill their granaries in anticipation of seven years of drought ahead, and it is good advice today, that during good times you strengthen your balance sheet and your financial position so you can weather bad times in the future.

Unfortunately, the United States has done just the opposite. At the end of three decades of magnificent growth and economic prosperity the U.S. government appears weaker financially than it has in its entire history. Just as Wall Street investment banks got in trouble by utilizing too much leverage, the U.S. government itself utilized increased leverage to live far beyond its means. The U.S. government, as well as its people, during prosperous times, have not been happy with the consumption they could afford, but rather have borrowed vast sums of money, and gone into serious levels of debt to finance purchases and consumption that they could not afford in the long run. It will be difficult for the U.S. government to continue its spending given that it now must begin to repay the debt that financed its past purchases. It will be extremely difficult for the U.S. government to take on the additional commitments required to slow the financial contagion occurring worldwide as they are already maxed out when it comes to the liabilities and the total risk exposure.

My analysis begins with the financial health of the United States and its capacity to act to help slow the financial crisis and prevent it from spreading to other countries and other asset classes and other markets. A good place to start is an examination of the federal government's liabilities. When most people discuss the federal government's liabilities, they think about its outstanding debt. Most people know that the U.S.'s total debt has just recently surpassed $11 trillion. Some experts argue that this is not the right debt level to study. They argue that the $4.8 trillion of the $11 trillion held by the public is the more relevant number. In more normal circumstances the experts would be right. If one U.S. government agency decides to invest in U.S. Treasury securities instead of holding cash on its balance sheet, it would make sense to net the total government debt of this double counting and talk about just the U.S. government debt held by the public.

But these times are far from normal. The dramatic difference between the total government debt of $11 trillion and the publicly held amount of $4.8 trillion is primarily due to the cash surplus that has been built up into Social Security and Medicare plans of this country. To suggest that these are assets of the government ignores why Social Security and Medicare have cash surpluses today. Most everyone realizes that Social Security and Medicare are not in a net cash positive position in the long run. The reason they have temporary positive cash resources is because of the demographics of the baby boom. Most of the baby boom is still working and paying into the system, but there is an enormous liability coming due once the baby boom begins to retire. This suggests that the total government debt is somehow reduced because Social Security and Medicare are sitting on these temporary cash stockpiles, even given the enormous liabilities these programs face in the future, makes no sense at all. Therefore the right number to use when looking at total government debt outstanding for the United States is the $11 trillion balance. This is a significant percentage of the total GDP of $14 trillion.

But that is not the extent of this government's total liabilities. The government has all but nationalized Fannie Mae and Freddie Mac. Fannie Mae and Freddie Mac have an additional $1.6 trillion of debt on their balance sheets and $3.7 trillion of additional mortgage guarantees for which they're liable. Today, when the U.S. Treasury stepped in and formally took over Fannie Mae and Freddie Mac they purposely left Fannie Mae and Freddie Mac stock outstanding, even though both were trading at less than one dollar per share. The reason is that the U.S. government did not want to have to absorb Fannie Mae and Freddie Mac's debt and liabilities onto the government balance sheet, and to date they have not done so. But, this is purely cosmetic. In actuality, everyone now knows that the U.S. government is standing behind all of Freddie Mac and Fannie Mae's debts as well as their mortgage guarantees. It is clear that this debt adds an additional $5.3 billion of liabilities to the U.S. government.

The General Accounting Office (GAO) published a report (Fiscal Year 2006 Financial Report of the United States Government, available for download at www.gao.gov/financial/fy2006/fy06finanicalrpt.pdf), which details all of the U.S. government's on and off balance sheet liabilities. There is an additional $4.7 trillion of liability of the U.S. government just solely for retirement plans and health coverage that they have promised their own employees and veterans so there is close to $20 trillion of debt and liabilities and, unfortunately, the big numbers are yet to come.

In the same GAO report, there is a delineation of the present value of the off-balance sheet liabilities the federal government faces today. The report shows that there is an additional $38 trillion of liability created in Social Security. The good news, if there is such a thing, is that all but $6.5 trillion of this liability is covered by expected future tax revenue from taxing people over 62, people 16 to 62 years in age, and even including projected tax revenue in the future from children ages 1 to 15. But Social Security is looking today at a $6.5 trillion shortfall and this is a real liability of the U.S. government. Part of this shortfall will be funded with the cash surplus Social Security has built up, but this presumes that the investment returns will keep up with general inflation and the increasing costs of retirement in the future.

You will find it hard to believe but Medicare is in even worse shape than Social Security. Medicare faces $40 trillion of present value liabilities going forward, but has only funded $16 trillion of these liabilities leaving a $24 trillion shortfall. What is Congress doing about this? Rather than trying to close the shortfall, Congress passed full pharmaceutical benefit coverage for seniors, Medicare Part D. This created an additional $10.2 trillion liability for the federal government, and keeping with their past ineptitude, Congress only allowed $2.4 trillion in premiums to cover this new generous program. So, just Medicare Part D has added an additional $8 trillion liability to the U.S. government. Here is what the total numbers look like:

Total United States debt outstanding	$11.0 trillion
Fannie Mae and Freddie Mac debt and guarantees	$5.3 trillion
Retirement and health care liability to federal employees and veterans	$4.7 trillion
Present value of Social Security shortfalls	$6.5 trillion
Present value of Medicare shortfalls	$32.3 trillion
Net of debt held by SS and Medicare	($5.2 trillion)
Total liabilities of U.S. Government	$54.6 trillion

This number, $54.6 trillion, should look shockingly large you. If it doesn't, you might want to express it in billions as $53,600 billion, or if that doesn't do it you can express it in millions as $53,600,000 million. Still not shocked? It is more than three and a half times the GDP of the United States and is close to the entire economic output of the entire world. It would take 100 percent of all taxes collected in the United

States—income taxes, sales taxes, federal, state, and local taxes, property taxes, and even Social Security and Medicare taxes—just to pay the interest each year on such a large liability.

So from a total liability perspective, the United States is not in good shape. Especially given that the United States is about to head into some tough times as these numbers do not reflect the full cost of the housing and mortgage crisis and the global financial meltdown. For example, the FDIC only had some $52 billion of assets available to it at the end of 2007 according to its own annual report online at www.FDIC.gov and yet has guaranteed more than $4 trillion of investor deposits at commercial banks. As more and more of these commercial banks become bankrupt under the weight of their mortgage loan exposures, it is a near certainty that the FDIC will need additional capital infusions. That required capital is not included in the total liability number above.

You might expect a country with such a weak balance sheet and so much debt outstanding and so many off-balance sheet liabilities would be careful not to make a problem any worse by running operating deficits or adding additional liabilities to its balance sheet. Just the opposite is true. Not only does the Congressional Budget Office (CBO) estimate that the country's operating budget deficit is more than $500 billion for 2008, it expects it to grow in the future as the country heads further into recession. Including additional costs from the crisis and allowing for bigger deficits during the recession years that are ahead suggests that the country is not far off from its first $1 trillion annual government-operating deficit.

Typically countries try to run surpluses during good times because they know that deficits usually result in recessions. The reason is simple. Much of government revenue is tied directly to the health of the economy as incomes and income taxes decline in recessions while the expenditures of a government may actually increase in a recession as more people need government services such as unemployment insurance and welfare payments.

As the country heads into recession it is not crazy to imagine that the government-operating deficit might exceed $600 to $700 billion, especially when you add in the losses from Fannie Mae, Freddie Mac, and the FDIC. This shortfall in government-operating revenues directly increases the amount of debt the country has outstanding. In another eight years there could be a further doubling of the total debt. And this number does not include the amortization of the liability due to the underfunding of Social Security and Medicare, which would push the annual operating deficit closer to $1.5 to $2.0 trillion per year. There are only two alternatives in reducing this deficit: 1) increase taxes; or 2) print money and increase inflation. Neither alternative is attractive because they each cause further declines in the economic growth rate. And, as the economy continues to contract, government revenue shrinks even further. This only stokes the deficit fire further.

What is most disturbing about the large government debts that have been run up as well as the substantial government-operating deficit is that it is not apparent where all the money went. The infrastructure of the country, the bridges and highways, are in disrepair and more than $1 trillion is needed to be spent to ensure that they are safe. Although a great deal of money has been spent by the government fighting the war on terrorism, there are many more terrorists in the world today than there were eight years ago. It is not as if the money had been spent to make the world safer, as a matter of fact the world has never been more dangerous.

No, unfortunately, much of the government spending in the past decade has gone directly into the pockets of big company shareholders as the government has dramatically increased its privatization efforts and turned over much of its operations to big business. In addition, big pharmaceutical companies and hospital companies have made a killing at the government's expense and under Bush's plan that Medicare not be allowed to negotiate the prices of pharmaceutical drugs is positioned to make an even bigger killing in the future. Although the country is spending trillions of dollars on national defense, few people realize that little of this money ends up in the hands of dedicated forces and their families, but a great deal is spent with the defense companies building new weapons systems, the privatization of the military, and the reconstruction efforts through private business of countries destabilized by U.S. bombing. Halliburton's stock has increased some 700 percent since the beginning of the war in Iraq, mostly due to its no-bid contracts there and in New Orleans after Katrina.

One indication of how the United States is bad off is to examine world opinion, which is at an all-time low. You might be able to explain why many Muslim countries of the Middle East have approval ratings for the United States of less than 10 percent of their population. But it is less clear why many of the United States' allies in Europe and in Asia and around the world hold to approval ratings of 25 percent or less (Talbott 2004). Most countries of the world disapproved of the invasion of Iraq because they did not believe in preemptive war, and they realize that Iraq had nothing to do with 9/11. Bush is held in low regard in almost every country of the world. Finally, as if this is not enough, U.S. mortgage losses are not contained just in the United States. Banks and sovereign governments the world over are taking substantial losses in the trillions of dollars as securities that they were promised as AAA-rated declined substantially in value. When discussing the health and strength of the country, it is appropriate to measure world opinion because it is a true gauge of how well that country might act as a leader of the free world to bring about change, and how strong the support of our allies will be for any programs the United States attempts to improve the global economy. If the world holds us in low regard it will be less likely to sign on to any potential solution to the global financial crisis.

Some experts point to the recent growth in gross domestic product (GDP) of the United States as an indicator that the country's economy is strong and vibrant and growing rapidly. This is illusionary. A total of

22 million jobs were created under President Bill Clinton and now under eight years of President George W. Bush less than 4 million net new jobs have been created. Although GDP growth has been positive throughout most of the Bush administration, this growth is suspect for a number of reasons. GDP as a measure of a country's economy itself has come under greater scrutiny as of late. Many experts argue that GDP doesn't measure the right thing after all.

For example, GDP growth goes up when companies pollute with dirty air and dirty water and then have to purchase pollution-control equipment to clean it up. It's hard to see how the average citizen is any better off than he was before the pollution was created, but this doesn't prevent GDP from increasing. Some experts argue that the U.S.'s obsession with status seeking and materialism is not helpful to the quality of life at all and yet dramatically increases economic output as measured by GDP. For example, a $15,000 Toyota can get you the same places as a $120,000 Hummer for a lot less gas, and yet if you drive a Hummer instead of a Toyota the GDP is $105,000 higher. A modest two-bedroom house will keep you as warm and dry as a million-dollar McMansion and yet GDP increases substantially if you opt for the 12,000 square foot McMansion. Americans, and their children, are seeking every day new ways to consume, they are constantly in search of new things to buy, but there is no study that says they are any happier. If greater materialism does not lead to greater happiness the entire concept of GDP maximization has to be reexamined. Some people argue that even defense spending in the trillions of dollars is wasteful as it creates bombs to be exploded against bridges that need replacing and tanks that become obsolete fighting weapons systems that have been sold to old allies who have become new enemies.

Not only does the GDP measure the wrong things, GDP is overly inflated and much of the growth it shows is phony because it is increasingly measuring things that it has not measured in the past. For example, mothers used to stay at home with their children and do a tremendous amount of work for free, which never showed up in the GDP. Now, the mothers work and their wages show up in GDP, but so does their expenditure for maids, child care, restaurants, fast food, etc. An economic number shows up in the GDP for all the hard work that stay-at-home mothers used to do for free. The number of women who are working in the United States has increased from 32 percent in 1968 to more than 64 percent today. A great deal of the supposedly increase in GDP of this country can be explained by this transformation.

Finally, GDP and its growth do not differentiate between products that are purchased for cash versus those that are purchased on credit. It doesn't seem right to me that a country is any richer when I purchase a house or car with 100 percent credit. And it isn't just Americans who have gone borrowing crazy, so has its government. Government debt has increased $5 trillion over the past eight years and that consumer debt, including mortgage debt, credit card debt, and student loan debt has increased from $7 trillion to $16 trillion over the same period. This increase in debt of both the government and the consumer means that any cumulative GDP increase that has occurred over the past eight years has been fully paid for with 100 percent debt; in other words, there hasn't been any real GDP increase at all, it has all been borrowed. Americans are now consuming it, but future generations will pay for it.

The United States currently has a negative savings rate. This is a testimony not only to its populace, which is obviously less frugal and more free-spending and less concerned about the future, but also of the country and what it means when the populace has lost interest and confidence in investing. Either the country is so corrupt that people conclude their investments will never be realized or the economies of the countries are so poor that there are no investments that will yield positive returns. Either way it is a clear warning message that something is terribly wrong with the country. Contrast this with China, which has a 40 percent savings rate on average among its populace. Although the percentage seems shockingly high compared to the United States, examining the absolute dollar levels is an even more shocking story. For you see, the average American household earns $65,000 per year and saves none of it, while the average Chinese household earns less than $3,000 per year and saves 40 percent of it. The Chinese are saving for their children's education, to invest in the infrastructure of their country, to build their own entrepreneurial businesses, and improve their villages. The American is doing none of that. The American is spending 100 percent of his salary on consumables, on himself. At the end of 10 years of work the American will have nothing to show for it. And the country will have declined substantially from a lack of investment.

There has been much talk about the U.S. trade deficit so I don't want to focus too much attention here other than to say at $1 trillion per year it is exceedingly large and another indicator of how weak this country's economy is. If products and services that the world valued were created, there would be a trade surplus. It is a problem because a trade deficit causes a weaker dollar. And the dollar is only going to get weaker as the housing and mortgage problem exacerbates. The reason is that the Federal Reserve will continue to print money to prop up failing banks and investment banks and this printing of money will cause greater inflation. The dollar has to weaken as inflation accelerates because it decreases the purchasing power of the dollar. There is little that can be done from an interest-rate perspective to help the dollar because interest rates are being held at an unusually low level of 2 percent in order to try to stimulate the weak economy. The fact that interest rates are already at 2 percent means they can't be cut further to help with the housing crisis and yet if they are raised substantially there is a great fear that it will stifle any possible recovery. The only question of the dollar is whether it will devalue as rapidly as the other major currencies of the world that are also inflating rapidly to pay off their bad bank loans.

The decline in the value of financial and real assets in America will also weaken America's economy. There is no way American residential real estate can decline by $8 trillion, commercial real estate by

$2 trillion, and the stock market by $6 trillion, and not have a sustained negative impact on the economy. There has never been a residential real estate decline of this magnitude that was national in scope, but home price declines will be much more hard-felt by the economy in the United States than typical stock market trade-offs. The reason is that housing is much more leveraged than stock ownership with homes typically purchased with 90 percent debt, stocks limited to margin debt of 50 percent, and the typical stock bought for less than 4 percent debt. Equally important, few Americans own stocks outright and even given their pension fund ownership and their 401(k)s, the typical American owns less than $1,000 in common stock. More than 73 percent of Americans own their own home. A home price decline is going to have a much broader effect on the general economy than a stock market decline.

Let me speak briefly about other problems the United States faces that if not threatening to the economy certainly makes it more subject to a substantial financial meltdown and global recession. Americans public education system is in ruins. The country has dropped from being one of the best-educated peoples in the world to having its education system rank near last among advanced countries of the world. People rarely take global warming seriously because it is such a long-term phenomena with global temperatures rising 1° every 30 years or so. But once you realize it is real and that humans are causing it, the real cost of fixing it will be on the United States and Europe because they are the worst offenders. The average American consumes 22 times more energy as citizens of a typical developing country, produces 18 times as much waste, and uses 20 to 40 times as much carbon dioxide per capita. They are not going to be able to stop producing carbon for free. There is going to be a cost associated with it. If you tax carbon emissions of industries, industries will raise prices of their goods so that the consumer feels this as a real cost. It may be necessary to institute this tax, but don't kid yourself, it is going to hurt the current economy.

Even now, Congress is envisioning a cap-and-trade system for carbon pollution that will cost more than $100 billion per year in new taxes. New jobs might be created to slow carbon's advance, but they are that funny kind of job that just gets the country back to where it was before it started burning carbon.

Economists believe that wars can be stimulating to an economy. Again, GDP increases typically during wars, but it is hard to figure out how taxing citizens to build bombs that destroy bridges is productive. The United States is now spending more than $1 trillion each year on its defense when the Department of Homeland Security is added to the Pentagon and intelligence community budgets. This is sapping wealth away from more productive enterprises. This expense is not creating anything of value to Americans. You can argue that Americans value security, but I would argue that there was more security before the country spent the $1 trillion invading countries, dropping bombs, killing civilians, and encouraging terrorists to organize and kill Americans.

Finally, the United States is not just economically in dire straits, the country itself faces an ideological battle it has not seen since its founding. Big corporations and their lobbyists have taken such a stronghold on the government that elected representatives no longer represent the interests of their constituents but solely the interests of big business and Wall Street. This influence can be seen in everything from gas prices to the lack of electric cars on the road, to pharmaceutical prices and health care costs to the housing crash, lobbyists infiltrate all levels of the government's decision-making process. And pollute it.

For 30 years elected officials have emphasized smaller government, lower taxes, and deregulation. Instead, government has gotten bigger, taxes are higher, and the deregulation that has occurred is the wrong kind, encouraging business to take unnecessary risks and to rip off the consumer in search of greater profits. It will take years to institute the required regulation needed to properly supervise financial markets and businesses and the country runs the risk that if the government does a poor job that any new regulation will be destructive to the economy rather than constructive.

Finally one of the greatest risks the United States faces is one that is never discussed. Compared to our European allies and other advanced countries of the world, Americans are subject to more religious fundamentalism than all of them. Religious fundamentalism is not limited to Islamic extremists in the Middle East. Religion in the United States, for whatever good it might do, now has gotten to the point that it is a damaging influence on good government.

Big corporations and their lobbyists have taken such a stronghold on the government that elected representatives no longer represent the interests of their constituents but solely the interests of big business and Wall Street.

Many religious people, with very good hearts and minds, are electing officials, congresspeople, senators, and presidents, and support the appointment of federal and local judges on one issue, abortion. They are building a government that does not work. If economic and security issues are ignored by a democracy that is narrow-mindedly focused on a single issue like abortion, it is impossible to explain how that country can improve its government and its economy going forward. It is increasingly scary these same religiously based voters depend on a faith that is not based on evidence and logic but just the opposite, one in which without seeing and without evidence is more highly regarded and more deeply rewarded than belief based on scientific evidence. By definition, there is no rational reasoning with people of this type of religious faith. They are true believers, but the country and the economy will suffer as a result.

Chapter 7

The United States Enters a Long Recession

Even the most stubborn real estate agent admits readily today that there is a housing price decline. Most agents, though, keep telling their clients that the worst is behind us and that prices are bottoming. For reasons described in an earlier chapter, this is not the case. I think that as of the end of 2008 the housing price decline is about half completed and that now housing price declines will move from subprime mortgages to prime mortgages in wealthier neighborhoods where most of the dramatic price appreciation during the real estate boom occurred.

This housing price decline is different from all others, not only because it is national, but because it started without a recession and significant job losses up front. Typically it is a weak economy and a recession that causes job losses to be so significant as to force people to either default on their mortgages or sell their homes at lower prices and move to more moderate shelter. Here, because the housing boom was caused by loose lending with aggressive bank terms, the price decline was possible without a recession and without significant job losses, at least to start.

In this chapter I will discuss the possibility that the housing price decline and the mortgage and banking crisis that ensued will cause a severe recession in the United States. In later chapters I will talk about how these housing problems, mortgage problems, and the recessionary environment might spread internationally.

Even today, there are still some experts out there who are not forecasting a recession for the United States. Their reasoning is simple. These experts believe that the housing and financial problems to date are an asset problem and will have little impact on the real economy of jobs and economic activity in the country. When these experts calculate how an asset class and its decline in price can impact the general economy they typically refer to what is known as the wealth effect. They make comparisons between what happens when a stock market declines and people's wealth declines as a result, and what that means for their spending going forward and its impact on the general economy and GDP. The wealth effect is nothing more than calculating how much slower GDP will grow each year as a result of a shock or a decline in the wealth of American citizens.

Similarly, housing experts talk about the wealth effect when applied to housing price declines. Today, through the end of 2008, there has been a decline in the total aggregate market value of all residential real estate in the United States from $24 trillion to approximately $19 to 20 trillion. If the American people feel they are $4 to $5 trillion poorer, how will that impact their spending and consumption?

Advocates of the theory that housing price declines have little to do with real economic output suggest that these declines have little impact on economic activity. They argue that the $5 trillion is not real because few people sell their house each year. It is a paper loss. Also, it is not $5 trillion that people invested in their homes from hard-earned equity, but rather it is simply giving back $5 trillion of profit that appreciated in the homes during the boom years. As a matter of fact, these profits were earned just since 2004 in the U.S. housing market.

So, there is an argument from many supposed experts that the housing price decline will have little impact on the general economy. Even if you point out to these experts that the banks will suffer losses in the trillions, they reply that there are no real losers in this disruption because for every loss to a bank there is someone who gains, when someone defaults on a mortgage by definition, they keep the monies and the boats and cars and vacations that it bought.

As you might have guessed by now, I am not of this school of thought. I believe the housing price decline will have a significant impact on the economy, its growth, and the stock market. Although I believe the wealth effect is real, especially for housing because of the great deal of leverage homeowners utilize and the breadth of ownership of houses relative to stocks, I don't see it as the key driver that transforms housing price losses into real economic output declines such as a decline in GDP.

I do believe that the value of residential housing in the United States at $24 trillion is such a large number that the country cannot experience 20 percent declines to date through to the end of 2008 or expected 30 to 40 percent declines nationally without having far-reaching impacts on the $14 trillion economy.

The first impact on the economy is a direct impact. Industries closely related to housing will suffer. And these industries are going to suffer for a long time. The home-building industry is already in a severe depression. Home builders building new houses will suffer even more than typical homeowners living in existing homes because new homes act as sort of a buffer of new supply to the market when there is great demand for housing. But similarly, when that demand disappears, and there is an increase in the existing home supply for sale by current owners, there is no need for new construction and new home building. It is one of those cyclical industries that goes from enormous demand to zero overnight. Demand for new homes doesn't go down 2 percent in a bad year but trades off 60 percent to 70 percent. Existing homes for sale make up more than enough of the supply for all the home-ownership demand.

Secondly, home builders have to build their new homes in areas with a substantial amount of raw land available. This prevents them from building downtown in the heart of many metropolises. They end up building far, far out in the suburbs. New home building was not significant on the coast of San Diego in Delmar or La Jolla where every square foot is already filled with homes and condominiums. But 1½ hours northeast of San Diego there was tremendous building in Temecula and Vista. When the housing market crashes, a lot of new homes on the market dramatically impacts prices. Also, as home prices decline everywhere, commuters realize that there is no need to live in Temecula and face a 1½-hour commute each day when they can now afford homes closer to San Diego. So new home prices and new home builders get clobbered.

There is a story that a small town just east of San Francisco by two hours and south of Sacramento by one hour saw its new homes that had sold for $720,000 a month earlier were auctioned off for $320,000 after the crash. Of course, construction companies and developers that focused on condo development downtown in many major cities like Miami, San Diego, and Las Vegas also took a beating. They were building condominiums as fast as they could because the market, with the banks lending to them, were willing to pay two to three to four times the cost of construction for a new condominium. When prices collapsed, so did the condominium projects, many of them in a half-completed stage of construction.

In addition to home builders and condo developers, the next obvious direct impact on economic health and GDP is that hundreds of thousands of real estate brokers will see their livelihood greatly impaired. It looks like housing sales volume will decline by as much as 30 percent, if home prices are off an additional 30 percent this means that real estate commissions will decline by more than half, and that presumes that in a competitive market with far too many real estate agents the traditional quite monopolistic 6 percent realtor fee structure is maintained.

Of course real estate brokers are not the only people who make a living off the housing business. Mortgage brokers, appraisers, commercial bankers, rating agency personnel, investors, and investment bankers all do well when housing and mortgage volume is booming. Most mortgage brokerage firms are now bankrupt, three of the five largest investment banks are out of business, and the boom is about to drop on a number of big and small commercial banks. Not only is reported economic activity lower when this housing activity disappears, but these personnel will be out of jobs and looking for either unemployment insurance or full-time employment elsewhere, which cannot help the general economy.

One of the largest industries in America is the construction industry where I have said that new housing construction will almost cease for some period of time. People are wondering when new home construction will come back. Coincidentally, just as this housing crash begins to abate in five years or so, the bulk of the baby boom will be retiring and many elderly Americans will have moved onto nursing homes. The retirement of the baby boom will have a dramatic detrimental effect on GDP. But few people realize that as elderly people move out of their homes and into nursing and assisted living facilities this dramatically increases the number of existing homes available for purchase. As Congress cracks down on illegal immigration, and the elderly move out of their existing homes and into nursing homes over the next 20 years, it may be the case that America will have very little, if any, new home construction for the sustainable future.

A final direct impact on the economy from the housing price decline is what will happen to the renovation business and the furniture business and the moving business. A great deal of the renovation work done to homes in America over the last two decades was improvement work in anticipation of flipping a house for sale. Now that sales have slowed, and that people are living in their houses for much longer periods of time, it only seems natural that renovation work will slow. It was also the case that during the absolute boom, that renovation work not only paid for itself, but was profitable. Unlike any time in recent history, if you spent $60,000 to renovate a kitchen and two bathrooms in your home, the value of your home increased by $100,000 to $120,000.

This is just the opposite of the standard rule on renovations, which is you will never get your money back from renovation as it reflects too much your own personal choice and tastes. Typically, renovations recoup anywhere from $0.30 on the dollar to $0.60 on the dollar, but are almost always money-losing propositions. There will be some trickle remaining of renovation work as people realize that they won't be selling their homes anytime soon and wish to remodel them. But once this work is done, you have to assume that renovation activity and its impact on the general economy will slow dramatically.

Companies that depend on new home construction and renovation activity will slow terribly. Although Home Depot and Lowe's have traded off on the stock market, it is a wonder they have not traded even lower. The only explanation is that they have been successful in bankrupting many of their small local hardware store competitors and that they now can charge exorbitant monopoly-like prices in the markets they operate. But even this pricing will come under pressure as people refuse to pay $42 for a piece of plywood or $18 for a hammer in a down housing market.

So negative wealth effects will translate lower home prices into a weaker American economy and lower home prices will mean less activity in the real estate sector, broadly defined, which will mean lower growth rates in GDP. But I believe that the biggest impact from the housing crisis on the real economy is rarely discussed in the media or in academia. I believe that the biggest impact on the real economy will be due to the bank losses caused by the housing crisis from the sharp decline in mortgage asset values. The reason is that I believe that bank losses are the real key to understanding recessions.

Many people believe that recessions are normal cycles in business activity because they have always occurred, people look beyond trying to find a cause or a solution and rather accept them as inevitable and part of normal business activity. Former Chairman of the Federal Reserve Alan Greenspan, partly in trying to avoid blame for the current housing and mortgage crisis, even talks about the current crisis being a 100-year event, like it was some sort of flood that occurs randomly every 100 years or so. There is nothing random about this crisis. It could have been avoided. It had real causes and enough people warned about the peril that it could have been avoided. Let me try to explain why I think bank losses are the key to understanding recessions.

The concept is so simple that you might choose to ignore it if it weren't for the strong set of evidence that supports my theory. Banks are highly leveraged. American banks historically have been leveraged approximately 10 to 12 times. This means that they had total assets equal to 10 to 12 times their total shareholder equity. How do they leverage their shareholders equity to buy so many assets? They take deposits and they borrow money and issue debt. The good news is that for every 1 percent extraordinary profit they earn on assets it means a 10 percent to 12 percent extraordinary profit to their shareholders. That is why it's called leverage.

But companies with such substantial leverage also have to understand that leverage works against them in a downturn. Many commercial banks in the United States are no longer leveraged 10 to 12 times. Now, they have achieved leverages of 15 or 16 times, and that is before all of their off-balance-sheet assets and leverage is included. Citibank had more than $3 trillion of assets under its control in 2007 but only $110 billion in equity beneath them, and that before they lost $55 billion of equity in bad loans. This is almost 29 times leverage.

You can see why this makes Citibank much more risky. Citibank has $3 trillion of loans and other assets to manage and yet if they lose just 5 percent on all their assets they bankrupt the firm. Given the diversity of assets they hold this is unlikely. But is it crazy to think that Citibank might lose 50 percent on a class of assets that make up 10 percent of their balance sheet? This also would bankrupt Citibank. And this is the risk the banks face now as they have written off more than $500 billion of losses already, mostly from residential real estate and mortgages.

So my simple theory as to how bank losses impact the real general economy goes as follows. When banks face substantial losses in one of their businesses, it threatens their rather small equity base and the solvency and sustainability of the firms. What banks do when they face such losses in any portion of their investment or loan portfolio is to pull back from almost all lending. Certainly they are less aggressive in their lending terms, and as a result they end up lending less money to business, investors, and consumers. Such a pullback in bank lending has to have a material impact on the economy. And don't forget the leverage effect. If the commercial banks ended up losing $1 trillion as a result of declining housing and mortgage prices, that is

When banks face substantial losses in one of their businesses, it threatens their rather small equity base and the solvency and sustainability of the firms. What banks do facing such losses in any portion of their investment or loan portfolio is to pull back from almost all lending.

a direct contraction of their book equity. Because they are leveraged 15 to 1, that means that unless they find a replacement for the lost equity through new equity issuance they may have to reduce their balance sheet and lend $15 trillion less. This is the deleveraging you hear about that is happening on Wall Street now. Can you imagine if the banks reduce their lending by $15 trillion what the impact of that will be on the general economy? Banks aren't just cutting back lending to homeowners to buy new homes, or to home builders to build them. They are reducing their lending in the areas of student loans, credit card lending, automobile loans, business loans, and small business loans. They have to get smaller or else they will not survive. So they won't be making any new loans to grow, and they won't be renewing many of their favored clients' revolving credit facilities. They are going to be calling in many loans. This has to be negative on the economy and the historical evidence is exactly that.

In 1982 and 1983 banks had substantial losses to farmers in the United States and to Third World countries that were substantial enough at the time to threaten their equity capital bases. They pulled back on their lending not just to farmers and the Third World, but all of their lending and caused a significant decline in GDP growth.

In 1990 and 1991 commercial banks in the United States experienced significant losses in leveraged buyouts, junk bond issuers, and commercial property development. Remember, this was back when brand-new overdeveloped and empty skyscrapers in Houston were called see-throughs because you could literally see all the way through them from the outside as they had no curtains inside, no furniture inside, and certainly no employees inside.

The greatest example of my theory of bank losses causing economic difficulties in a country occurred outside the United States in Japan in 1993. Housing prices collapsed in Japan in 1993 when their national housing prices declined by 50 percent and houses in their major metropolitan areas declined some 75 percent. Prices returned in Japan to where they were before their housing boom, not coincidentally exactly what I am predicting for housing prices in the United States.

As you can imagine, Japanese banks were devastated. They had financed not only the housing boom and a commercial property boom, but many of the operating companies in Japan had begun to invest in real estate as a side activity. There is no question that technically speaking from an accounting perspective all of the major Japanese banks were officially bankrupt by 1994. The only thing that kept these banks in business was that they were in bed with their government. The Ministry of Finance (MOF) for the Japanese government controls the banks and determined when they had to recognize real estate losses. To prop up the banks and prevent bank runs and to keep the banks from claiming bankruptcy, the Japanese government thought it wise to not force the banks to recognize their losses from real estate. What happened as a result is a travesty. People lost all confidence in the banking system and the lack of transparency meant that investors and businesspeople did not know which bank was solvent and which wasn't and where the bad losses resided. As a result, the Japanese economy went into a recession for the next two decades of which they were just beginning to grow their way out of when the U.S. housing crash hit in 2006 and 2007. So, regardless of whether banks hide their losses or recognize them, the impact of substantial bank losses has an enormous detrimental impact on a country's economy. It should not be lost on Americans the similarities between Japan in 1993 and United States today. Obviously, the country sustained substantial housing price declines, mortgage asset price declines, and substantial bank losses. To the extent that the administration in the United States has gotten so close and comfy with big banks they may refuse to force the banks to recognize their losses, the economic impact will be as bad but much longer lasting. By trying to hide the losses, American regulators, congresspeople, and presidents can end up causing a global recession, which will last for many years.

In 2001 the high-tech and Internet sector of the economy took a substantial hit. Although many people are familiar with the impact on the highflying stocks in the tech sector, people had never realized how substantial the loss was to the commercial banks that financed this sector. Although not necessarily causal, the recession that followed was due in part to the commercial banks retrenchment and lack of lending after these high-tech losses.

So now the banks face enormous losses that might approach $1 to $2 trillion. The commercial banks in America typically hold as much as 40 percent of their assets in residential and commercial mortgages and real estate properties. To the extent that their equity base is only 4 percent to 5 percent of total assets, you can quickly calculate that a 10 percent decline in the value of their real estate and mortgage portfolio could bankrupt many banks in the United States. The largest commercial banks are most at risk because they held more residential mortgages on their books while the smaller banks mostly packaged mortgages and passed them up through Fannie Mae to be sold to mortgage investors. Also, the larger commercial banks were more involved with the enormously complex mortgage products like CDOs and off-balance-sheet vehicles like Structured Investment Vehicles (SIVs) that because of their complexity, poor structuring, substantial rating declines, and use of leverage are seeing the most rapid declines in price.

But even small community banks are not off the hook. Although smaller regional banks were quick to sell residential mortgages upstream to mortgage packagers like Fannie Mae, they often involved themselves in substantial loans to local real estate developers and builders. Construction loans are a big part of a small regional bank's business and to the extent that a great deal of residential and commercial construction has now ceased, some of it with half-built buildings in the ground, these regional banks will face very substantial losses. These regional banks also have significant exposure to mall developers that are suffering as retailers begin to go bankrupt and will suffer substantial loan losses as the economy softens and the general business climate deteriorates.

The sheer magnitude of the size of the potential losses means that it will take years for the banks to deleverage and to replace their threatened equity capital base. No economy can effectively grow without a healthy banking climate as banks provide the necessary capital for new business formation, new building growth, new home growth, and new factories and other business development.

Another argument made by the naysayers and those still in denial as to whether there will be a recession is that everything is temporary, that these are not permanent losses but only cyclical losses. Nothing could be further from the truth. These losses from the bank's perspective are indeed permanent. These mortgages are not going to spring back to full value. Housing prices that have declined are not going to reinflate. The reason is that the bubble is bursting and is deflating a boom and returning to more normal pricing. The banks in the future are not going to lend 11 times your household income to buy a house. They might lend three to five times your income if you have a good job with demonstrable income, if you have a good credit score, if you are willing to put down a substantial down payment, and if you have some verifiable means of demonstrating your job and income. This is a return to normalcy. Bank's losses are not going to be reversed. They are permanent. The effect on the general economy is permanent.

So the real question is not whether there is going to be an impact on the general economy and GDP from the housing price declines, but rather why hasn't it happened already and why hasn't it been more substantial? Why is GDP still growing through the middle of 2008?

As to the question of why has the U.S. economy not fallen into recession and negative growth already there are a number of answers. Remember, this business cycle is just the opposite of all prior business cycles. Here the housing price declines occurred first, and that caused resulting economic weakness and job loss. In more typical housing cycles, you had the job loss first, so you would expect the economy to contract sooner in the cycle. Housing prices are going to take five to seven years to reach bottom, and so it is going to be a long drawn out process as this lower housing activity and the bank losses are reflected in the general economy. It is as if you are watching an automobile crash in slow motion. For those of you who work on Wall Street in the stock and bond markets and are used to instant gratification and news and information being incorporated in a stock or bond in minutes, this can be very frustrating.

A second reason why the economy did not deteriorate immediately upon the housing price declines can be seen when you track through who experienced the real losses in this housing crash. A homeowner with no mortgage who never bought or sold a home during the last 20 years has only enjoyed paper profits and paper losses and there is no real cash gain or loss from living in the same home during this period. But for those people who speculated and flipped houses and constantly moved into ever-larger homes with smaller down payments, they enjoyed a substantial profit. If someone bought a house for $200,000 in 1997 and sold it in 2005 for $400,000, that is a real cash profit and a benefit. If they then purchased a new larger home for $1 million and financed it with 100 percent bank debt, they still have no loss even as that new house declines in value so long as they are willing to walk away from their loan and leave the new house with the bank. What this example shows is that for the vast majority of home purchases and refinancings during the period, it was not the homeowner who suffered a monetary loss, but the bank who suffered the real cash loss. Even people who didn't sell their home but just refinanced their home and bought second homes, cars, boats, and vacations were all better off and if they default on their new large mortgage, again it will be the bank that suffers the cash loss not the homeowner.

So why hasn't the economy contracted quicker? The answer is that the average homeowner who either flipped houses or refinanced during the boom hasn't suffered a cash loss yet. Net, net, they've made money on the deal and have money in the bank. It is the banks that have suffered and the secondary effects from their pullback in lending that has not been felt yet in the general economy. But, as people spend the last of their cash windfall they got from their refinancings over their overpriced home sales, and at the rate of consumption they are doing currently it won't be long until these homeowners burn through these cash windfalls, the economy will suffer because there is no new bank lending to replace it. The banks are not going to be doing any more new boat financings. The banks aren't going to be doing aggressive new automobile financing. The gig is up. Once people burn through the monies they received from refinancings or home sales there is no more coming down the pike. The game is over.

Just because the economy does not go down today, does not mean it is not going to decline in the future. Finally, almost 2½ years into this housing price decline there are increases in the unemployment rate. Unemployment in the third quarter of 2008 was 6.1 percent and increasing. It is this unemployment that will lead to dramatic reductions in GDP growth. If your definition of a recession is two consecutive quarters of negative GDP growth, I can assure you that your definition will be satisfied, but it may be as late as early 2009. Once the recession kicks in, there is no guarantee that it will be short-lived. As a matter of fact, I believe it will be a very long and very deep recession. I believe the tens of trillions of dollars that the banks will not lend in the future around the world will have a devastating impact on the global economy. And then the feedback cycles begin. As people are laid off in the construction and real estate industries, they end up consuming less and people begin to get laid off in other supporting industries. Automobiles, already in trouble, head south. People delay taking vacations. People delay buying cars. People stop buying boats. Retailers suffer, restaurants suffer, layoffs continue. As layoffs accelerate, economic activity slows, generating further layoffs.

Business investment slows as business inventories build. Businesses lay off more employees.

I don't believe it is clear to any economists what stops this vicious downward cycle. Keynesians used to believe the government could step in and spend monies to stop such a devastating feedback loop. But today's economists believe that consumers and businesses are more fully rational and understand that phony government spending must be paid for with increased taxes or inflating the currency and so are less likely to fall for a government stimulation plan.

Milton Friedman once told me that eventually, even in a depression, unemployment will get so bad and wages will be so low that eventually there will be new hiring as people find productive uses for the newly unemployed and low-wage labor pool. I'm not sure I believe that. Milton Friedman tried to argue that wages were inflexible during the Great Depression and this prevented a quick recovery. I don't see it. The Great Depression occurred before the formation of most labor unions in the United States and certainly most workers were not in unions at the time of the Great Depression. I am no expert on the history of the Great Depression, but even I remember pictures of people carrying signs saying I will work for food. That doesn't sound like labor inflexibility to many. Laws were passed that tried to support wages, but it is hard to imagine they were immediately effective.

I am much more pessimistic than Milton Friedman. I believe that capitalism is based on trust. And that when

I believe that capitalism is based on trust. And that when that trust is violated, and contracts are not certain to be honored, and loans are not certain to be repaid, and when businesses hide losses and when banks cannot be trusted with deposits, there is a risk that all economic activity will stop.

that trust is violated, and contracts are not certain to be honored, and loans are not certain to be repaid, and when businesses hide losses, and when banks cannot be trusted with deposits, there is a risk that all economic activity will stop. People will take their money out of banks and put it in their mattress. People will stop buying new things. Companies will cut production and workers. Companies will cut investment. It is not at all obvious to me how a country gets out of such a negative spiral. This is the risk that occurs. The biggest businesses and the largest banks and investment banks were allowed to run crazy for decades with little to no government regulation. The price must now be paid. I can only hope that the price is not too severe and that the country can pull out of these difficulties. But I also hope that the lesson is learned. In Chapter 15, about the deeper causes of the housing boom and crash, I will point a finger squarely at the lack of regulation in America and the damage corporate lobbyists did to the government, the people, and the country.

Chapter 8

The Global Economy Catches the Contagion

U p to this point, the focus has been on the U.S. housing market in the U.S. economy. I was not being xenophobic or ethnocentric but rather realized that the U.S. housing crisis and the mortgage meltdown in the United States has been the cause of this very substantial global problem. But from a larger perspective, it is a much more important question to ask if this contagion is capable of spreading to other countries and to the world.

The focus begins on Europe for one simple reason, the United States and Europe, although representing only 12 percent of the world's population account for nearly half of global GDP and economic output. Goods may be manufactured in China and services may be outsourced to India but the ultimate consumer of those goods and services most likely lives in the United States or Europe. If consumption slows dramatically in the United States and Europe, it is impossible to explain how the rest of the world economy can hold together. Many of the other countries have become expert at manufacturing or providing services or raw materials to consumers in the United States and Europe, but today, have not developed substantial enough domestic markets and domestic consumption to prevent a global recession if the United States and Europe slow their consumption.

There are experts who have tried to argue that in the modern world the United States and Europe no longer dominate. They have tried to argue that the growth of the BRIC economies, namely Brazil, Russia, India, and China has been so dramatic that there has been in fact a decoupling of their growth rates and the health of the global economy from that of the United States and Europe.

It is true that China and other developing countries have seen dramatic growth in their economies, but if measured properly these countries have relatively small economies relative to the United States and Europe. A great deal of their economic growth depends on exporting to the United States and Europe.

The best way I have found to diffuse this decoupling argument is to utilize an interactive graphing tool available on the *Wall Street Journal* online homepage. If you go to their markets data center and look at their data on international markets you can easily plot stock market changes by country and contrast and compare them. It becomes quickly apparent that the stock markets of the countries of the world move fairly closely in unison. The exception is oil-rich countries such as Nigeria and Russia, which strengthen when oil increases in price while oil-consuming nations like the United States typically suffers when oil prices increase. But, in the long run, even this disparity will come into line if the United States and European economies soften as the demand for oil will decline, the price of oil will decline, and even Nigeria and Russia will suffer from a global slowdown. From the

Wall Street Journal site, a simple way to see that there is little decoupling of the world economy from the U.S. economy is to plot their world stock-index versus their world stock-index after excluding the U.S. stock market. Again, these two indices plot almost on top of each other and the correlation is so strong that it is hard to argue that the global economy has decoupled from the United States.

There are four possible ways that the contagion that began in the United States as a housing and mortgage crisis and the eventual U.S. recession can spread internationally to other global markets.

First, foreign banks and foreign sovereign governments experience losses directly from holding U.S. mortgages and U.S. mortgage-backed securities. This is the most immediate means in which a contagion ignited in the United States can spread quickly overseas. And it is already happening. Before U.S. banks started having a problem with U.S. mortgages and CDOs backed by U.S. mortgages, German, Swiss, French, and Danish banks were reporting significant losses due to their holdings of U.S. mortgages and mortgage-backed securities. These losses were substantial because U.S. investment banks, commercial banks, and Fannie Mae and Freddie Mac had effectively sold a large percentage of U.S. mortgages and U.S. mortgage-backed securities to foreign governments around the world. Some of the biggest buyers of the most complex and risky CDO securities were foreign countries, their central banks, and their commercial banks.

To the extent that foreign banks have significant losses because they hold U.S. mortgages, this story is much the same as in the United States as to how this might cause economic problems and lead to global recession. As stated previously about U.S. banks, foreign banks with substantial losses in U.S. mortgages are going to see their equity capital bases threatened and will pull back from lending. This reduction in the amount of lending to both consumers and businesses and a withdrawal from the aggressive terms previously available assures that these countries will take a hit to their economic growth prospects. Given that

Europe was growing less rapidly than the United States for the past decade, typically at a level of less than 2 percent per year, means that it takes less of a hit to drive GDP growth negative and thus have an official recession after two quarters of negative GDP growth.

Unlike the United States, the European Central Bank initially decided not to substantially cut interest rates. This means that a recession in Europe will probably occur sooner and be deeper initially than what happens in the United States. Eventually, the United States should have as deep if not a deeper recession since most of the mortgage problem resides there. In addition, most of the European governments did not offer any type of stimulus package like the United States did. While a temporary Band-Aid that does little to solve the underlying problems exposed in the housing and mortgage prices, a large monetary stimulus does postpone the economic impact. Witness the 2.9 percent growth in GDP in the United States in the second quarter of 2008. This number would have been much closer to zero percent growth without the U.S.'s economic stimulus package.

The losses experienced by foreign banks have to have real economic impact in some form. If the banks are left to struggle on their own, their pullback in future lending will be recessionary. If governments increase taxes to fund these bank losses, these increases also will hamper economic growth. Most likely, and what I have seen to date, these foreign countries will do just what America has done, have their central banks inject capital into their struggling money losing commercial banks and then fund that injection by printing more currency. The countries of Europe have already announced plans to inject some $2.3 trillion into their banks. Just as in the United States, when foreign governments print more currency, it causes inflation in the country as there are more units of currency chasing the same amount of real goods, prices of all goods have to increase. This is the coward's way of funding bank losses. The central bank does not have to admit to the magnitude of the problem, the governments of the world do not have to take responsibility for a lack of regulation and supervision of the commercial banks, and the governments of the world do not have to approach their constituents and tell them that their taxes are being raised. Taxes are not raised directly, but in effect that is what higher inflation is, it is a higher tax. The reason is that typically, especially in the United States, workers are not able to negotiate higher wages as rapidly as the prices of food and energy prices escalate during inflationary periods.

Europe is different from the United States in many ways. One important difference is that unions today are much stronger in Europe than in the United States. Typically, unions in Europe have automatic escalators in their wage agreements that guarantee wage increases to accommodate for any increases in general inflation. Such union agreements make it more difficult to stick the worker with the true cost of the banking crisis because his wages escalate automatically with the inflation caused by printing more money. In the United States, most workers have no such protection and, it is the worker who ends up paying the cost of our central banks bailing out losses at our commercial banks. This is what Milton Friedman meant by flexible labor agreements. That if there was ever a problem in the economy, regardless of whose fault it was—banks losing money, government corruption, or business management mistakes—you could always pass the cost down to the worker through either lower wages, wages that did not keep up with inflation, wages that did not improve as productivity improved, or if that didn't work, job layoffs.

So the primary means by which the U.S. mortgage crisis can expand to Europe and the world is because commercial banks and central banks around the world held U.S. mortgages and U.S. mortgage-backed securities and suffered losses in some cases as great as their U.S. counterparts. As of the end of 2008, there is already weakness in the global economy directly because of the global losses in U.S. mortgages. Germany looks as if it is already in recession, the United Kingdom is on the brink, and Japan is reentering a recession having just escaped a multi-decade downturn. Europe entering recession before the United States should not be surprising given that their growth rates were less than the United States to start, they offered no stimulus or rate cut, and their central bank was quick to print money and give it to their commercial banks, regardless of the inflation caused and its negative impact on the economies of Europe.

The second means by which this contagion can spread overseas is if foreign countries begin to have their own housing crash and housing price declines. There are a number of similarities between what happened in the United States during its housing boom and what happened in worldwide housing markets. Although much of the rest of the world was spared exposure to the crazy exotic mortgages that mortgage brokers in the United States were pitching such as zero down payment, interest-only, and negative-amortization loans, there was enough similarity between what happened worldwide and what happened during the U.S. housing boom that it makes an ensuing global housing crash inevitable and with it a global recession unavoidable.

When I wrote my first book in 2003, *The Coming Crash in the Housing Market,* I faced a great deal of criticism because in the book I argued that the housing boom and eventual predicted crash were going to be national in scope unlike all previous residential real estate declines, which had been limited to a particular city or region of the country. In my subsequent 2006 book, *Sell Now! The End of the Housing Bubble,* I had to admit that I was wrong. The boom in the coming housing price crash was not national. I realized it was going to be international.

In the book, *Sell Now!,* I showed that the housing boom was not limited just to the United States. Cities all over the world had seen the real price of homeownership or condominium ownership explode since 1980. A 1,000-square-foot condominium in a premier location in Manhattan had seen its real price triple from $420,000 in 1980 to more than $1.2 million by the end of 2005. Manhattan was not unique in the United States. San Francisco saw real price increases of 150 percent during the same time period. San Diego, Boston, and Los Angeles witnessed double increases in their real home prices.

A similar 1,000-square-foot condominium in a desirable neighborhood in London went up even faster than Manhattan, escalating from $350,000 to $1.2 million during the period. Dublin, Ireland, realized the fastest percentage increase as the real prices for thousands square foot apartments there went from $100,000 to nearly $800,000. Madrid was not far off as a similar condominium there went from $80,000 to $650,000. Milan, Italy, and Sydney, Australia, more than tripled in real prices and Paris and Stockholm at least doubled in real price. Given that real home prices had not increased in the United States for 100 years, and given that incomes of average workers around the world had not exploded, such appreciation sets the stage for what should be a resounding global collapse in condominium and house prices around the world.

You might argue that Dublin and Madrid deserved big home price increases during the past 25 years because they have had dramatic economic growth and improvement in household incomes. But, these typical homes in Dublin and Madrid are now in real dollars more costly than living in Paris or Amsterdam and close to the price of a similar apartment in Milan. Not to disparage Dublin and Madrid, but that is fairly rich company as far as the quality of life goes. I still would want to have dinner in Paris more than Dublin, all other things being equal.

I lived in Ireland for a year in 2003 and I witnessed firsthand the Irish miracle that led to its dramatic increase in economic output. Even then, I was shocked to find that the average home in Dublin sold for €240,000 and the average home outside of Dublin sold for €180,000 when the average income in Ireland was approximately €30,000. Ireland had made a great deal about its high-tech boom, but the one I saw were many high-tech manufacturers that designed and produced their laptops and computers in other countries and then did the final packaging and assembly in Ireland so as to be inside the European

Union border. These were not high-tech, high-paying jobs, because many people just poured packing popcorn on top of laptops to which they had attached a new corporate logo. I didn't see how €30,000 jobs were going to support €240,000 home prices. As in the United States, the ratio of home prices to average incomes had gotten completely out of whack. At least in the U.K. when a couple applies for a mortgage they only consider 50 percent of the spouse's income when determining qualification, unlike America where they count 100 percent of both people's wages and earnings.

The fact that sophisticated metropolitan and cosmopolitan European neighborhoods and cities accelerated the fastest in home price appreciation supports our earlier arguments that it was aggressive bankers in the cities that helped cause and fuel a house price explosion craved by home buyers who were more concerned with status and the neighborhood they lived in than making the mortgage payment.

The United Kingdom and Ireland and many other foreign countries do not have a long-term fixed-rate mortgage market. You couldn't get a 30-year fixed-rate mortgage there even if you wanted to. About 95 percent of the mortgages in the United Kingdom are floating rate. This certainly looks like a recipe for disaster. As rates increase in the future as grist returns to the global financial sector, mortgage interest rates in these countries will float up making mortgage payments more difficult. Because interest rates were artificially low worldwide, foreign banks had the same problem as U.S. banks with their qualifying formula. Short-term floating rates in the first year were used to justify lending amounts of money that would be impossible to pay back if rates ever increased in the future.

It is a fact that those European countries, like the United States, that had dramatic declines in nominal interest rates from 1996 to 2004 such as Australia, Ireland, Spain, and the United Kingdom, also had large home price appreciations. Countries such as Austria, Germany, Japan, and Switzerland had lower or no decline in interest rates and saw little home price appreciation. As in the United States, real interest rates did not change materially in these countries. What was happening to interest rates was that inflation was burning out of the economy. If real interest rates didn't change, housing prices shouldn't either. The fact that they did is most likely due to the problems that bank-qualifying formulas have in handling varying levels of inflation, as discussed earlier about the United States. As inflation varies, banks' inadequate qualifying formulas end up restricting lending to borrowers during periods of high inflation thus generating credit histories of low default rates and foreclosures, but then when inflation comes down and nominal interest rates come down, these banks end up over-lending and thus cause foreclosures and default rates begin to spike.

So you can expect significant declines in home prices in the United Kingdom, Ireland, Australia, New Zealand, and Spain as well as in any other foreign countries that have seen dramatic real home price appreciation. Things have to return to normal given that banks are now not going to be doing such crazy lending. To the extent that housing prices declined dramatically in these countries it will ignite the number of mortgage defaults and foreclosures and cause significant losses to their commercial banks, the same as what is happening in the United States. This is just now beginning as the United Kingdom reports that home prices are off some 6½ percent from their peak and Ireland reports a 4 percent decline. Home prices as a multiple of income at the peak seem just as bad in London and Dublin as they do in San Diego, and before this is over they should

You can expect significant declines in home prices in the United Kingdom, Ireland, Australia, New Zealand, and Spain as well as in any other foreign countries that have seen dramatic real home price appreciation.

expect similar home price declines north of 35 percent to 40 percent. This is not just a guess, their banks will not have the funds to make such aggressive loans in the future and their interest rates are already beginning to trend up as inflation heats their economies. Because nearly all of their mortgages are floating rates, this higher inflation and higher interest rate environment will immediately result in higher mortgage payments. All of the homeowners in these countries will experience the sticker shock that adjustable-rate mortgage payers face in the United States. Many people will see their scheduled mortgage payments increase 30 percent to 50 percent making payment completely unaffordable and guaranteeing a dramatic increase in defaults.

Not all countries in the world got caught up in the loose credit extended by commercial banks around the world. Canada comes to mind as a fairly conservative country with what Americans would call good Midwestern values and never bought into the concept of borrowing 10 times your income to purchase a home. The banks were never crazy enough to lend the money and homeowners were not crazy enough to sign the mortgage notes promising to pay it back. Home prices in Canada as a result never appreciated dramatically like the United States or parts of Europe. Real prices of homes in Toronto increased less than 10 percent in real terms cumulatively over the entire 25-year period from 1980 to 2005. This is a real price increase of approximately 0.4 percent per year as compared to 10 percent to 20 percent annual increases in some cities in the United States.

Even Canada had its pockets of rapid home price appreciation. Areas of Vancouver, especially on Victoria Island, in which vacation and second homes saw an explosion in prices are now subject to price declines as rationality returns to those markets. Toronto, which is building more new condominiums this year than any city in North America, had buyers finance their purchase with what are called 107 percent mortgage deals. These mortgages not only require no down payment from the buyer, and finance 100 percent of the purchase, they also allow the real estate agent to take 3 percent of the purchase price out as a fee and the home buyer to take home 4 percent of the purchase price at the closing just for signing the mortgage note. These terms are so crazy and so unlike the rest of Canada that they guarantee that the Toronto condominium market will see some softness and price declines have already begun there. Condo prices in Toronto will return to the cost of replacement construction, something closer to $180,000 than $360,000.

The third means by which the U.S. contagion and its weak economy can be exported to other countries is through exports themselves. Countries that have substantial exports to the United States, and depend on exports to the United States and Europe as a significant portion of their economy will suffer as the United States and Europe's economies begin to weaken.

China is the most dramatic example of this, but it also applies to India and somewhat surprisingly to Germany, which in percentage terms is one of the biggest exporters in the world. Germany's strong export economy in combination with its immediate bank losses due to U.S. mortgage holdings has caused Germany to be one of the first countries of the world to enter a recession because of this contagion.

With regard to China, people have misrepresented the magnitude of the problem. Some experts are trying to claim that China is a $6 to $7 trillion economy and is large enough with its own vibrant domestic economy that it can be independent of the United States and Europe. But this is not the case. China's economy is measured at $6.5 trillion in purchasing power parity (PPP) terms. This is an economic method to try to translate the Chinese economy measured at the current exchange rate in U.S. dollars and allow for the fact that those dollars buy much more in a low-cost environment in China. In other words, the actual size of the Chinese economy is only $1.6 trillion measured at today's exchange rates, but, according to PPP reporting, this is the same purchasing power as if the Chinese economy were $6.5 trillion in size.

But purchasing power parity is not the right measure to use when analyzing how independent China's economy is or to see how big it is relative to other economies of the world. The question is not what constitutes the standard of living of the typical Chinese person, which PPP does a good job of answering; rather, it is to try to determine how big and independent the Chinese economy is and how much it depends on United States and Europe. From this perspective, PPP is the wrong way to go. The correct measure of China's economy, when considering its influence on America and America's influence on it, is the $1.6 trillion number that is determined by utilizing current exchange rates. Americans don't care about the standard of living in China or what a typical Chinese can purchase, Americans care about the power of the Chinese economy to move markets, to help the U.S. economy, and Americans live in dollars, real dollars, not purchasing power parity dollars in China.

What is apparent is that the Chinese economy, while rapidly growing and successful, is still relatively quite small compared to the $14 trillion economy in the United States and the $16 trillion economy of a unified Europe. In other words, it's hard to argue that such a small economy could be completely independent of the larger world economies and this is proven by the fact that almost half of China's GDP is created by exporters who export products to the United States and Europe. If Europe and the United States economy suffer, you can be sure these exporters will suffer. China has developed rapidly not because Chinese companies produce wonderful goods that they trade in exchange for goods manufactured in the United States, but rather because so many European and United States companies have relocated their factories there. Most of the manufacturing done in the world is now done in China. Most of the trade coming out of China is intra-company, as if IBM manufacturing is in China and IBM corporate, the importer, is in Armonk, New York.

Not only will the Chinese exporters suffer tremendously as the United States and Europe face a significant downturn, the rest of the Chinese economy will also suffer. These manufacturing and export jobs in China are some of the better and higher paying jobs in China and the people who hold these jobs employ many other people in China to make products for them and provide them services. If manufacturing slows in China because of less demand from United States and Europe, you can be sure those people laid off from the manufacturing facility in China will be consuming fewer Chinese goods and services.

> *Not only will the Chinese exporters suffer tremendously as the United States and Europe face a significant downturn, the rest of the Chinese economy will also suffer.*

The fourth method of spreading the contagion is through currency movements. Predicting currency markets is a relative business. As we have seen, some countries' currencies are depreciating even faster than the U.S. dollar, making it appear that the dollar is strengthening relative to them. The Mexico peso is a good example. While the dollar and the U.S. economy are very weak, the Mexican economy and peso are even worse off. Oil prices are headed down, which is not good for an oil producing economy like Mexico, tourism is way down with narco-terrorism up, exports to the U.S. are off the repatriation of dollars from Mexican-Americans to their homeland has slowed tremendously as unemployment in America has hit industries hiring immigrants, such as construction and remodeling, the hardest.

There are four ways in which the problems in the United States can contagiously spread internationally. First, many foreign countries and their commercial banks will face direct losses as a result of their holdings of U.S. mortgages and mortgage-backed securities. Second, you can expect housing prices to decline rapidly in those countries that experienced unsustainable housing price booms. Third, exporting countries to the United States and Europe will see their economies decline as consumer demand declines in the United States and in Europe. And finally, currency movements will amplify losses in countries that they themselves will be threatened by the crisis. Not only will companies and banks come under pressure, but entire countries will be threatened with bankruptcy and their currency declines will amplify the negative returns experienced by foreign investors.

Much of this process has already begun, and in the spirit of this book, readers should be warned that the worst is yet to come. Housing prices in the United Kingdom and Ireland have just begun a decline that could easily match some of the worst cities in the U.S. experience. Although global banks continued to report losses from U.S. mortgages, the inflationary impact of their central banks giving them newly printed currencies are just now being felt in their economies. And even though China's stock market has seen a trade-off of 60 percent at the end of 2008, it is uncertain that the worst is over for those countries that are large exporters to the United States and Europe.

Chapter 9

Too Big to Fail— The $400 Trillion Derivatives Market

The crazy aunt in the attic that nobody is discussing is the $400 trillion derivatives market. It is the primary reason that mortgage losses in United States cannot be contained (some say it has grown in excess of $600 trillion) to just the commercial banks and investment banks that held the mortgages or mortgage-backed securities. In an enormous spider web of interconnecting financial contractual relationships, the derivatives market, especially the credit default swap (CDS), market ensures that substantial losses to any large financial player will be felt by all in the global financial system. Rather than diversifying us, the derivatives market amplifies it and transmits it globally to all regions and countries of the world. The derivatives market is the reason why the U.S. government deems many firms too big to fail, even those that appear to be rather small and inconsequential players in the global financial markets. The reason is that their derivatives' exposure prevents the government from containing the effects of their bankruptcy on the world markets as a whole.

It would take a book much longer than this one to fully describe the derivatives market. Whatever brief descriptive comments I make here will be considered simplistic by those who make a living in the derivatives market, and enormously confusing to laypeople who seek a better understanding of this very complex financial market. Having said that, here goes.

A derivative is a financial contract, typically between two parties. It derives its value from another unrelated financial security or asset. For example, a stock option is a derivative security because its valuation is dependent on the company's underlying common stock value.

Most derivatives today are not really securities in the sense that you think of options or futures. Rather, they are just simple contracts between two parties who agree to enter into a financial arrangement based on some underlying security or asset value. When the derivatives market was just starting off, the securities were fairly straightforward and fairly harmless. If I were a company that borrowed money for 30 years on a fixed-rate basis and you were a company that borrowed money for 30 years on a floating-rate basis there might be agreement in a contract between us that I pay your floating rate of interest and you pay my fixed rate. This is a simple interest rate swap. Or, you might borrow money in Euros and I might borrow money in U.S. dollars and yet we might enter into an agreement where I'd take over your repayment in Euros and you take over my repayment of dollars, known as a currency swap. Interest-rate swaps and currency swaps are fairly straightforward transactions and make up a large percentage of the total $400 trillion derivatives market. Four hundred trillion dollars is simply a notional amount because it refers to the total size of the contract to which interest rates or currency exchange rates are applied. The exposure in total is nowhere near $400 trillion, an enormous number, but rather just the difference in either the fixed versus floating rates on that number or how much the Euro and U.S. dollar currency rates change based on that number. If the entire $400 trillion derivatives market solely consisted of interest rate swaps and currency swaps, the real money at risk in the contracts is probably not more than $2 trillion in total.

But this is not the case. As part of a $400 trillion derivatives market there is now a $65 trillion credit default swap market. These credit default swaps have a much larger percentage of the total notional amount at risk than a simple interest rate or currency swap. You should be much more concerned about the volatility of $65 trillion of credit default swaps than you would be about either $65 trillion of interest-rate swaps or $65 trillion of currency swaps as they result in much larger payoff relative to the full notional amounts.

A credit default swap, or a CDS, is a simple contract in which you make a payment to me each year, say $100,000 per year and I agree to pay you $10 million if a particular company has a credit event and enters bankruptcy. So, if you held $10 million of a risky debt security in a troubled company like AIG, and you wanted insurance in case AIG went bankrupt, you could pay me a market-determined premium, let's say $100,000 per year, and I would pay you $10 million if AIG went bankrupt. You have completely hedged the risk of bankruptcy for AIG. You may lose $10 million on your AIG note, but due to your credit default swap with me, I will make you whole by paying you $10 million.

Credit default swaps, when properly utilized, allow holders of risky securities to diversify their risk to other parties in exchange for cash payments. Because this is a hedging device, and an insurance product, it would seem to have value to many participants in the financial markets, and judging by the rapid growth of the credit default swap market this appears to be the case.

But, the devil is in the details. Theoretically, if this is how all credit default swaps worked, no one would be the poorer. But there are serious problems in the credit default swap market. Essentially, the credit default swap market has created a completely unregulated insurance market. Pretty much anyone, including small hedge funds, can act as an insurance provider and guarantee that others will not lose money on their risky investments. But the normal insurance business is a heavily regulated one, especially at the state level. There is a good reason for this. In the insurance game, individuals and companies pay premiums each year to make sure they are protected from high-cost, but low-risk events, which happened once in a long time.

The only thing worse than paying premiums and never experiencing a reimbursable loss is to pay premiums to a company that cannot afford to reimburse you for your loss. In fact, you could end up paying premiums for years on end and then when you go to make your claim find out the counterparty is either not substantial enough to make payments to all claimants, has been poorly managed or fraudulently managed, or has gone out of business themselves, possibly for the same event type risk that you were trying to insure against. This is why the insurance business is regulated. Regulation is to ensure that all insurance providers are adequately capitalized given the risks of their insurance portfolios, that they have adequate sources of financing even in tough times and it may remain a going concern for the foreseeable future. Without regulation, anybody, including you and me, could hire two associates, get a phone and an Internet connection, and start selling insurance knowing full well that we wouldn't be in business long enough to ever pay off any clients. It wouldn't really be an insurance business, it would be an insurance premium collection business never intended to make any cash payments to policyholders, knowing from the start that there was not enough capital to do so.

Because the credit default swap market is almost completely unregulated, this crisis is exactly what has resulted. Small hedge funds can write credit default swaps to provide insurance to others, and can do it in such large volume that it is unlikely the small hedge fund would ever be able to pay in case of a default. It is not coincidence that company defaults on their corporate bonds occur exactly at the same time that financing alternatives evaporate for hedge funds and other financial players. Liquidity tightens for everybody at the same time during rough times.

Consider this example. Imagine if you ran a hedge fund with $100 million of assets. Suppose you go out and write credit default swap contracts in a size such that you guarantee $2 billion of Lehman Brothers debt. In the marketplace, you may receive premiums equal to $20 million per year for taking on this risk. This represents a 20 percent return each year on your $100 million of assets, and you haven't done anything. As a matter of fact, you agreed to take on a risk that you can't possibly responsibly ever pay off. If Lehman Brothers goes bankrupt, as it eventually did, you would owe your credit default swap partners $2 billion, but I already said that you only have $100 million of assets. This is not completely a theoretical example, as currently a large Swiss bank is suing a $100 million hedge fund for writing $1.2 billion in credit default swaps.

Even large companies like AIG can get in trouble with credit default swaps. Supposedly, AIG wrote insurance on approximately $440 billion of credit default swaps. Because AIG is a traditional insurance company, the country's largest, you can assume that they were in the risk-taking insurance-providing side of most of these credit default swaps. They were basically collecting premiums to guarantee against defaults by major companies around the world. It is not a coincidence that AIG got into serious trouble in the financial markets the same weekend that Lehman announced its bankruptcy. If Lehman was one of the companies that AIG was guaranteeing wouldn't go bankrupt, they would have enormous cash liabilities once Lehman claimed bankruptcy. If Lehman was 2 percent of their total $440 billion credit default swap portfolio, AIG on the Monday morning after Lehman's bankruptcy announcement would owe $9 billion to its credit default swaps, more than AIG makes in an entire year, and this is just one bankruptcy.

So why would AIG get into this business? The same reason the small hedge funds got into it, for the profits. If AIG were earning an average $200,000 premium on each $10 million on its $440 billion credit default swap portfolio, then this translates into $8.8 billion of cash profits each year to AIG. This amount completely dominates AIG's total reported profits as a company for the year.

But AIG was not the largest player in the credit default swap market. Why didn't bigger players like J.P. Morgan get in trouble in the credit default swap market? The analogy I like to use is a sports bookie and how he manages risks at a big hotel in Las Vegas. A sports bookie in Las Vegas puts out a line and takes bets on either the Giants or the Bengals in a pro football game. But, he keeps his order book balanced. If too many bets come in on the Giants he adjusts his line accordingly to make betting on the Bengals more attractive. If he does his job well, at the end of the day, before the game even starts, he is completely hedged and loses no money regardless of which team wins the game because his order book is balanced. His profit is perfectly hedged equal to the vig he charges, typically equal to 10 percent of all losses.

Not that J.P. Morgan would like this comparison, but in my example J.P. Morgan is the Las Vegas sports bookie. They most likely did a much better job of balancing their credit default swap exposure. Not only were they diversified over a broad range of names, they didn't just play one side of the transaction like AIG. For some of their deals they acted as the insurance provider and for others they purchased insurance to minimize their firm's risk exposure.

Hedge funds are perfectly situated to benefit most from an unregulated insurance market like the credit default swap market. This is because hedge funds themselves are completely unregulated, there is little transparency, and there are no requirements that firms providing credit default swap insurance be adequately capitalized. In addition, there is no central clearing of derivative transactions and few collateral requirements. What a perfect combination, an unregulated market like derivatives in which the major players are unregulated and nontransparent hedge funds with no collateral requirements.

> *Hedge funds are perfectly situated to benefit most from an unregulated insurance market like the credit default swap market.*

Hedge funds are secretive and go out of their way to stay out of the public light. Given their lack of financial reporting, this makes it difficult with any degree of certainty to say exactly how many are playing this credit default swap game and how much of their profits are due to it. But just because market participants like hedge funds are secretive and nonreporting does not mean that I cannot speculate as to what is going on in the darkest corridors of the world of finance. It would be wrong not to speculate because the evidence is mounting that something is terribly wrong with both the derivatives market and with how hedge funds are regulated. Because of this speculation, Congress may eventually decide to properly regulate hedge funds and shine a bright light of transparency on their operations. There is some evidence from the marketplace that suggests that the credit default swap market is not operating as originally planned and that hedge funds may be operating by a completely different set of rules than you and me.

One clue that came up during the Bear Stearns bankruptcy was that even though Bear Stearns only had $190 billion of external debt, there was close to $2 trillion of credit default swaps written to guarantee it. It is hard to imagine why you would need more than $190 billion of credit default swaps to guarantee the entire amount of Bear Stearns debt outstanding. It looks like there is an enormous amount of naked speculation occurring in the credit default swap market that has nothing to do with hedging debt holders' exposure to Bear Stearns default risk.

Some other clues that all is not right in hedge fund land: hedge funds, over the years, have done much better than the market in general, even after allowing for their rather exorbitant fees and profit sharing. This of course violates the first rule of modern finance and efficient market theory that says that no one party, much less an entire industry, should be able to beat the market consistently. The fact that the same hedge funds appear in the upper quartile of performance year in and year out is further evidence that something is wrong. This is another violation of efficient market theory. According to efficient market theory, it cannot be that one or two firms continually outperform the market place, even when the industry as a whole returns market rates of return.

Another piece of evidence suggests that the majority of hedge funds are not performing this miracle of extraordinary performance through savvy stock picking or just being smarter than the average Joe. There are now computer index funds that are able to replicate the average hedge fund returns each year. These index funds do no human-influenced stock picking nor communicate with anyone about research ideas or undervalued assets. They simply hold the percentage of cash, debt, and a short or long position in the equity markets and they are able to replicate the returns of the hedge fund industry quite well. This says that the majority of the hedge fund industry's returns are not alpha extraordinary returns due to human brilliance of its managers, but rather simple beta returns that are nothing more than an asset allocation that returns the markets risk and return.

So if hedge funds are returning better-than-average returns each year, how do they do it? Well to the extent that they are just manipulating beta returns, in essence, what they are doing is just holding riskier assets and riskier portfolios; in other words, more concentrated and leveraged ownership than a well-diversified portfolio. Other things might be going on however. The fact that many of hedge funds do much better in good times and so much worse in bad times suggests that they are utilizing debt leverage in their capital structure. Leverage exaggerates returns during good years, but hampers returns during bad times.

Although I have no specific evidence of this because it is impossible to get inside a hedge fund and they refuse to open their financial reporting, there are other ways to generate consistent excess returns, especially in an unregulated market with a company not subject to any financial supervision or reporting. The two most obvious methods are market manipulation and insider trading. Both methods are as old as Joe Kennedy Sr., who was expert at both before the Securities and Exchange Commission (SEC) outlawed them and made him its first commissioner in order to crack down on these market irregularities. President Franklin Roosevelt said at the time, sometimes it takes a thief to catch a thief. Hedge funds are perfectly positioned to do both because in addition to being unregulated and nonreporting, they deal in information, they communicate with each other constantly and with the investment banks that are doing the major merger deals on Wall Street, and many of them focus in one narrow industry or a few select stock names so that a small hedge fund can be a large percentage of the average daily trading volume in a stock. This requirement is primed for market manipulation. You only have to be familiar with the penny stock exchange in Denver to see how someone who represents a substantial percentage of the daily trading volume in a particular stock can decide for themselves whether the stock goes up or down and which of its customers will receive profits and losses. Corporations have complained about hedge funds attacking their stocks, but to date there has been little investigation of either potential market manipulation or insider trading by the hedge funds.

But there is a legal way for hedge funds to report unusual profits. Just like collecting insurance premiums in the credit default swap market, hedge funds can offer all sorts of insurance for unlikely events in the future. All asset classes have probability distributions associated with the returns. On average, even risky assets do well in most years until there is a one off event that causes a significant decline in the value of the asset. Fannie Mae and Freddie Mac paid the interest on their debt every year and yet even with their implied government guarantees always needed to pay a 30- to 50 basis-point premium for borrowing money. There was always a small risk that Fannie Mae and Freddie Mac would get into trouble and the U.S. government would walk away from its implied guarantee, something that turned out not to be the case once Fannie Mae and Freddie Mac were nationalized.

So, if you are a small hedge fund and you want to make money all you have to do is short or sell these long-tail, low-probability, high-cost events. Long-tail events are those events that rarely occur, once in a blue moon, so to speak, but when they do they can have devastating consequences for all.

Someone will pay you to guarantee that Lehman Brothers will not go bankrupt.

Someone will pay you to guarantee that the U.S. government won't go bankrupt.

Someone will pay you to guarantee that Argentina won't go bankrupt.

Someone will probably pay you to guarantee that interest rates will not see 15 percent next year or that oil will not trade above $200 a barrel.

In each case, you can legally collect all sorts of premiums on the insurance you're providing, although in most cases you never have to make a payout. And, in the unlikely event that a long-tail probability event occurs, oil does go to $200 and you do owe billions of dollars in payment to your counterparties, you simply fold up shop and leave. Most hedge funds consist of five guys and a couple of computers, so it's easy to pack up the shop and head to the airport. Most of the assets of a typical hedge fund fit in the elevator each evening as they head home to see their hedge fund wives.

The original reason that hedge fund managers argued that they should be unregulated and not subject to SEC reporting requirements was that they'd only deal with sophisticated investors, those investors with substantial financial assets and financial savvy to clearly understand what they were getting into and the risks associated with the type investments hedge funds were likely to make. But, in retrospect, this test is not enough. For once you allow unregulated nonreporting entities enter into a functioning capital market they can do great damage to the functioning of that market if they indeed end up pursuing insider trading or market manipulation techniques or enter into contracts they can't possibly honor. It is not their sophisticated investors that suffer, it is all investors—specifically those counterparties who happened to end up trading with them. You would not want to buy a stock from a hedge fund if you knew that the hedge fund was trading on insider information and already knew the results of an earnings release for the company that wasn't due out until tomorrow.

But it isn't just the direct counterparties that suffer from illegal activity in unregulated hedge funds, the entire market suffers. Because no one knows exactly whom they are trading with in a sophisticated capital market, you just draw general conclusions over time that something doesn't feel right. Call-option contracts have a way of increasing in value the night before mergers are announced and put-options have a way of growing in value just before companies publicly announce depressed earnings. You can't point your finger at any one hedge fund or market participant, but you know there is something fundamentally wrong and unfair in the market. They say if you sit at poker table for more than five minutes and can't figure out who the sucker is, it's you. Similarly, why would it make sense for you to trade securities in the market place if other participants have unfair and illegal advantages? It doesn't, so you won't. You end up holding your assets out of markets like this. Markets such as this are rigged. They

But it isn't just the direct counterparties that suffer from illegal activity in unregulated hedge funds, the entire market suffers.

are nothing new. They exist all over the world in every small podunk developing country in the world. But it is sad, if such activities are condoned in the United States simply because hedge funds are the largest financial contributor to elected representatives in Congress and a future president's reelection campaign.

It is also argued that the derivatives market, and specifically the credit default swaps market, needs no regulation. The reasoning here is that it is simply a compilation of a number of contractual relationships between two unrelated parties. It's just a bunch of contracts floating out there, each one between two separate parties.

An analogy will help you see the fallacy of this argument. The airline route chart or map for the United States that shows all available daily flights across the continent is a similar network of two-party transactions. No airplane travels between more than two cities at one time. There is always a departing city and arriving city. And yet, the resulting network of airline flights is enormously complex and tremendously interdependent. You can't leave on your flight from Chicago to Houston unless the plane arrives on time from Dallas. If too many planes arrive at the same hub at the same time delays result. So, here is an example of a compilation of simple two-party transactions that are so voluminous and so interdependent and so complex that they result in a network or spider web of interconnectivity that absolutely needs to be regulated. Could you imagine getting on an airplane if there was no ground control or air control? Do you think the planes would run on time without regulation?

This simple analogy also helps us understand counterparty risk better in the credit default swaps business. Counterparty risk in the derivatives business is the risk that the person or company that you have contractually agreed with on a derivative contract disappears or bankrupts itself before the end of the contract. Imagine what would happen if AIG with its $440 billion of separate two-party derivative credit default swap contracts was suddenly allowed to go bankrupt and not honor these derivative contracts. The analogy in the airline business is to understand what happens when a major node of that network fails. I have seen what happens when Chicago's airport is shut down due to snow in bad weather. Of course, it doesn't just impact flights into Chicago, it impacts the entire network. Shortly after delay postings begin to appear in the Chicago airport, they begin to appear nationwide in San Francisco and Atlanta and Dallas and elsewhere. This is the definition of a network and interconnectivity. Similarly, if AIG were allowed to drop out as a major node in the credit default swap derivatives network, there is no telling what the impact will be to the entire network. Certainly its direct counterparties will feel the loss, but because they will have unexplained and unexpected losses themselves, there is no guarantee that they won't further impact other trading partners.

This is the reason why the U.S. government stepped in and bailed out Bear Stearns, AIG, and Fannie Mae and Freddie Mac. They were not too big to fail, especially with the government backing of the implied guarantee behind Fannie Mae and Freddie Mac's debt. But, they were all major nodes in the credit default swap derivatives market and their bankruptcy, and their refusal to honor counterparty transactions in the derivatives market would be exactly analogous to Chicago airport snowing in again—not for one hour but forever.

The derivatives market and specifically the credit default swap markets that were created to diversify risk and make the mortgage function better, ends up causing risk to increase during those periods of uncertainty when you most want to control it. Because of the potential failure of substantial counterparties, the derivatives market and the credit default swaps market are allusions of risk diversification. The government must step in and guarantee the survival of all major counterparties and because of their importance as nodes in the overall network, the creation and functioning of the credit default swaps derivative market is nothing more than socialism. As people have described, the largest financial institutions have been turned into for-profit risk-taking enterprises when times are good and experiments in socialism and government guarantees and moral hazard when times are bad. Because of the interconnectivity of the credit default swaps derivative market, all of these large financial institutions have an implied guarantee from the U.S. taxpayer because they are too big to fail. So, an entrepreneurial invention like the derivatives market ended up socializing the American capitalist. I will discuss in Chapter 15 the reforms necessary to return America to its rich capitalist foundation in which companies are motivated to make profits, but allows companies who mistakenly err and lose money are allowed by the system to go bankrupt.

Chapter 10

Local Governments
Feel the Pinch

R eflective of the title I have chosen for this book and of some of the evidence presented in the previous chapters is that what began as a simple decline in housing prices is going to have repercussions and ramifications far from the world of real estate. It's probably not surprising that such a significant decline in Americans' total well-being could have a serious impact on the United States and the global economy. But now I'm going to discuss just how far reaching the impact of the housing price decline reaches.

I think it will come as a surprise to many of you if I told you that one of the primary losers in this real estate decline are the state and local governments around the country. And the means and mechanisms by which they will suffer from the housing crash are not intuitively obvious.

I think it will come as a surprise to many of you if I told you one of the primary losers in this real estate decline are the state and local governments around the country.

First, the last place you would expect to see an impact from a decline in credit quality of 30-year mortgages is with money market instruments that are short-term in nature. And yet many myths of values across the country reported short-falls in their cash accounts that they had invested in short-term instruments.

The most egregious examples are known as auction rate securities. This example was another invention of Wall Street to supposedly garner greater returns for money market investors, but in actuality they merely generated excess fees for investment banks and commercial banks.

The idea behind auction rate securities is to take your illiquid long-term corporate bonds and mortgage-backed securities and package them into a pool and sell them to investors looking for safe liquid short-term returns. If it can be done, it is a windfall because typically longer-term debt securities yield much more than short-term liquid securities. The reason is simple: they tie up your funds for longer; they have less liquidity; and they face much greater bankruptcy risk over the period in short-term money market instruments such as treasury bills.

The investment banks knew they had to provide liquidity to this pool of illiquid long-term securities. The idea they came up with was to guarantee that there would always be a bidder for any redemptions, thus assuring liquidity in the pool. As the bidder of last resort, the investment bank told their money market investing clients that if no one showed up to bid at the monthly auction, the investment banks would make the investors whole.

Municipal and state governments do not have the same reporting requirements as publicly traded commercial banks and investment banks, so there is still no idea of how badly hurt are these local governments by the housing crisis and the mortgage banking meltdown. But, a number of local governments have reported being taken by auction rate notes. It turns out that a number of auction rate notes pools included mortgage-backed bonds in their mix. By July 2008, when it was time to demonstrate the liquidity of these auction rate notes, auctions were held and no bidders showed up. Rather than honoring their commitment to redeem the money in these auction rate pools, the investment banks reneged on their promise and ended up freezing the accounts. It took Andrew Cuomo and a number of states attorney generals to threaten the investment banks to get them to agree that they had used manipulative and illegal selling practices in pushing auction rate notes on the municipalities and other short-term investors, that they had lied when they said the investments were as good as money market instruments or cash. As part of the agreement with the states the investment banks and commercial bank issuer's agreed to refund the investors money.

So, here is a completely unintended consequence of the contagion. Who would've guessed that the housing price decline in California and Florida and across the nation could impact the investment portfolio of municipalities across the country, and specifically, whoever would have thought that it would be their short-term cash investments that would be impacted. It makes no sense. But isn't that the nature of this entire episode?

Because municipalities have not reported yet for the 2008 fiscal year, their total losses due to the mortgage crisis are unknown. It appears that most of their auction rate note problems will be refunded by the issuers, but they will probably lose some monies in legal fees and court costs. These local governments have also not reported on their other losses and mortgage-backed securities. Of course, some municipalities across the country, like Birmingham, Alabama, have been forced to make public statements because they are bankrupt and don't have the cash to run their operations. But the vast majority of the problems resulting from investment in mortgage-backed securities won't show up until 2009 when these local governments begin to formally report.

Although the direct loss of value in their investment portfolio due to declined values in mortgage-backed securities and auction rate notes is the most direct and immediate of the housing crisis impact on the books of state and local governments, it by far will not be the largest impact. The most significant impact on local governments will be that one of their primary sources of revenue, property taxes, will take a large and direct hit as appraised values on property are readjusted downward. This adjustment will have far-reaching impacts for everyone because property taxes fund the majority of educational budgets across the country. School districts are already under budgetary pressures, and this is happening as property taxes have exploded across the country. It is hard to imagine how they will adjust to declining property values and lower property tax revenue.

In 2008, in an attempt to avoid a budgetary crisis, many municipalities sent out word that their property appraisals going forward would on average increase only 5 percent to 7 percent as opposed to the double-digit increases people had seen in earlier years. This news was not received warmly. Everybody who could pick up a newspaper or read a for-sale sign in front of a house on their street knew that property values were down, not up. There have been property tax revolts in states like California and Arizona, but expect many more as appraisals do not adjust downward quickly enough to reflect declining property values.

Although the public school system in the United States has deteriorated over the past three decades, the spending per student has increased dramatically as home appraisals have exploded and property taxes have kept track. But the local governments and the school boards have done a poor job of spending the windfall in property taxes they received. Teacher salaries did not appreciate relative to inflation, the school district did a poor job of attracting young people into the profession, insisting on onerous and unnecessary education degrees, and worst of all, overhead increased dramatically. In most school districts, teachers complain that there are more than 25 students for each teacher in each class. But what they have failed to mention is that there are huge numbers of support personnel from administrators to coaches to assistants to special ed teachers to guidance counselors to school psychiatrists that never see the inside of a typical classroom. The ratio of students to teachers in many schools is greater than 25 to one, but the ratio of children to adults, including all overhead personnel, is usually more like five or seven to one. Local governments have dramatically increased the schools' budget and overhead but have done little to improve the students' in-classroom experience and to pay and motivate the best teachers.

How will this system survive the cuts in its budget? It's not likely that the administration types who manage school budgets are going to fire themselves first. Typically what they will do is reduce teacher salaries and reduce the number of teachers and then complain to parents and the community that they do not have adequate resources to effectively run the school. This is an old trick. It really is a form of extortion. Whenever a community has a decline in local taxes the first thing they do is cut services that the public desperately needs. When the department of motor vehicles (DMV), is forced into a budget cutback do they fire any of the hundreds of people employed in the back office? No, they cut back the number of service employees working with customers at the window from 10 to 7, thus guaranteeing long waits at DMV. In effect government is saying don't you dare threaten to reduce our budget or we'll hurt you.

So as this contagion spreads, declining home prices impact property taxes, which hurt the budgets of the public school system. I don't think it's too far a stretch to say that the education system is critically important to this country's ability to compete in the global economy. One of the reasons that wages have stagnated in the United States is that workers have been put in competition with low-paid workers around the world. Only through education will American workers be able to acquire the high-skill, high-paying jobs in the global economy. Isn't it ironic that something as crazy as a housing price decline might end up not only harming the education system but the competitiveness of the entire country in the global economy? Here's a beautiful example of how contagious this financial epidemic.

Many cities in California and Florida are facing home price declines of 50 percent or more. It is doubtful that the communities will allow property tax appraisal declines of 50 percent. The way property tax appraisals work in most cities is that they are consciously and purposely set at a level below the true market value of a home so the city does not have to get into many unproductive disputes with the homeowners. Any shortfall in funding is then adjusted by just increasing the property tax assessment itself.

In a declining home price environment this is more difficult to do. People will see their home prices at levels lower than the appraised value of their home for property tax purposes. In a recessionary environment in which homeowners are having difficulty paying their mortgage and their home heating bills each month it is hard to imagine that they would be supportive of increasing the property tax rates in their communities. And some wealthier communities in California have property taxes on homes that are as much as $5,000 to $6,000 a year, not an inconsequential amount. It's easy to remember a time in the not too distant past when $5,000 a year would rent a fairly nice home in a good neighborhood, now it just goes to pay property taxes.

The revenue decline at local governments due to the decline in property appraisals is a serious problem. An even larger immediate problem state and local governments face, exacerbated by the housing price decline, is the dramatic increase in their retiree expenses. Although private sector workers in the past 20 years have been moved from defined benefit pension plans to defined contribution plans, most government workers have retained their defined benefit plans. The percentage of workers in the private sector that have defined benefit plans has been reduced from 60 percent to 10 percent. This means that regardless of what happens to the investment performance of the stock portfolios of local governments they still have to meet a defined benefit for the retirees that is assumed to grow with general inflation.

Public sector workers have done much better in America than the typical private enterprise worker. Because they have been much less subject to the pressures on workers from globalization, public sector workers have done a much better job of protecting their unions, their wages, and their benefits. Public sector employees are much less likely to see their jobs shipped overseas or for their employers to be so highly motivated toward cash savings that they outsource a significant percentage of their jobs. Private sector unions declined from 35 percent of American workers in the 1950s to just under 9 percent today, government workers have seen their union membership maintained at approximately 40 percent membership.

The average American working in the private sector today earns $26.09 an hour, including all benefits. The average government employee in America earns close to $39.50 an hour in total compensation including benefits. This is not to suggest that government workers are overpaid or that they do not deserve the wages they are making. But it is clear that they have done a much better job preserving their earnings capacity relative to the private sector worker. It is disconcerting that the public servants are making more per hour than the master they supposedly serve, the American worker (Talbott 2008).

Many local governments are going to have serious problems over the next two decades. They have promised their employees generous retirement, health care, and pension benefits that are going to be an enormous difficulty to fund. Because of the generous terms of their retirement packages, many teachers, fire fighters, police officers, and municipal workers can retire as early as age 40 with 20 years of service and guarantee half their salary in pension for life. In addition, all of their medical expenses are guaranteed for life.

Even before the current housing and economic crisis, many municipal employees were taking advantage of the generous retirement terms and retiring early. Many retired from their government jobs in their 40s or 50s and took second careers to supplement their incomes. But the current crisis makes the problem even worse. Again, I can argue that because their stock investments and home values have declined they may choose to work longer rather than retire early. But many will find they can maximize their income by retiring from their government jobs and seeking employment in the private sector. In essence, they garner an attractive government pension and whatever wages they might earn in the private sector.

This could not occur at a worse time for local governments around the country. Just as Social Security and Medicare face increasing deficits as they try to fund Americans retiring and living longer with larger health expenditures, local governments will face the same problem. But for them, the problem is amplified because their workers will work fewer years, retiring at younger ages, and end up living much longer lives. The math simply doesn't work. No individual can work from the ages of 20 to 40 and then expect an employer to pay half his salary and all his medical costs if he plans on living to 100.

Of course local governments are not run as for-profit businesses. Their only source of revenue is the taxes they assign to their citizenry. In the past, if they ran shortfalls due to rising expenses, they simply tax their citizens more. This won't necessarily work in the future. The reason is that state and local taxes are at an all-time high today. As a matter of fact, state and local taxes together including state and local income taxes, sales taxes and property taxes, combined, are larger than all federal taxes combined, both federal income taxes and Social Security and Medicare taxes. Think of that. This is a world where income taxes had been equaled in magnitude by Social Security and Medicare taxes and now you have to add them together to reach the magnitude of the local taxes that you pay.

There has to be a limit to how much local tax people will pay. As retirement expenses explode for these local governments they will find it increasingly more difficult to pass these higher expenses onto their citizens. The fact that local taxes already equal all federal taxes and that they are at an all-time high does not bode well for these local governments' retirement expenses, which are due to explode soon. Property taxes will decline as property appraisals head down due to housing price declines. Similarly, sales tax revenues and local income tax revenues will also decline as the recession hits middle America. Revenues will be declining, expenses will be rapidly escalating, and there will be a limit as to how high a tax the typical American can pay. Already, many Americans are moving from high tax-rate states to low tax-rate states such as Nevada. If this becomes an exodus the retirees of the exiting state will have real difficulties as local bankruptcies are not out of the question.

Local governments have a problem similar to large automobile companies. It got to the point with GM, Ford, and Chrysler that no matter how many cutbacks they made in production and hiring, their cash shortfalls only got worse. The reason is that most of their cash was going to their retirees. As they shrunk the size of their companies to try to find more profitable niches the smaller worker base was not able to fund the huge amount of retiree costs.

Similarly, it will be difficult for local governments to cut back expenses to remove themselves from this cash crisis. The reason is that so much of their expenses will be retiree costs. Already, a small town outside of San Diego is seeing 75 percent of its total budget going to retiree costs. These types of intractable problems are what cause local government bankruptcies. In bankruptcy, a local government may renegotiate its commitment to its retirees. Short of bankruptcy, there is little that it can do with this dramatic increase in its expenses.

Local governments are essential to the proper functioning of an economy. In addition to the invaluable resource of education, they are responsible for a great deal of the infrastructure in a community without which it would be difficult to pursue commerce. As local governments cut back on services provided to their citizens in an attempt to balance their budgets, local economies will suffer.

In Chapter 13, I talk about how this current crisis is impacting various investment alternatives. Based on this chapter, you should probably avoid making investments in local governments and municipalities. If you haven't been scared off of municipal investments yet, let me also say that most municipal bonds are guaranteed by third-party monoline insurance companies, many of which will be claiming bankruptcy themselves because their other business is guaranteeing mortgage-backed securities. Finally, many of these municipalities and local governments have lost their underwriters as the investment banks who previously served that role have themselves gone bankrupt. It is not a pretty picture, but it is demonstrative of how far-reaching this contagion can reach into this society.

Chapter 11

From Wall Street
to Main Street

A crisis that began with housing has now spread to Wall Street and caused the global financial system to encounter great stress and put many of the largest and strongest financial institutions under the threat of bankruptcy. To demonstrate the power of this contagion, Wall Street's problems will now reflect back and cause serious consequences on Main Street.

I thought it was well understood how a freezing of the lending markets and losses at this country's largest commercial banks and investment banks could harm this economy and the welfare of Main Street. I assume Treasury Secretary Hank Paulson also thought it was well understood because he did not have a good answer prepared for Congress when he was asked in the bailout hearings why Main Street should even care about bailing out Wall Street. At the risk of being overly simplistic, let's examine the direct and secondary links surrounding Wall Street's well-being, the general economy of the country, and the well-being of average citizens on Main Street.

The most direct impact on financial institutions that suffer such large losses as they have in the mortgage and mortgage-backed securities area is that they will pull back on their lending to all sectors of the economy. You might argue that you are not currently in the market for a bank loan so such a pullback does not directly impact you, but you would be mistaken.

Consider homeowners who are comfortable in their houses and are not currently looking or seeking to move. They have no need for mortgage financing. They're happy in their existing home and plan to live there for decades. The value of their property can be directly impacted by the lack of mortgage financing coming from the commercial banks and Wall Street. As mortgage financing dries up, or as rates increase for what are considered riskier mortgages, values of homes come down. Few buyers today buy homes for cash. Almost all buyers depend on mortgage financing. If there is no mortgage financing there are no new buyers. Even if you don't intend to move in the near future, the market value of your house will decline if mortgage financing dries up for potential buyers. This should be important to you once you realize that many people each year are forced to sell their homes because of unusual circumstances. Medical emergencies, divorces, and loss of jobs leave many homeowners forced to sell their homes at unexpected times. At such times, if there is little mortgage financing available and home prices are down significantly, you may be in the uncomfortable position of being underwater on your mortgage. You may well owe more on your mortgage than your home is worth. Because potential buyers will not be able to find adequate mortgage money from the banks and Wall Street you may end up losing a substantial portion of your home's equity or possibly even default on your mortgage.

But it isn't just mortgage loans that will dry up. Banks will pull back on all consumer lending. They have already begun to pull back on credit card lending. Banks are finding all new reasons to increase fees and interest rates on credit card balances and many people are facing annual interest rates of more than 30 percent per year on their unpaid balances. There are many families that have multiple credit cards and have total balances exceeding $10,000. Although the housing market was booming, people used their homes like ATMs to make additional purchases of assets and also to pay down their credit card and other personal debt. Now that that game is over, credit card debt is exploding, even at much higher rates. Because much of credit card debt is securitized, just like mortgages were, and the buyers are highly dependent on suspect ratings from the rating agencies, this market has also begun to freeze up. The total outstanding amount of all credit cards in the United States is less than $2 trillion and pales in comparison to the $12 trillion mortgage market. But, if the banks decide to start pulling credit on credit cards and demanding repayment in full, families will have no place to turn.

Another unsuspecting victim of the housing and mortgage collapse is the student loan industry. Privatized under Ronald Reagan, commercial banks make the vast majority of loans to students to allow them to attend college. But, like mortgages and credit cards, much of this bank debt is packaged, securitized, and sold upstream to long-term investors. This securitization process is under great pressure and many student loans are not being made. There are countless stories of first-year university students who are being turned away at the door because their student loans never came through.

Talk about a major economic impact. The primary reason that America is not more competitive in the global competitive marketplace is that the education system has labeled workers as not as well-educated as other advanced countries.

Another unsuspecting victim of the housing and mortgage collapse is the student loan industry.

Everyone agrees that the key to increasing the competitiveness of Americans in the global economy is to encourage enhanced education. This credit crisis is having the opposite effect. Instead of student loan programs expanding, they are retracting and many capable students are not finding the money they need to attend college.

The automobile industry, the largest manufacturing industry in the United States, was already suffering before this credit crisis began. High gas prices and the failure of U.S. auto manufacturers to retool their lineup of cars to get better miles per gallon meant that U.S. manufacturers have continually lost market share to foreign manufacturers. As gasoline approached $4 per gallon in 2008, the American consumer finally gave up. New truck sales at American manufacturers declined some 58 percent, gas-guzzling SUVs are off 30-plus percent, and American car companies could not figure out how to produce a small well-made car that conserved gasoline and made a profit for the car company.

The car company's problems have exploded with the credit crisis. Not only has bank financing dried up, but the car companies are having difficulty securing financing for their credit subsidiaries. GMAC, the financing arm of General Motors, is most directly impacted by the housing crisis because they own ResCap, a home mortgage-financing subsidiary that is experiencing large losses due to the housing crash. But all of the Big Threes' credit subsidiaries are finding credit much tighter, even at much higher rates. At one time General Motors or Ford could offer low 2 percent per year financing on its cars because its credit subsidiary could borrow short-term at that percent in the credit markets. Now, all of the Big Three are near junk credit status and their financing subsidiaries borrow at much higher cost. As credit dries up in the automobile industry it does not just impact the monthly cost of buying a car, alternatively all auto loans may dry up and you may only be able to buy automobiles for cash. Car sales have already declined in the states, but if auto companies had to rely on cash sales only, their sales would drop dramatically. Their lease divisions already are facing significant losses because the resale value of the vehicles turned in at the end of leases is turning out to be much less than anticipated. And the automobile industry, including the tire industry and the auto parts industry, is still a large employer in the United States and important to the health of the overall economy. With overhead and benefits factored in, union jobs in the automobile industry can earn as much as $70 per hour and even nonunion jobs can earn as much as $35 per hour when overtime and benefits are included. The loss of such good-paying jobs can be extremely harmful to the economy.

So far, all I have talked about is the direct impact of banks lending less money to consumers. Consumers are also going to feel the economic hit as banks and investment banks extend less capital to small and large businesses. Banks are big lenders to business and Wall Street through the commercial paper market and the issuance of corporate debt is also a big funder of corporations' liabilities.

Most every corporation in America has debt of some kind on its balance sheet. Over the past 10 years corporations have become even more dependent on debt financing as nonfinancial business debt has grown from some $7 trillion to nearly $11 trillion. Although successful companies have predictable cash flows generating from their businesses, these annual cash flows are not sufficient by themselves to fund major investment and expansion opportunities. Big new plants that require lots of American workers need financing. It would be too expensive and too complex to try to find private investors to make equity investments in such plants. It is an obvious solution for a bank or Wall Street to extend loans or debt financing to a company to expand its operations and to pay the loan back with the increased revenues and earnings from the new plant.

If the source of credit is turned off to American corporations, much of their planned expansion will cease. Not only will it be more difficult to raise debt capital to fund the expansion, but the secondary effects on the economy will lower consumer demand for products and there will be less perceived need by the company for expanding its products and services. If American companies stop expanding, they have no need for new workers. Unemployment figures are always net figures. There are always people being laid off from jobs and people getting new jobs and it is the net figure that contributes to unemployment. If you stop the flow of credit, this net figure on unemployment will explode as there will be few new job opportunities to replace those that are naturally ending.

Even small businesses typically carry some bank debt on their books. Small companies without operating plants still have needs to finance their general operating expenses. Revenues may come into a small business in lumpy forms and they may need help smoothing out their expense payments through loans. Many small businesses factor or sell their receivables and inventory to raise needed cash for operating purposes. If you cut off the supply of bank capital to the small businesses of America many would go bankrupt. They are healthy businesses, and they do have sufficient cash flow to pay all of their debts, but restricting asset access to bank loans would cause many of them, even many successful companies, to declare bankruptcy. The reason is simply that small businesses have uneven and unexpected cash expenses associated with them and they need the help of banks to smooth out those expenditures and finance them until their revenue streams kick in.

Consumers on Main Street will be directly impacted as banks slow their lending in mortgages, automobile loans, student loans, and credit card loans. These same residents of Main Street will be secondarily impacted as Wall Street and the commercial banks make fewer bank loans and less debt capital available to large corporations and small businesses across the country. Without debt capital these businesses will find it difficult to expand and many of the smaller businesses will be unable to maintain their existing operations. Job layoffs will result and job hiring will slow, causing unemployment to spike. Once unemployment trends up, it is only a matter of time until the overall economy and consumption slows, thus impacting everybody's livelihood. Everybody becomes worse off as fewer goods and services are consumed by the society. Layoffs transmit throughout the society regardless of whether industries or businesses had any bank debt outstanding as consumer demand for their services declines.

> *Consumers on Main Street are going to be directly impacted as banks slow their lending in mortgages, automobile loans, student loans, and credit card loans.*

It doesn't stop there. As previously discussed, the stock market itself will trade off considerably because of the direct mortgage losses of its financial institutions as well as the resulting recession and economic decline across the country. Although Main Street is not as big a purchaser or holder of common equities as Wall Street, people do hold equity securities in a number of important places. Some people hold common stocks in individual accounts and count on them for their retirement purposes. These stocks become even more important in a period of falling housing prices as individuals realize they cannot depend on their house sale to fund their retirement needs.

Many 401(k) retirement plans are heavily weighted in common stocks. Advisers recommend this because they believe that 401(k)s are long-term investments and stocks should on average outperform other investments such as bonds. The stock market is currently off some 30 percent and could easily be off close to 40 percent before this market turns. Already drastically underfunded relative to the true cost of retirement, 401(k)s cannot afford a 40 percent hit to their assets.

For those of you lucky enough to still have defined-benefit corporate pension plans you may not be completely sheltered from the impact. The great majority of these corporate and union pension plans are invested in the stock market. For them to take a hit as large as 30 percent to 40 percent of their total assets would mean that the majority of these pension plans would become severely underfunded. The federal government offers a guarantee plan for individual pension plans that are underfunded through the Pension Benefit Guarantee Corporation (PBGC). But resources are limited at the PBGC and certainly the PBGC could not be expected to withstand such a systemic shock to the pension system that the collapse of so many pension funds all at one time would cause. The federal government could make additional contributions to the PBGC to ensure its solvency, but it would have to get in line behind the FDIC, the Federal Home Loan Mortgage Board, Fannie Mae and Freddie Mac, and all the other guarantees that the federal government has been making lately.

The story I am describing is one in which the value of people's homes declines, at the same time that their stock market portfolio value declines, at the same time that reignited inflation causes a market value decline in their bond portfolios, at the same time that their 401(k) and pension benefits are threatened. Americans are poor savers. As a matter of fact, in 2008 America had a negative savings rate. As discussed in Chapter 6, the typical person in China making an average $1,600 a year saved 40 percent of his income last year while an American earning about $45,000 a year was unable to save a single dollar. Now this American awakens to find his retirement pool, which includes the value of his house as well in his actual retirement savings, have all declined dramatically overnight. It may be too late for him to create enough savings for a comfortable retirement, but he is going to be forced to save more. There is no way Social Security is going to be adequately funded enough to pay retirement benefits to all who retire.

As Americans begin to save again you may think that that is a good thing for an economy. And in the long run, all other things being equal, it is. But Americans, remember, have been the consumption engine for the entire world. If Americans start saving 10 percent of their disposable income rather than consuming it there will be a multiplier effect through the entire global economy. Every dollar that is consumed gets passed through the economy to other Americans who consume a majority of it and save a little. But every dollar that is saved gets taken out of the broad economy and does not have a multiplier effect. As the country moves from greater consumption to greater savings it has a negative impact on economic growth immediately. Some experts argue that the increased savings might generate increased investment in the future, but I never believed this argument. I believe increased investment is due to the increased investment opportunities that are related to new technologies, education, and the human spirit. If people have good ideas, there will be money made available in the form of savings somewhere in the world to fund them. Just because a country's citizens decide to save more for retirement does not mean this is a better investment idea or investment alternative, and it does not mean that greater growth will result. Certainly immediate consumption and immediate GDP will decline.

Hopefully, you are beginning to see the importance of credit in a capitalist society. It is the magic of capitalism and the free markets that all the activities that I described in this chapter not only stay in balance but they do so almost invisibly because small and subtle differences in supply and demand of credit in each of these markets causes the market to adjust. Major distortions in the supply of credit, however, will have meaningful impacts on livelihoods in this country. The fact that many of Wall Street's debt markets have completely frozen with nobody able to borrow money, including large financial institutions, without posting collateral means that the impact of Main Street could be severe. You can understand why Main Street has difficulty comprehending this because it is never happened before. Even in 1929, the crash was caused by margin calls on stockholders and bank runs caused the ensuing depression. Bank credit eventually dried up but there was never a single episode of such magnitude that occurs today.

But this does not mean that Secretary of the Treasury Hank Paulson's false choice to take his bailout plan of giving $700 billion to Wall Street or suffer a severe credit crunch across the country is necessary. It is important to recognize how painful a credit crunch could be, but also understand that there may be little you can do to eliminate all the pain ahead. Regardless of what actions government takes, it is most likely that the country will be in for a serious and substantial economic downturn for a number of years. And, indicated in later chapters, the Paulson plan may not be the only alternative, may not be the best alternative, and may end up doing more damage than it promises.

So in determining how badly Main Street wants to help Wall Street in this crisis please understand that there is going to be pain regardless of what you do, that Wall Street deserves to bear the brunt of this pain, that even though many of the financial institutions on Wall Street have burned themselves through their equity capital they still have significant debt capital from debt investors they can lean on and that today, I have found no reason why a bailout of Wall Street by Main Street is necessary. In fact, if the banks' debt investors took a small, say 15 percent haircut to their principal accounts, this problem would go away without any taxpayer monies being needed. It is true that the banks on Wall Street have suffered most of the losses from the housing price crash but it does no good for Main Street and the American taxpayer to write checks to make them whole. Managements and poorly performing companies in a capitalist system must be allowed to go bankrupt. There is no other way under capitalism.

Chapter 12

Demographics Magnify Contagion

The reason that the problems discussed today are so serious is because they are so long-lived. Nominal prices of houses will continue to see decline in the United States for another two to three years. But even after that, for another three or four years, house prices in the United States will not keep up with general inflation. They may show a small nominal increase in price, but because the percentage increases are less than the inflation rate, the real prices of homes will still decline.

Similarly, the ensuing recession in the United States is not going to be minor or something the country grows out of quickly in months. It is going to be years until the U.S. economy turns around. You can't take $5 to $6 trillion of wealth away from residential property and $7 to

$8 trillion of wealth eliminated in a stock market decline and expect an economy not to go into a long, prolonged, and serious recession. A broken financial system that is too highly leveraged and not transparent in combination with a government that is corrupt and takes bribes from big business is proof that the recession will be long-lived. Although you would expect the stock market to turn up before a turn in the economy, in anticipation of the rebound, it is unreasonable to think that this will occur quickly. So this is about a stalled economy for at least the next three to four years and possibly five to six years.

Take a look at the outlook for the United States in the next 5 to 20 years to determine whether the losses suffered today are permanent or merely a temporary speed bump in the continued growth of this country.

$1946 + 62 = 2008$

This simple arithmetic expression gets at the key problem facing the United States in the future. It suggests that those individuals who came to be known as the baby boomers who were born in the postwar era after 1946 are just now, in 2008, reaching the age of 62, at which they can retire and receive Social Security benefits. The baby boom continued from 1946 to 1964, so those boomers retiring in 2008 are just the first wave of a large demographic shift of productive workers leaving the economy and entering retirement.

The retirement of the baby boom will have a dramatic impact on all measures of economic output in the United States. The baby boom has been one of the most productive generations in the history of the world. Taking advantage of government subsidized scholarships and school loans, baby boomers were able to educate themselves and secure high-paying employment in all sectors of the economy with tremendous added benefits from newer technologies and globalization.

The baby boom represents 28 percent of all the adult population in the United States. As boomers retire, their enormous productivity will be lost to the economy. In addition, it is only natural to assume that their consumption will drop dramatically upon retirement. Therefore, the economy will not only lose their productive capacity, but there will be much less demand for other products and services provided currently by others in the economy. The secondary effects of losing such a large percentage of the workforce and the total productive output will be enormous.

Some experts argue that because of the current housing and economic crisis these baby boomers may end up retiring later. If this is true, it may help the arithmetic that holds the solvency of the Social Security program together, but it does little other than delay the negative economic effects of their retirement. It is not clear to me that they will indeed retire later. I can construct an argument where I believe that many of the baby boomers may end up retiring sooner than they had planned. Although the retirement assets and the value of their homes have been diminished considerably because of this crisis, so has their motivation for working. As a direct result of this serious impending recession, many of these baby boomers will lose their jobs. It is usual for companies to lay off the oldest employees first because they are often the highest paid. If the baby boomer gets laid off from his job in a recessionary environment it is not clear that he will be motivated to find a new job or that he will be successful. If you think it's hard finding a job when you first get out of college at 22, try looking for a job at 62. It is also the case, due to globalization and other concerns, that when successful people lose $100,000-plus jobs at major companies, it is difficult for them to find similar paying jobs in the market. Someone used to a cushiony executive job at $100,000-plus is not going to be motivated to work at Kinko's for $7 an hour with no benefits. Because few employers will offer a 62-year-old job applicant benefits, the 62 year old is going to see a significant reduction in gross pay including his benefits. He may decide not to participate in the productive economy at all.

So the problem is twofold. It is hard to imagine a 62 year old as highly motivated to seek new employment. But it is also hard to imagine employers actively seeking out 62-year-old job applicants with high-paying jobs and meaningful benefits. Of course, there will be those who are so unfortunate that they will be required to continue working because they will have seen most of their nest eggs lost in this crisis. My prediction is that the toughest job to get in the future will be the elderly person greeting you as you enter the local Walmart.

In addition to a direct reduction in economic output from the baby boomers retirement and the ensuing reduction in their consumption, the baby boomers themselves are going to be deleveraging. They are not going to be acquiring assets; they're going to be selling assets. The amount of total consumer debt has doubled in the past 10 years. As homeowners default on their mortgages, this consumer debt will decline. But it still needs to be pared down by an aggressive reduction in assets. People have already begun to sell their second homes, their second cars, their pickups and SUVs, their snowmobiles, their boats, etc. This trend will continue. There is no reason why Americans need more than one billion credit cards, which is more than nine credit cards for every adult in America. The double whammy of this crisis is that not only will banks not be lending as much in the future, they will insist that Americans carry less debt and Americans will have to sell assets to deleverage. This is bad for an economy because it means that all those businesses currently selling fairly large assets such as boats and cars to the baby boomers and others will see a dramatic decline in sales.

Part of the rescue plan from this crisis is going to involve some means of seeing that many Americans get to stay in their homes and avoid foreclosure. The FDIC is already doing this with mortgages that they took control of in the bankruptcy of IndyMac, and the United States has said they will ease mortgage terms to allow more people to stay in their homes after the nationalization of Fannie Mae and Freddie Mac. The Democrats assure us that such a plan would be a part of any federal bailout of the commercial banks and their mortgage portfolios.

Although compassionate, this may not be a good idea. It is true that the reason why many Americans got into difficulty is that they were spending too much for the homes they purchased. Yes, the banks gave them the money, but American citizens signed the mortgage notes and agreed to repay the loans. It may not be a good idea to help them stay in a home that is larger and nicer than they can afford.

And here's the key. Even if the government subsidizes their ownership by giving them a below-market rate of interest, it's still a large amount of consumption on behalf of the homeowner and not investment. When you live in a home you are in effect consuming the potential rental income you could earn by leasing it to someone. Therefore, living in your primary residence is not investing in real estate, it's pure consumption. The entire country, because of the real estate boom, is essentially overinvested in their primary residences. They are living in homes that are too large. This has to be bad for the economy. All of that investment capital is not going to productive investments that generate jobs, create wealth, and stimulate the economy; rather this capital is sitting in the bricks and mortar under your feet of your primary residence. It is totally unproductive capital. You can argue that it is productive because the home brings you feelings of security and happiness, but it is not the investment nature of your primary residence that brings these joys, it is the consumptive nature. You have invested a tremendous amount of money in your self, not in the country or in new businesses.

Another way to say this is $24 trillion was invested in residential real estate by 2005. This is mostly primary residences and vacation and second homes that are not leased out. People are consuming the entire rental stream by living in these abodes. This is $24 trillion of capital that could be better utilized anywhere other than in primary home ownership. People should live comfortably, but they should also understand that if they live in a $1 million house instead of a $250,000 house, that is $750,000 of capital that is not being invested in productive enterprise. In this regard, a decline in the price of homes is good as it shifts the balance back to productive enterprise, but, to the extent that government will subsidize homeowners to stay in their homes and not move to more reasonably priced and affordable homes, it is a problem.

The final direct impact on the economy of the aging baby boomers is that more and more Americans each year will face health difficulties because of aging. The miracle of modern medicine is the years added to your life, but as my mother says, they get added to the wrong end of your life. Living longer, while an admirable goal for the individual, becomes the next expensive proposition for the state.

You can expect consumption of health services and pharmaceuticals to increase in the future, but because of the loss of wealth due to this crisis, more and more aging Americans will not have adequate resources to pay for their medical care. As Americans live longer and exhaust their life savings, they will be wards of the state and their significant health-care expenses will have to be picked up by the general populace.

This of course is amplified by the retirement of the baby boomers, but even Americans currently over 62 years old will dramatically feel the impact. By the year 2050 there will be something like 20 million Americans over age 85. This will represent a considerable strain on this country's resources.

Social Security and Medicare are near bankruptcy. Medicare is funded through 2020 and Social Security through 2040. Americans cannot depend on these systems to adequately fund the dramatic increase in retirement and medical costs for retirees going forward. Even now, a young middle-income worker in America is paying 13 percent of his wages to fund Social Security and Medicare. In many cases this percentage is greater than his income tax bill. And, even with this funding, these programs are in deficit. As projected medical costs increase dramatically in the future for longer-living Americans, it is unclear how America will end up paying for it. To further tax young Americans, those most likely to never see any Social Security or Medicare benefits, is not only a moral problem, it may be entirely counterproductive. At some point, federal, local, Social Security, and Medicare taxes become so onerous that people choose not to work as aggressively as they might.

There is an entire program of successful investing that says you should dedicate your investment dollars to those countries that, demographically speaking, are quite young. The dynamic economies of India and China are young with approximately 65 percent of their population under the age of 40. With America's baby boomers retiring, the United States is rapidly aging. Japan, as one of the oldest populations has seen its economy in the doldrums for the last 15 years, magnified by bad government decisions and the bursting of their real estate bubble in 1993. If this theory is correct, then GDP growth and booming country stock markets are a result of young people increasing their productivity and declining nations are a result of older people retiring and exiting the productive economy. If true, this theory does not bode well for the United States.

Because of the housing crash and the stock market decline, many retiring baby boomers are facing a shortfall in their retirement nest eggs. At the same time they are experiencing real losses in their 401(k) plans and company defined-benefit pension plans due to the stock market's decline, they are seeing their home price values decline substantially. Many senior citizens use their homes as bank accounts in which they flipped out of their long-term home and into a nursing care facility with the proceeds generated from the home sale funding their medical and retirement needs going forward. Given that house prices have declined substantially, this is much more difficult to do.

Because home prices are not appreciating rapidly anymore, and because the stock market is also significantly down, Americans may have

Because home prices are not appreciating rapidly anymore, and because the stock market is also significantly down, Americans may have to resort to something they haven't done for some time: Save.

to resort to something they haven't done for some time: Save. The savings rate in the United States is currently negative. I always felt that the reason it was negative was twofold. One, Americans were generating such incredible capital gains each year on their homes that they felt they didn't need to save. Second, if Chinese and other emerging growth companies' workers are willing to make products for you at $0.50 per hour and you are earning $20 an hour in an advanced country's economy it only makes sense that you would borrow as much as you could, save as little as possible, and consume as much of these low-priced attractive goods as you could. And that is just what happened; credit card debt, auto loans, second mortgages used to fund other purchases of assets have all exploded as Americans have treated themselves to the inexpensive goods created by the low-wage countries of the world.

But now that their homes are declining in value, and they have taken such hit in the stock market, Americans will have to start saving again. Most economists mistakenly believe that this is a good thing. They don't seem to understand that as Americans save more they have to consume less. In the long run, this is a good thing because Americans consume too much. But the shift from consumption to savings will be painful for the U.S. economy. If Americans begin saving more and consuming less there will be a direct impact on the GDP of the country because fewer goods and services will be purchased.

I think the mistake that economists make about encouraging savings over consumption is that they assume that savings is good, all other things being equal. But in this case, all of the things aren't equal.

Consumption will decline. If you had two countries and they were both consuming the same amount of goods and yet one country was also saving an additional 10 percent of their total incomes you have to expect the greater savings country to do better in the long run. But it is not clear that a country that saves more and consumes less will have greater GDP output currently or in the future. Just because a country has a high savings rate does not mean it has a high growth rate. Growth rates of countries depend on how well organized their business and governments are, how motivated and educated their people are, and the quality of ideas that the people discover and invest in. Savings money, much like any other funds in the world, is rather fungible across countries and will seek out those countries with the greatest investment opportunities. America can end up saving more in the future and still face a fairly bleak economic outlook. The savings will just naturally flow to higher growth countries where there are better investment opportunities such as India and China.

Of course, just because the baby boom retires does not mean that the U.S. economy ceases to exist. There are willing workers younger than the baby boomers who are capable and willing of stepping up and filling their productive shoes in the economy. But, there are clearly fewer of them so there will be a GDP decline.

Can this younger generation step up and be as productive, or more productive, than the baby-boom generation. Certainly, there are some extraordinary performers in the younger generation who have worked hard to attain an excellent education and utilize many technological advances to maximize their productivity. But, this may not be the story of their entire generation.

One of the results of our government's corruption by big business and wealthy lobbyists is that less and less opportunity has been made available to middle-class families and their children for education, health care, and job advancement. Now there is greater income disparity than any time since 1900. The opportunities of an Ivy League education are still there for some, but mostly it is for the children of the wealthy. The best predictor of a child entering first grade as to his future educational and business success in his life is the income of his parents. The model of America as a meritocracy is damaged and the country has unfortunately adopted the old European model of inherited wealth, status, position, and privilege that Americans so desperately despised at the time of this country's founding.

This means that many young Americans have not had the opportunities to develop that they should have. There is nothing healthy about an economy that dedicates its best educational resources to address the wealthiest 10 percent of its people. Everyone in a growing and developing economy needs a chance to seek education as a means of advancing herself and to not provide this opportunity to all means that your economy will eventually decline. You can never predict where the next Warren Buffett or Bill Gates will come from, but in probability, if everyone is given the same opportunities, it is unlikely that they would come from the wealthiest 10 percent of Americans. As a matter of fact there is only a one in 10 chance that they will if opportunity is really open to all. If there is no investment in the middle class, who knows how many Buffetts and Gates will be overlooked in the future?

The magnitude of the decline in the population of Americans younger than the baby boomers would be even more extreme except for the dramatic recent immigration movement of some 21 million people to U.S. shores. The vast majority of these immigrants are Mexican. Although extremely hard-working and vigilant and much concerned about their families, these immigrants have been under-invested in as a class. They came from a country with a much lower standard of living and have less educational attainment than a typical American. Minorities already represent a population majority in California and by the year 2050 minorities will represent a majority across all of America. This is a wonderful thing. America has a chance to eliminate the hyphens of African-Americans, Hispanic-Americans, and Asian-Americans and finally see everyone together as simply Americans.

But solely from a GDP and wealth perspective, you would have to presume that it will be difficult for these new immigrants to be as productive as the baby boomers who are retiring. The children of immigrants are working hard to receive better educations, but it is not easy given the decline in the quality of the public school system and the reduction in funding for college scholarships and student loans. This argument has nothing to do with the bigger decision as to whether immigration is good or bad for the United States. I am only stating a simple point, that because of the vast amount of immigration that has occurred to date, and the fact that the majority of those immigrants come from less-developed countries, you can expect the GDP, and the GDP per capita, to decline as these workers replace the highly productive baby boomers in the workforce.

The rest of America's youth don't have it much better. As I said, there are a significant proportion of young people today who are doing everything right, getting a great education, working hard if not harder than their parents, and securing valuable productive employment in the real economy. But you need only look around to see that there are also a large number of young people who have lost their way. And the problem is not limited solely to disadvantaged youths.

Many children from well-to-do families are relying much too heavily on their parents largess rather than carving out a niche in the marketplace for themselves. Although it is normal for an 18 year old to enjoy himself at college and expect some support from his parents, today there are 25 and 30 year olds who are living off their parents paycheck and, if not still living at home, occupy condominiums and homes that were purchased by their parents. The fact that children spend an average 5½ hours in front of the television set, not including their time surfing the Internet, chatting with their friends on their cell phones, and playing video games, should concern you. There is a record number of obese children in America and depression and other mental ailments are on the rise.

Contrast this situation with India where children wake at 7 AM each day, study two hours in the morning, go to school for eight hours, and come home and study until 11 PM, often with their mothers bringing their dinners into their bedrooms so they don't have to stop studying. I would argue that this is overdone, that part of being young is being immature and having fun with no responsibilities, but solely from an economic perspective it is clear which model will benefit over time.

So I see the next generation as divided between those young adults who are highly motivated and well educated and guaranteed a productive and successful life, those who had everything going for them and are slowly wasting away, and those who are under-invested. You can disagree on how the percentages break down among these groups, but it is hard to imagine this group in its entirety completely replacing the baby boomers and their enormous productivity.

Finally, in trying to predict the future, a great influence on the health of America's economy is what the outlook is for the entire world. The good news over the past 30 years is that much of the emerging world has been moving to a more free-market capitalist system that dramatically reduces poverty and increases output. It would be a travesty if this economic crisis were responsible for a setback in the economic development of the Third World. But there is no question that the economies of the Third World will come under great pressure as consumption slows in the United States and Europe, the global economy is sent into a recession, and commodity prices decline substantially. How these emerging country governments deal with greater economic uncertainty and whether they stay on the narrow path of free-market capitalism and greater growth and prosperity for their citizens is not known. Countries in Latin America have taken a sharper turn toward socialism, and not without reason. These countries received the worst exposure to capitalism; they were introduced to the greediest corporations who quickly bought up and monopolized their basic utility industries, including their water companies, their electric companies, and their telephone companies, amid tripling and quadrupling prices.

The openness of ideas possible under global trade during the past 20 years has also contributed to a healthy world economy. Again, it would be a shame if the progress made in bilateral and world agreements and trade fall apart because of the economic debacle facing the countries of the world. But, as governments lose tax revenues during a global recession and their businesses decline, the pressure to reject imports becomes greater. America's leadership on this issue has been greatly diminished as world opinion about America has been substantially negatively impacted by not only the Iraq war, but now by America selling its junk mortgage securities to the countries and banks of the world.

Although the world is never completely safe, the decline of oil prices and the increasing instability and aggressiveness of Russia is a threat to all peace-loving countries of the world. China also has been aggressively building its defense industries and funding its military. The declining availability of clean water in many countries of the world, the continued reduction of fossil fuel supplies, and the overheating of the planet either begs for a great new technological innovation or a serious reduction in the population of the planet. It appears the planet in its own unique way is telling us there are too many occupants on earth. Global warming is what it is, it will only get 10 times worse as China, India, and other populous countries reach the same stage of development as the United States.

So, investors in the United States who have made a lifetime of a buy-and-hold strategy in which they ignore all stock market downturns as being solely temporary might have to reconsider the current downturn. This might be a much more severe global economic decline and America may be poorly positioned to achieve its leadership position in the world going forward. Certainly the United States will be a major player in the future, but it is not crazy to think that its per capita real GDP will be declining for years to come. Buy and hold is a great investment philosophy if you are certain the country you are investing in will not only survive in the future but prosper. I believe once the Dow reaches its trough at something like 7,000 to 8,000, it won't decline further, but neither will it increase radically in the future. I am looking at a decade of stagnant economic growth in the United States and after that much depends on whether Americans regain control of government and get government to properly regulate businesses. The current corrupt model of government in the United States is not one that encourages a healthy economy. Free markets are great for creating wealth, but without regulation and the rule of law there can be no free markets.

Chapter 13

Which Investments and Which Countries Will Weather the Storm the Best?

The actual contagious nature of this crisis is not entirely evident until there is a thorough examination of where best to put your money during these difficult times. A detailed examination of alternative investments around the world will make clear the expression that "Cash is king!" during hard times.

Many investors living today have never really had to survive really tough financial times. It is getting rarer and rarer to meet someone who was old enough during the Great Depression to recall how tough that was, especially on investors. Although there have been recessions since, none has been of such a devastating magnitude as the current crisis. The current crisis is unique not only in its severity and its projected length, but in how far-reaching its effects will be felt worldwide.

The reason that people prefer to hold cash during difficult financial times is because most every other asset group faces significant risk of loss to their principal account. Regardless of the promised interest rates and promised returns, capital losses on a bad investment can make total returns negligible or negative. It is never worth risking 10 percent or 20 percent of your capital to garner an extra one percent return per year.

People have great difficulty understanding this concept. Investors have grown used to double-digit-type annual returns. But, if during bad times you can preserve your capital and its purchasing power, you are actually doing quite well relative to other asset classes, which may be declining in value.

The benefit to staying liquid and holding large amounts of cash even though it is low yielding is that you are prepared to take advantage of asset prices when they sink. The advantage of being liquid and cash-intensive is that other potential asset buyers coming out of a boom will be highly leveraged and unable to take advantage of low-asset prices during a crash. And banks will not be lending. Therefore, someone who has substantial amounts of cash and equity available to them will be able to find huge bargains in the different asset classes. Of course, as always, it is difficult to call the exact bottom as markets crash. But, when asset prices have declined some 50 percent to 60 percent there clearly is relative value there, and if you are patient enough you can achieve real absolute value over time.

Let us walk through an asset-by-asset analysis to demonstrate how widely spread this contagion is and will be and how attractive holding low-yielding cash as an alternative might be. First let us examine common stocks and the equity markets. Stocks are riskier than bonds. This is simply because bondholders get the first claims on a company's cash flow and any remaining cash flow goes to the stockholder. In times of economic weakness, you would expect cash flows to the stockholders to be much more volatile than cash flows to the debt holders because of the financial leverage above them. Bondholders have less upside in good markets and supposedly less downside in bad markets.

To some extent, this is happening in the equity markets in the United States where the stock market is off approximately some 40 percent at the end of 2008. And the bottom does not seem to be close given that the recession in the United States due to the housing crash is just starting now. Of course, financial institutions have been the big losers today with the financial institutions index off some 56 percent. Home builders have seen a dramatic loss in market capitalization of some 60 percent. More than 80 percent of mortgage brokerage firms have gone bankrupt. But the losses are not limited just to the residential real estate industry.

As banks experience greater losses and curtail their lending, and real estate and home-building companies lay off workers, the general economy begins to suffer. Homeowners have less money available from second mortgages and refinancing of their mortgage loans to not only buy homes, but to buy cars, boats, and vacation packages. Many homeowners find themselves in houses bigger than they can afford and thanks to adjustable-rate and option-pay mortgages many homeowners see their mortgage payments jumping by 50 percent or more. This puts a cash squeeze on homeowners who are already spending in excess of 50 percent of their take-home pay trying to keep their mortgage current. They had little cash-flow cushion when things were good, now they have no cash cushion. They pull back on everyday consumption items trying to save money. Restaurant company stocks suffer, retailers stocks nosedive, even Starbucks closes hundreds of stores as people realize they can get by without their $4 coffee fix each day.

As the economy continues to weaken, common stocks of other industries begin to suffer. People start buying fewer big-ticket items like automobiles and boats, but also start consuming fewer services. They put off the purchase of big items to the future. Businesses do not need to expand to meet the consumer demand and hold off on big investments in new plants. When this occurs, even the deep cyclical companies such as earthmoving companies begin to feel the hit. When business investment slows, heavy machinery companies and big construction companies suffer tremendously.

The next sector to take a beating due to this recession is the high-tech sector. The financial industry is a large purchaser of computer hardware and software and computer services. But it is not just the financial industry that will slow its purchase of computer hardware and software. All industries, facing cash shortfalls and an inability to borrow at attractive rates from banks, and the commercial paper market will pull back on all investment spending like computer systems. Just as car owners will realize they don't have to replace their two-year-old car with a new car every two years, business owners will become quite satisfied with two-year-old software and not feel the need to replace it annually. High-tech stocks are typically high beta stocks, meaning that they have much more volatility than the market average stock. This is another indicator that you would expect their stock prices to do poorly as the recession deepens.

Given the severity of this crisis I would recommend not holding any common equities. There are some experts who think that defensive stocks will do fine during this recession. But traditional defensive stocks like health-care companies are not going to make it. Even though you consider health-care expenditures as a fairly nondiscretionary cost, health-care expenses have gotten to be such a large percentage of people's budgets today that they will cut back even on suggested medications. Another typical defensive stock category is the food sector, including food producers and grocers. Although expected to do better than most sectors, I think this recession will be so severe that people will cut back in this area as well. This may be the first time you see shoplifters, not at an apparel retailer at the mall, but at the local grocery store. Brand-name food producers will yield to generics as shoppers migrate from brand label retail stores to Walmart during these tough times.

It is sad to say, but the best performer in the common equity group will probably be addictive products such as liquor and tobacco. It is the nature of addiction that it must be satisfied in bad times as well as good, and liquor has the extra advantage of numbing some of the pain from the current recession. Movie studios have also done quite well in previous recessions as people desperately seek out some form of escapism from the world collapsing about them. But, it is my expectation, that although these defensive stocks will do relatively better than the other stocks, they also will have absolute negative returns and over the next couple of years low-yielding cash will outperform them as an asset class.

The next asset class to review is bonds. Chapter 10 discussed the difficulties municipalities will face because of this crisis. It is safe to assume that you would not want to hold municipal bonds or short-term money markets dependent on municipal bond holdings. People have to be careful during difficult times like these not to go out yield shopping. These buyers, when shown a range of alternative investments, pick the highest yielding in an attempt to garner income. As municipalities have greater and greater troubles funding themselves and face greater and greater risk of bankruptcy and defaulting on their bonds, those municipalities that are at the greatest risk will begin yielding the highest returns in the marketplace. A troubled municipality or housing authority or an airport facility will offer 50 basis points or 100 basis points more than a comparable tax-free bond because it faces an increased risk of bankruptcy. If your research only consists of picking municipality (aka muni) bonds with the highest yield you will be shifting your portfolio into the riskiest bonds at their time of greatest stress at highest risk of bankruptcy. Although it is difficult to predict exactly which muni bonds will have problems, given their lack of thorough financial reporting, the best strategy here is to stay away from all of these types of bonds no matter how attractive their yields are, even given their tax-free status with regard to the payment of interest.

Many people who shift assets away from high-risk equities make the mistake of putting their money in corporate and federal government bonds. Again, in an attempt to garner greater yield they are inclined to invest in longer maturity bonds. In this environment, that would be a terrible mistake. Many brokers sell treasury bonds as being completely risk-free. This simply is not the case. When you purchase a fixed-income security like a current coupon treasury bond, you are locked into that interest rate for the life of the bond. If inflation comes back, and market interest rates increase, the market value of your bond declines. If you have to sell the bond prior to maturity you will not receive offers equal to par. It would not be unusual to see offers at 30 percent and 40 percent discounts to par if inflation reignites. You will have lost 30 percent to 40 percent of your principal.

Even if you decide to hold your bond to maturity you cannot avoid this loss. This is more difficult to see because you'll definitely get back the $100 you invested at maturity in say 10 years. But because inflation has reignited in the economy, $100 won't buy what it used to. You have been locked into a fixed-dollar return on your dollars but that $100 has lost its purchasing power. And the loss can be quite substantial. If inflation increases to 8 percent per year, in just 10 years your $100 might only be worth $40 in purchasing power. You will have thought you made a safe investment in the U.S. government and yet still have lost 60 percent of your purchasing power. Not a good investment.

The same thing happens with corporate bonds. Again, you might be enticed to buy a high-rated corporate bond instead of a U.S. Treasury bond because of its slightly higher yield. But if you are lending money on a long-term basis of more than three or four years to either a company or the government and they promise you a fixed rate of return for the period, it is you who run the risk if inflation reignites.

You will suffer the loss of purchasing power because your fixed coupon did not keep up with the rate of inflation.

One way to avoid this problem is to invest in short-term debt securities. Two problems with that approach. First, in difficult times, everybody has the same idea so yields on such securities are minimal. In the current crisis, yields on three-month treasury securities even went negative for a time. This means, even in nominal terms, you are paying the U.S. government to hold your money for you, they are not paying you interest for the use of your money. In real terms, after adjusting for inflation, the real return to you is quite negative, say −4 percent per year.

Second, although you might think you can avoid bankruptcy risk by lending shorter and shorter terms to corporations and banks, there is a bit of a prisoner's paradox involved. In such difficult times it is almost as hard to predict which company might announce bankruptcy tomorrow as it is to predict which company might announce bankruptcy on a day 10 years from today. This is the same dilemma faced by the prisoner in the famous philosophical paradox who was told by the King that he will lose his head sometime in the next 30 days but when it happens it will be a complete surprise to him. The prisoner reasons that if he makes it to the 30th day he can't lose his head because it wouldn't have been a surprise to him. Tracing back through the 30 days, the prisoner convinces himself he can't be beheaded on the 30th day, the 29th day, the 28th day, etc., until he finally convinces himself he cannot be beheaded on any day, at which point the King's executioner walks into the cell and beheads him. Trying to predict corporate bankruptcies one day or one week or one month in advance can result in the same outcome.

The best investment in times of great capital risk and greater inflation risk are Treasury Inflation-Protected Securities (TIPS). These are bonds issued by the U.S. Treasury, which return a modest real return but are augmented by a return exactly equal to whatever the inflation rate is. Because the U.S. Treasury guarantees you the inflation rate, the principal you invest in them maintains their purchasing power and trade almost always at or near par. In such difficult times it is hard to think of an investment category that is guaranteed to return your principal plus the inflation rate and guarantee that you will maintain your equivalent purchasing power of your principal.

It's funny, but housing itself has typically been good for a hedge against inflation. Although common stocks themselves have been poor performers during inflationary periods, the housing stock has appreciated at least as much as general inflation on average. Unfortunately, in the current environment, given that housing is still overpriced relative to fundamentals, you cannot benefit from this long-term correlation. But, depending on what neighborhood you are in and when prices bottom out, housing itself will become an attractive investment. Remember, to buy a home and live in it and consume the rental income by doing so is not investing, that is consumption. I'm talking about making a housing investment in which the rental income pays not only the mortgage interest but also any maintenance and property taxes needed. If this is the case, and you buy at the trough of the market, in the long term, you would expect housing itself to appreciate at the general inflation rate thus protecting your purchasing power. But, most cities in America are still 20 percent away from a true bottom so this investing strategy involves additional patience.

Commodity purchases should also be good hedges against dollar inflation. The reason is that you are buying a hard asset with dollars, in effect you are shorting the dollar, which is going to inflate, and buying property. Hard assets like commodities typically go up in price during periods of high inflation. It's not necessarily that the commodities themselves that are more useful are in greater demand, it is much more likely that the currency used to measure their value, in other words, the U.S. dollar, is declining in value. That is, if you measured these commodity prices relative to each other they wouldn't change materially, but it is the inflating dollar that is distorting their prices. Having said that, if you get into commodities during inflationary periods it can be a good strategy for preserving your purchasing power.

The purest commodity play to just protect purchasing power is an investment in gold. The reason is that there are vast reserves of gold in the world, few commercial uses for it, and limited new mining completed relative to the amount of world reserves. This means that gold makes a good currency; it's difficult to inflate the total amount of gold available to the world quickly. Gold might be an even better currency than the U.S. dollar since the Federal Reserve can print more dollars and inflate the currency anytime they desire. In the long term, you would expect gold to be a good hedge against dollar inflation. Unfortunately, the volatility of gold prices makes it a difficult means of hedging against a short-term inflation burst. Before you invest in gold, you have to determine whether the current market price, say $750, is itself a fair value for the metal or whether it is facing some sort of price distortion. For this reason, TIPS are a more straightforward means of protecting your principal and protecting against future unexpected inflation. The old rule of thumb on gold is that one ounce should just about approximate the value of a fine man's suit, which appears to be just about right today with gold at $750. If you are looking to invest for 5 to 10 years, gold should work as an inflation hedge.

Commodities other than gold, such as copper, steel, pork bellies, are influenced by economic activity. Greater production and greater consumption in the general economy creates greater real demand for these products and as such you would expect real prices to decline during an economic recession. But the price decline will be disguised because prices of these commodities are quoted in nominal dollars not real dollars. There will be two countervailing influences. These commodities will inflate in price because of the printing of dollars in general price inflation but their real underlying price may actually decline as industrial production and demand slows in the recessionary economy. Suffice it to say that these real commodities, other than gold, are too unpredictable in periods of high inflation and weak economies to be able to project their nominal price movements. I would stay away from them.

Any high-risk investment such as venture capital investments or private equity or hedge funds should be avoided. Venture capital will slow dramatically as the initial public offering exit strategy ceases for most venture firms. It will be the exception to the rule to find a small high-growth company that can access the public markets and because of this venture capitalist returns will decline quite substantially. Private equity firms, which are quite risky normally from the high degree of leverage in their investments, will face even more demanding times. Their model of business buying companies and leveraging them up will no longer make sense in a world in which debt capital is expensive and banks put severe limits on the amount of leverage on a business. There will be some buying opportunities as stock prices collapse, but it will take a smart private investor to differentiate between real buying opportunities and companies near collapse. The last thing you'd like to do to a company facing a recession and declining revenue growth is to own it on a leverage basis. Again, leverage multiplies returns in an up environment, but magnifies losses in a declining recessionary environment.

Hedge fund investments are also broadly discouraged because hedge funds themselves are going to come under great pressure. Regulatory reform will force them to become more transparent and that transparency will force them to make money the old-fashioned way, honestly. By removing the old boys' network of insider information and preventing market manipulation of individual stocks and getting them out of the CDS market, hedge funds managers will see their returns dramatically lowered. Again, the leverage they utilize will work against them in a recessionary market with declining asset values. Many hedge funds, once regulators become involved,

Any high-risk investment such as venture capital investments or private equity or hedge funds should be avoided.

will become obsolete as there will be no need to leverage average market returns and there will be no demand for small hedge funds to collect premiums in a new highly regulated credit default swap market.

Although I have made these comments about these different asset classes with regard to the United States, the same general asset class comments can be translated to most every country. Regardless of what country you live in, cash is going to be king until these asset classes reach their bottom. Credit is going to be tight the world over because the entire global financial system is threatened by losses resulting from U.S. mortgages.

European countries are facing a double whammy. They have already entered recessionary environments in many cases because their central banks were quicker to inflate their currency and rescue their commercial banks from U.S. mortgage losses. But, to date, much of their economic weakness is due to their bank's exposure to U.S. mortgages. Housing price declines in many European countries are just beginning. As England, Ireland, and Spain experience eventual housing price declines of 25 percent to 35 percent in magnitude, their banks will realize significantly greater losses, their financial systems and financial institutions will increasingly become more insolvent, and their remaining banks will pull back dramatically on lending. This will push these countries into even deeper recessions. I would not be surprised to see Europe's GDP contract by as much as 10 percent or more over the next four to five years in real terms. Clearly this is not an environment in which you would like to invest. As a matter of fact, a GDP decline of 10 percent is many people's definition of where a recession stops and a depression begins.

Australia and New Zealand have overpriced housing markets similar to the United States and the United Kingdom, so expect about 30 percent drops in the price of homes there. The resulting bank losses will cause significant economic declines in these countries as well.

As the United States and Europe enter into severe recessions driven by lower bank lending and less consumer demand, this will cause global demand for products and services to contract dramatically. The United States and Europe still represent more than half of the total global GDP. And much of European and American consumption is end-product demand by consumers. Other countries may manufacture a great deal of the components that go into the product consumed in the United States and Europe, but the predominance of pure consumption still resides in the United States and Europe. As the U.S. and European economies go, so go the world economies.

This is particularly true in the emerging markets. Take Africa, for example. Although Africa's economy has been growing at a remarkable 5 percent per year, to date it is mostly due to increased demand for commodities from Africa. Commodity prices have grown so rapidly that many African nations are seeing tremendous increases in their GDP even though their unit production of these minerals and resources has not increased. This all stops in a global recession. Real commodity prices, after allowing for general inflation, will come down as global demand for products and services comes down. Africa will be exposed for the simple fact that it has done little to advance the education of its people, their skill set, or their productive capacity. Even oil-rich countries like Nigeria will see a dramatic reduction in revenues as the demand for oil declines with a decline in the global economy. People around the world will drive their cars less, they will consume less heating oil as they readjust their thermostats in their homes and industry will utilize fewer fossil fuels as they cut back production.

With regard to the BRIC economies, Brazil, Russia, India, and China, you would have to think that Brazil is positioned relatively the best. I say relatively because even Brazil will see dramatic reductions in its output as the global economy slows. Brazil has been successful in developing a domestic economy and has tried to wean itself from foreign oil, but it is still highly dependent on exports and will suffer along with the global economy. Russia, like Africa, to date is almost solely dependent on commodities, specifically oil and gas. Oil and gas has made Russia a rich country, but as the price of oil declines, so will Russia's fortunes. Russia's corrupt government has prevented the development of a true entrepreneurial class and new business formation. Russian oligarchs and billionaires are not developed from the ground up like Bill Gates, but rather are anointed from the top down by Vladimir Putin. With Russia's oil and gas wealth, they have missed a real opportunity to build out their physical infrastructure and legal and constitutional systems of justice that would spread wealth to all Russians. Don't be surprised if Russia goes bankrupt.

India has been growing at 7 percent to 8 percent per year and has provided a nice investment return over the past decade. Unfortunately, people are now starting to realize that a great deal of this investment boom was funded by India's commercial banks. You would have to expect that in a period of tighter credit, this investment spending by commercial banks will slow or cease. Anyone familiar with India will be surprised that India was staying close to China's growth rates given the huge amount of bureaucracy in India as well as the difficulties of getting an overly democratic federal government to achieve any strategic direction at all. Now that the commercial bank investment will slow, the underlying power of India's new economy will be tested. Many experts claim that the well-educated of India's elite classes have been successful in attaining high-tech service jobs through outsourcing over the Internet, but this model is not easily transferable to the great population of India who remain captive in small villages with poor educational opportunities across the continent. It would not surprise me to watch India's growth record turn negative and have some contraction in GDP.

That leaves China. If this were the beginning of this crisis I would have to tell you that I would be fairly negative on investing in that country. Although China has enjoyed double-digit growth rates in the past, its stock market, its real estate market, both commercial and residential, and parts of its economy had been subject to asset bubbles driven by a populace that has never seen a credit crunch or asset price downturn. Just like home buyers in the United States during the boom, the Chinese could not get enough of common stocks, condominium apartments, or office building development. China's stock market has now traded off some 70 percent from its peak and thus eliminated much of the bubble from its pricing.

If I were to pick one country that should do well going forward given its current stock price levels, I would have to choose China. Although I dislike its centralized government approach and in the long run do not believe it is the most efficient method to organize a government and an economy, I cannot but be impressed by the Chinese work ethic and their wholehearted belief in hard work, savings, investment, and growth. Anyone who saw the opening ceremonies for the 2008 Olympics will agree with me that this is a force not to be ignored.

China also will experience slower rates of growth but should remain in slightly positive growth territory during this crisis. The reason China appears as an attractive investment opportunity is because of low relative valuations relative to the potential growth of the economy. The United States has 310 million citizens and the market capitalization of all of its publicly traded companies is approximately $8 trillion. The Chinese have 1.2 billion citizens and the market capitalization of all their publicly traded companies is approximately $2 to $3 trillion. Obviously, the Chinese economy is not as developed as much as the U.S. economy. But that's the point, isn't it? The upside in investing in China is that eventually there is no reason why the Chinese can't attain the same productivity and incomes per capita as the Americans. Chinese-Americans in the United States have attained even higher average incomes than white Americans. So, if China attains the same GDP per capita as the United States this means its total GDP for the country will approximate $60 trillion. It may take 30 or 40 years for this to be accomplished, but it represents tremendous growth from today's $1.6 trillion economy in China. Not all of this growth will be reflected in the market cap of China's currently publicly traded companies, but a great deal of it will. The easiest way for capitalist companies to show growth is not by stealing market share or even improving worker efficiency, it is simply by just selling more products and services. And this is what the Chinese expect to do. It is not without risk, but if I wanted to make a long-term investment in this global market facing this economic crisis, I would put my money in China at current stock price levels.

Other smaller emerging markets such as Eastern Europe and countries in Asia are themselves too risky to merit additional investment during this crisis. Country bankruptcies are not impossible. The smaller country economies will suffer as their exports decline and their governments revenues will shrink as they lose export fees, import tariffs, and tax revenues during the recession. The Ukraine, Hungary, Rumania as well as the former Eastern Bloc countries of the old Soviet Union have all been mentioned as possible bankruptcy candidates.

So, to summarize: cash is king, TIPS, gold, and China are the best bets I can suggest during these coming hard times. Cash and TIPS have the lowest risk and you might benefit tremendously in a tight credit market if you can buy assets at low prices during the trough. Gold and Chinese stocks are riskier investments but can work out well even if the recession is long and inflation reemerges. But, the message I wish to leave with you is that this is a short list of assets expected to perform okay during this period. The vast majority of asset classes and of countries in the world are going to face tough times ahead.

Chapter 14

Stop the Bleeding

I have described the housing crash and the mortgage and banking crisis as a car wreck happening in slow motion. I can continue the car wreck analogy to see what reforms are necessary to the correct problems like this from occurring in the future.

After a car wreck, the immediate need is to attend to the victims and stop the bleeding. The analogy here is to address the more immediate reasons for the freezing of capital markets and the damage to the global financial system. In a car wreck, attention can then be focused on cleaning up the scene of the accident, or in this case, the longer-term reforms necessary to clean up the financial system as well as the regulatory system.

Finally, when there is a bit more breathing space, with regard to the car accident, the root cause can be determined, possibly a brake manufacturer with poor quality controls at the factory. The broad philosophical question might be why a brake manufacturer would not take his responsibilities more seriously given the threat to human life and suffering that he can cause by manufacturing a faulty product.

In Chapter 16 I take such a broad view. I want to explore the real root causes of the housing boom and bust and its impact on the global financial markets and ask more philosophical questions as to what this means with regard to how the country is organized productively, what the government is organized to do, and whether as a people Americans are on the right track to achieve long-term goals. You may think that such a broad view is unwarranted, but if I can't examine U.S. society and its citizens' motivations and desires when the entire global financial system is close to crashing, when is it appropriate to do so?

So I will focus initially on how to stop the bleeding by taking a look at what can be done to prevent the seizing up of capital markets in the United States and around the world. U.S. Treasury Secretary Henry Paulson has convinced Congress to pass a $700 billion plan in which taxpayer money will be utilized to buy out risky and highly discounted mortgages and mortgage-backed securities from financial institutions. Secretary Paulson did a great disservice by presenting this as the only feasible alternative and by not allowing enough time for discussions of alternative plans. I will first examine the shortcomings of the Paulson plan and then see if there is another plan that would work better.

The Paulson plan's main deficiency is that it defines the current crisis as if it were solely a liquidity crisis, not a capital-loss or bank solvency crisis. His plan presumes that the reason that banks aren't selling these deeply discount mortgage assets on their books is that there is no bid for these properties. If this were true, then its having the federal government step in and buy these assets from the banks may indeed provide them greater liquidity. But all of the efforts of the Federal Reserve and the U.S. Treasury to dramatically increase global liquidity have failed to date. In September 2008 the central banks of the world injected more than $300 billion of new liquidity into the banking system and yet borrowing costs between banks increased. In effect, interbank borrowing disappeared except for a collateralized market in which securities were pledged in exchange for a loan. The market was saying that even banks would not lend the other banks without a pledge of equal value collateral. Markets just didn't trust the banks and their ability to survive even one more night.

And this is the fundamental mistake that the Paulson plan makes. In attempting to provide liquidity to financial institutions they create a ready market for these damaged mortgage goods and mortgage securities. But by creating a liquid market, they cause the financial institutions themselves to have to recognize losses in these securities. Banks today are slow to recognize all of their losses claiming that there is no good liquid market value established in the active-trading market place. The reverse auction process that Paulson suggests in his plan would create just such a liquid market and a market value would be established thereby making it impossible for a bank not to recognize its losses.

And these losses could be quite substantial. To date something like $500 million of losses have been claimed by the banks, but their losses will be much greater in the long run. The $12 trillion mortgage market will see losses of at least $1 to $2 trillion but that will not be the limit of the banks exposure. The banks have substantial holdings in leverage buyout debt, which was used to finance the purchase of companies by private equity firms. These debt investments by the banks will suffer tremendously as credit dries up, because leveraged buyouts incorporate a high degree of leverage in their capital structure. In a world of tighter credit and higher interest rates with greater risk premiums, those companies are less likely to survive. Already, leveraged buyout loans are being sold at 20 percent and 30 percent discounts to par.

In addition to residential real estate, banks have a large exposure to commercial real estate, which now will come under pressure as the economy softens. As retailers announce plans to open fewer new stores and many retailers claim bankruptcy, malls come under pressure with high vacancy rates, development stops, existing loans to mall developers become threatened. Construction loans, a staple of the banking industry, come under great pressure as there is no take-out mortgage loan after construction is complete. Tenants who had made previous occupancy commitments end up walking away from their down payments. Office building vacancies increase and new office building construction slows as the economy slows. Even apartment buildings, which you would think would do well as homeownership declines, come under pressure because rents decline as the economy suffers. If it costs less to own a home it should cost less to rent a home. This decline in rental values puts enormous pressure on the apartment building loans that banks hold.

In addition to real estate, banks primary exposure from a loan perspective is to corporations. Corporate loans get into trouble for a number of reasons sometimes unrelated to the economy, such as too much leverage that you see in leveraged buyout loans and some junk credits. But as the economy softens, a number of well-managed firms will come under pressure. Banks will face losses as companies default on their loans and banks will face additional funding requirements to weak companies because revolvers they have written will be drawn down. As a last line of defense many companies have unused revolving credits at banks that they only draw down in times of trouble. The bank makes substantial fee income during good times, but ends up being the lender of last resort during bad times.

In addition to real estate and commercial loans, the bank's entire portfolio will come under attack. As discussed in Chapter 13, municipal bond holdings will be threatened, and private insurance will provide little good if the private insurance company goes bankrupt. Commercial paper holdings of the banks will also be threatened as spreads widen in the commercial paper market.

So, the dilemma facing the banks is real and is not just due to a liquidity crisis. It is not that everything would be fine if the bank just had more cash. Banks are facing real losses throughout their portfolio that threatens their solvency. The Paulson plan does little to address this problem. As a matter of fact, you could argue that the Paulson plan makes it worse by forcing banks to recognize losses quicker due to the establishment of a true market price for their mortgage securities.

So the first fundamental problem with the Paulson plan is that it addresses liquidity and not bank losses and bank solvency. The second major problem with the Paulson plan is that it tries to do good too quickly. It doesn't give the markets the chance to identify which banks are poor performing and which might deserve to go out of business. Although all banks had some trouble during this crisis, clearly some banks did a better job managing their exposure to overpriced homes and mortgages than others. The Paulson plan wants to go in and save all the banks regardless of how poorly managed they were. It even looks like the Paulson plan might provide more benefit to the worst performers because these companies would have the biggest exposure to the doomed assets that Paulson intends to buy. It is as if the government is giving the most taxpayer money to the worst managements.

These financial institutions are highly leveraged with debt. But perhaps there is a silver lining in this. Banks and financial institutions in the United States are leveraged anywhere from 12 times debt-to-equity to more than 25 times debt-to-equity once off-balance-sheet activities are included in the calculation. Investment banks here in the United States are leveraged more than 30 to 1 debt-to-equity and banks overseas in Europe are leveraged as much as 35 to 1. What possible silver lining could there be in this news?

Consider Citibank as an example of a highly leveraged bank. They have seen their equity capital decline due to losses in the mortgage business from $110 billion to just more than $55 billion. But when all their off-balance-sheet activities are added to their balance sheet their total assets exceed $3 trillion dollars. This means their overall leverage is greater than 60 to one and increasing as they take further write-downs on their assets. Certainly this is a recipe for disaster. It means that if Citibank had as much as a 2 percent loss on its total assets of $3 trillion it would threaten its entire $50 billion equity base. But the silver lining is that Citibank is highly leveraged with debt. They have more than $400 billion of debt holders who have invested in their company. These debt holders have been earning an unusually high return relative to treasuries over the years because of their desire to expose themselves to slightly greater risk of holding Citibank debt than holding U.S. Treasury debt. Now it is time for them to pay the piper.

Let's say that by the time this cycle completes, Citibank's equity will be negative $200 billion. Under the Paulson plan, Citibank sells assets they have marked down in price to the U.S. Treasury but their fate does not change. They still face a negative book equity of minus $200 billion. They have exchanged the valued assets for cash and freed up some capital on their balance sheet, but they have done nothing to help the book equity of their firm, which demonstrates their insolvency.

But the answer to Citibank's troubles is not in Washington. The answer to Citibank's troubles is right on its balance sheet, on the liability side of the balance sheet. Although it is unreasonable to imagine their depositors taking a loss on their short-term cash deposits at Citibank, there are more than $400 billion of debt investors at Citibank who faced exactly this risk when they invested monies with the bank. If the debt investors at Citibank who number $400 billion take a 50 percent haircut to their principal, then Citibank book equity quickly turns positive, which may be sufficient to do business going forward. Especially if the business of Citibank over the next year is to further deleverage and sell assets to repay debt investors.

This is how capitalism works. This is how finance works. This is how bankruptcy courts work. And this is how the FDIC should work. The Paulson plan is an impediment to letting the markets operate. The market should determine who the worst managed firms are and who has the greatest exposure to mortgage problems and who is insolvent. It would be fairly simple for the FDIC to work with bankruptcy courts to institute an accelerated bankruptcy provision in which Citibank could be back in business in two weeks albeit under new management with a new investment and leverage strategy and with substantially lower debt as debt investors take the haircut that is warranted.

Paulson has tried this before. In his Bear Stearns rescue he got in so quickly and guaranteed $29 billion of assets that no Bear Stearns debt holder had to take a single dollar haircut even though there were $190 billion of debt on the Bear Stearns balance sheet. The whole idea of someone investing in Bear Stearns debt is that they get paid unusually high returns relative to risk-free treasuries during good times but if they've done a poor job in analyzing their investments they lose money if Bear Stearns goes under.

In the case of Fannie Mae and Freddie Mac the story is the same. Here, Paulson exposed the American taxpayer to a potential $500 billion to $700 billion loss on a $5.2 trillion mortgage portfolio. But he did it so quickly and before the losses were recognized in the debt markets that he in effect saved $1.6 trillion of debt investors in Fannie Mae and Freddie Mac from experiencing a single dollar of losses. These debt investors never had a guarantee from the U.S. government that their debts would be repaid. They knew they were dealing with private businesses. Fannie Mae and Freddie Mac were not agencies of the U.S. government. This is the reason that Fannie Mae and Freddie Mac bonds and their bond investors always garnered an extra third to half a percentage point more in return than holding treasuries. They were being paid to take the risk that Fannie Mae and Freddie Mac wouldn't go bankrupt.

Now that Fannie Mae and Freddie Mac are bankrupt, Mr. Paulson steps in and prevents them from experiencing any loss. The Congressional Budget Office (CBO) estimated that the total potential loss to the taxpayer of acquiring Fannie Mae and Freddie Mac was only $25 billion. If this were true, then the $1.6 trillion of debt holders to Fannie Mae and Freddie Mac could have written off less than 2 percent of their investments and American taxpayer involvement could have been avoided. Of course, this isn't true. As I said, the loss will be much closer to $500 billion to $700 billion. But, there is no reason why the debt investors at Fannie Mae and Freddie Mac should not suffer this loss. It would represent an approximate one-third haircut to their principal investments and is a direct result of any benefits they received from investing in risky securities such as Fannie Mae and Freddie Mac over the years and doing such a poor job in understanding and analyzing that risk.

People talk about Secretary Hank Paulson and his attempts at preventing moral hazard. They say that by allowing the stocks of Bear Stearns and AIG and Fannie Mae and Freddie Mac to decline near zero he is preventing any moral hazard from occurring in the future. Moral hazard is simply the risk that people will come to expect to be bailed out of their bad investments. But what these people fail to see is the huge problem of moral hazard that Secretary Paulson is creating in the debt markets. In each of these cases, Secretary Paulson is basically telling the debt markets you have nothing to fear, that the U.S. government will come in with U.S. taxpayer money and bail you out before you suffer one dollar of loss as the debt holder. This is a terrible signal to send to debt investors.

> *But what these people fail to see is the huge problem of moral hazard that Secretary Paulson is creating in the debt markets.*

So a much better plan than Paulson's, which avoids a true recognition of the weak players in this entire drama, is to allow the markets to operate, not just the equity markets but also the debt markets. Don't try to go in early with taxpayer money and permit any loss in the debt markets. Don't make out of hand equity investments in the banks before their debt investors are asked to take a haircut. Allow companies to compete, and allow the weak sisters to bankrupt. Because these are financial institutions and are necessary for the proper functioning of the capital markets, have in place a system, working with the FDIC, that quickly resolves these bankruptcies. Make sure the debt holders take the proper haircuts required to reestablish these financial institutions on much firmer foundations going forward. These companies were overleveraged. The people who should suffer for that are the people who caused it, the people who lent the money to become overleveraged. Once these firms are solvent, allow them to reenter the market place, preferably under new management and begin the longer-term business of deleveraging their balance sheets. This can be accomplished once they accept bankruptcy because their worst assets will be off their balance sheets.

Now that the Paulson plan has passed, the next step is for it to demonstrate its ineffectiveness with regard to freeing up credit and getting interbank lending going again, and then focus on what an effective approach to this crisis should look like.

In the bankruptcy process, some banks will be identified as being worth more dead than alive. There will not be any good assets or good management or good strategic plan to keep alive. In these cases, find good banks, well-managed banks to take the assets over. There should be willing buyers because the banks deposit bases are so valuable. Banks today make an enormous amount of money off depositors and the consumer lending arms of their businesses. With J.P. Morgan's acquisition of Washington Mutual, the deposits and their relationships with consumers are extremely valuable. Great synergy is created when Washington Mutual's depositors can be plugged into J.P. Morgan's banking services and credit controls.

You might ask, why didn't Secretary Paulson think of this alternative? I have to believe that he did. The cynic will say that Paulson comes from Wall Street and understands how powerful the debt investment community is not only on Wall Street but in Washington DC. People point to hedge funds as being big players in Washington, but the debt community dwarfs the hedge fund community by 100 fold in size. If Paulson were wearing the hat of his old job as CEO of an investment bank he would want to keep these debt investors happy, and, if he were wearing that of a Washington regulator reporting to Congress, he would want to keep the same debt investors happy as they are some of the biggest contributors to Congress.

But there is another important influence that affected Secretary Paulson's thinking in this matter. That is the credit default swap (CDS) market. The credit default swap market has grown from a small $140 billion market 10 years ago to a $65 trillion market today. Initially viewed as a hedging tool, this market has degenerated into a pure casino in which people make bets on which companies will go bankrupt next. The size of the market far outweighs any benefit it might give debt holders who are trying to hedge their exposure to risky investments.

For example, Bear Stearns went bankrupt when it had $190 billion of debt outstanding. But, in the credit default swap market, there were more than $2 trillion of contracts guaranteeing that Bear Stearns wouldn't go under. This makes no sense. Some percentage of the $190 billion of debt investors in Bear Stearns might want to hedge their risk exposure by buying insurance in case Bear Stearns announced bankruptcy. But the fact that $2 trillion of this insurance was written says that most of the buyers were purely speculating or gambling. The insurance writers were looking to an annual windfall of premiums from companies that never face bankruptcy and the buyers were looking to win if indeed companies like Bear Stearns claim bankruptcy.

The fact that the market was $65 trillion in size and that there is only $26 trillion of corporate debt outstanding in the United States demonstrates how speculative this market has become. The primary reason that Secretary Paulson could not allow individual investment banks or AIG or Fannie Mae or Freddie Mac or any of the major commercial banks to claim bankruptcy is because these bankruptcies would trigger payment of trillions of dollars in the credit default swap market. Again, a cynic might suggest that it is the hedge funds that write a great deal of this credit default swap insurance and would be the biggest losers, and given that they are such big contributors to Washington some hanky-panky might be involved. But ignoring conflicts of interest, it would have to be destabilizing to see trillions of dollars of payments triggered by the bankruptcies of a number of large financial institutions.

Therefore, Secretary Paulson saw his unenviable task of juggling all of the near bankrupt companies and financial institutions on Wall Street and trying to prevent the major bankruptcy from causing fallout in the credit default swap market. Given the magnitude of the mortgage banking losses and the ensuing recession with its corporate losses the task was too great for Paulson. Bankruptcies were inevitable. The problem should have been identified as a credit default swap problem and been resolved. Direct intervention in the credit default swap market by the government is required. Although it may seem extreme to some people for the government to take action against speculating in the credit default swap market, imagine how extreme it feels to taxpayers to be asked to contribute $700 billion to void a loss to the same speculators. Before uninvolved taxpayers can be asked for trillions of dollars to make whole these speculators, the government needs to identify who exactly is benefiting and why.

An examination of the credit default swap market is entirely warranted and needed. First, all transactions in the credit default swap market should be cleared with one counterparty so that net exposures can be understood. Certainly, once everyone's exposures are netted against each other, the potential loss is not anywhere near $65 trillion dollars. Once the total net exposure is known for each of the market disciplines, then it makes sense to assign losses more to speculators than to hedgers. To the extent someone really wants to try to minimize their exposure to a holding of Fannie Mae or Freddie Mac debt, this action should not be penalized. But, if a small hedge fund was writing billions of dollars of insurance business it seems perfectly reasonable to ask the speculators to suffer losses before hitting up the American taxpayer to make them whole. The credit default swap market was an unregulated market with no transparency and no prevention of complete destructive speculation. It is ridiculous to ask the American taxpayer to make whole these speculators.

So once it becomes apparent that the Paulson plan is not going to work and only saves the highly leveraged, poorly managed financial institutions and protects speculators in the credit default swap market, it will make much more sense to look to an accelerated bankruptcy process to identify the true weak managers and asking their debt investors to take the loss. If these bankruptcies trigger speculative investments in the credit default swap market, the government needs to step in and determine true hedging activity versus merely speculative activity and reward the first and punish the second before any taxpayer funds are threatened.

Of course, no action is going to stop all the bleeding immediately. A severe recession is coming. There is no denying that. The largest financial institutions have made bad investments of historic proportions and are looking at trillions of dollars of losses on their balance sheet. That cannot be denied. Homeowners have consumed way beyond their means and borrowed tremendously on the values of their homes to justify new car and boat purchases and extravagant vacations. This will all stop. This decline in consumption alone will cause a recession. But the banks also will pull back in lending and add to the recessionary fire.

And there will be a period of slow growth for years. The reason is that all of America, and much of the world, needs to deleverage. Americans have been enticed by easy money to borrow and consume way beyond their means. Household debt has doubled in the past five years going from $7 trillion to $14 trillion. Bank debt has doubled during the same period to $16.5 trillion, nonbank financial debt has increased from $7 trillion to $11 trillion and government debt has doubled from $5 to $11 trillion. Everything is overleveraged, and leverage must be paid back. The only way to pay back leverage is to sell assets to pay down debt and the leverage. This will be extremely difficult in a world in which everyone is trying to deleverage at the same time. There will not be ready markets for assets. From the consumer's perspective, he can expect to get bad prices for his Jet Skis, vacation homes, and bass boats. From the banks' perspective, even after they clean up their mortgage problems, there will be weak markets for commercial paper, commercial debt, municipal bonds, junk bonds, and leverage buyout debt. There just won't be any buyers. Everyone will be deleveraging together. Businesses will slow their expansion plans as they try to get their debt levels under control.

But just as the scene of a car accident must be cleaned up, similarly, the financial system in the regulatory structure must be cleaned up if Americans are to prosper and prevent a similar occurrence in the future.

In the latter half of the first decade of the 21st century, it did come to pass that the U.S. government did authorize $700 billion of taxpayer money to be given to its largest financial institutions to avoid Armageddon.

This authorization occurred even though it was reported that millions of phone calls and e-mails have been received in Washington from constituents and that 95 percent to 97 percent of these communications were strongly against the plan.

The entire idea of democracy is for elected representatives to act on behalf of their constituents. Books such as *Profiles in Courage* have been written describing instances where legislators answer to a higher calling than that of their constituents in deciding how to vote. Is that what was happening here?

If so, the only plausible argument that congresspeople could raise is that they understood better than their constituents the ramifications of not passing this bill. But, the President of the United States had come on prime-time television just the night before and said that without this authorization there would be utter chaos in the markets and that the country would face the prospects of a severe recession. Sarah Palin, the Republican vice presidential candidate, went so far as to say if this bill were not passed there would be a repeat of the Great Depression of the 1930s. Even with these warnings, the American people were strongly against this plan.

No, maybe the answer was much simpler than elected representatives pursuing a noble cause. Perhaps, they were pursuing the same cause they have followed for decades, to line their own pockets at the expense of their constituents. For you see, it was a combination of these elected representatives and greed and corruption in American business that led us to this financial precipice.

Certainly, the future outlook for the American economy is bleak. This book details how the crisis, which began with a housing boom and bust in the United States, has spread to other classes of investment assets, to other countries of the world, and to the general global economy. But, U.S. Treasury Secretary Henry Paulson, Federal Reserve Chairman Ben Bernanke, President George W. Bush, and the U.S. Congress and Senate wish you to believe that their $700 billion plan is the solution to stopping the suffering.

It is common when presented with a very difficult problem and a potential solution to err in the form of quick action and support for the proposed solution. The more important question to ask is whether the proposed solution will do good, or make matters worse, or whether there is another as yet undisclosed alternative solution that might have a better chance for success.

Chapter 15

No Future without Reform

I t is important to understand that this crisis did not happen by accident. Experts such as former Federal Reserve Chairman Alan
Greenspan who suggest that the causes of this crisis were as random as a 100-year flood do a great disservice to us all. To say that this
was simply a confluence of random events that occur naturally in all
business cycles suggests that there is nothing to be done to prevent future
similar events.

There was nothing random about this. Although some experts saw
it coming in advance and tried to warn citizens in the United States
and beyond, after the fact, and after careful analysis, it is fairly easy to
draw conclusions as to the real reason for this disaster.

Throughout this book, I have said that this problem started with the housing boom and crash. Certainly the suggested reforms must address the root causes of the housing boom and crash, but reforms cannot stop there. There are additional reforms needed throughout the financial system that allowed overpriced houses to translate into a potential meltdown of the entire global financial system.

Deregulation across-the-board was a primary motivating factor in not only the housing boom and bust but in how the financial system and the government reacted to the crisis. This was not just a problem of too loose lending and too much money being lent by banks to homebuyers. An entire industry was created by overly aggressive real estate agents and appraisers and a mortgage brokerage industry that were more concerned with closing deals and putting home buyers in new houses. Deregulation and lack of supervision from government had deteriorated to the point that no one thought it irregular that real estate agents were asking appraisers for estimates of their independent appraisals prior to signing deals with them, and no one thought to check to see if mortgage brokers were fraudulently changing the reported incomes on home buyer applications for credit.

Wall Street and the commercial banks felt no obligation to tell their investing clients about the potential problems in their mortgage investments if housing prices turned down and basically were selling their investors whatever the market would bear. In hindsight, it seems almost criminal that the rating agencies, Moody's, S&P, and Fitch, were taking out tens of millions of dollars of fees paid by issuing banks to tell these investors that their mortgage investments were rated AAA and were thus secure. Mortgage investors, including sovereign governments and pension funds, are not without blame as many depended solely on the credit rating of their investments without any further due diligence or credit analysis. There are many hours in the day to play golf if all you have to do to properly structure an investment portfolio is just buy AAA-rated securities.

Not all new regulation can come from Washington. Some policing of real estate agents, appraisers, mortgage brokers, and bankers must occur at the local level. If people in local communities don't care about fraudulent activities in their communities, they really can't complain when losses result. It is the inattention to the rule of law and to the policing of fraudulent and illegal activities that helped cause this problem.

There is a great deal of reregulation work that must occur in Washington if this problem is to be avoided in the future. Many problems occur in the financial system because people are making bets with other people's money. To the extent that homeowners were given the opportunity to own million-dollar homes in an up-market with little to no down payment, they essentially had a free option on the upside with little downside exposure.

If you wanted to eliminate a great deal of volatility in the system and provide more stability to the housing, mortgage, and banking industries it would be easy to pass a law requiring at least a 20 percent down payment on any future home purchases. Of course, this would cause further declines in the prices of homes as they would have to reach a level at which people felt they were a good investment of their own money, not just the bank's money. It is unlikely that Americans would be willing to face additional losses to the values of their residential real estate properties.

So, such a proposal probably will not be enacted. But it should be. Think about it. If individuals can buy homes in the future with no money down, there is a risk that the same type of irrational pricing in the housing market will reoccur. If people have to invest 20 percent of the purchase price, and could lose it, they will be much more careful to not overpay for the property.

If individuals can buy homes in the future with no money down, there is a risk that the same type of irrational pricing in the housing market will reoccur.

Because Americans are currently overleveraged with debt, very few currently have the cash reserves necessary to make such a required 20 percent down payment. Therefore, you can expect home prices to decline an additional 10 percent to 15 percent beyond the 20 percent declines that are expected nationally if such a law passed. It is the right thing to do. It will stabilize the markets. But don't bet on it happening.

Banks need to be much better regulated. There is no reason why a depositary institution that is supposed to be protecting the deposits of its client base should be allowed to leverage itself from 15 or 35 to 1, anywhere in the world. Such enormous leverage, even with the best of management intentions, guarantees a tremendous amount of instability in the banking system, volatility of earnings, and frequent threats to banks' solvency from loan losses that requires them to pull back their lending efforts. Because the banks are so highly leveraged, you can expect to have much more violent business cycles and many more recessions in the future as banks suffer losses that threaten their equity bases.

The entire reason for having governments is to identify problems that individuals and individual corporations may not see or to take actions that benefit the overall society but may not benefit any one particular corporation or entity. Governments of the world, including the United States, should make it illegal for banks to hold any assets off balance sheet, and their combined leverage should never exceed 10 to 1 debt-to-equity. This would mean that fully 10 percent of the banks' assets and holdings would have to go bad before their entire equity base is threatened. This is much more reasonable than a bank leveraged 35 to 1 that faces 3 percent losses of its total assets and finds itself insolvent. If all the banks of the world were leveraged at 10 to 1 or less, there might be less violent swings in the business cycles of the countries, many fewer bankruptcies of financial institutions, much less contagion of problems across countries of the world, and generally a much healthier environment for investment and greater economic prosperity.

Of course this won't happen without government involvement. The reason that banks are so highly leveraged today is that they feel it is in the interest of their management and stockholders. Management relies to a great degree on stock options for compensation and so have little downside investment in their company and yet enormous upside if the company does well. Such incentive stock option plans for management should also be examined in any reform package. Stock options should be replaced with stock grants that have real value on the downside, and employees should not be granted stock for free but should have to pay for a portion of it so they have real skin in the game and understand the risk of losing shareholder capital. Rational shareholders may come to the conclusion that greater leverage is in their interest because it multiplies the power of their earnings on the upside and given a fixed limited investment on the downside. This is why the decision about the proper amount of leverage in a society cannot be left up to individual shareholders. Government regulating leverage in the financial industry is a wonderful example of how good government can create tremendous value to society through limited intervention.

Certainly there must be greater transparency and reporting throughout the system. The idea that the entire hedge fund industry does not have to report financial information is ludicrous. The only reason I can think that someone would resist reporting financial information is that they are breaking the law. It would not surprise me to find out that if hedge funds are required to report financial information on a timely basis, a number of them are generating profits by maintaining inadequate capital, over-leveraging themselves, making promises they cannot honor, manipulating stock prices, or simply insider-trading. The best reason to fight against having to publicly report financial information is to avoid disclosing illegal activity. To assume that hedge funds can constantly outearn market returns violates common sense and all theories of efficient market returns. Many of the same hedge funds do well every year, which further suggests that something is not right.

Let them report and disclose what risks they are taking, what assets they hold and how they finance themselves, and then evaluate whether to invest in them or allow them to continue in business.

Other financial institutions should be subject to the same reporting and leverage requirements as the commercial banks. There is no reason why investment banks and nonbanks and mortgage providers should be allowed leverage of 30 to 1 and live outside the regulatory structure.

Possibly the biggest issue facing regulators going forward is what to do with the credit default swap (CDS) market. This is now a $65 trillion market. For a $14 trillion U.S. GDP, this number is mind blowing. The problems created by the CDS market must be addressed now or these problems will come back to haunt us.

The first step would be to have a central clearinghouse for all counterparty trades in the CDS market. This step, combined with complete transparency, would allow participants to judge counterparty risk appropriately. But, the assumption of counterparty risk cannot be left to the individual companies entering a contract. The failure of a large financial institution can threaten the entire system. Again, government cannot stand back and let Citibank enter as many CDS contracts as it wishes. By doing so, Citibank becomes too big to fail. They become too important a node in an ever more complex interconnected network of CDS contracts. The government entity that clears all counterparty transactions in the CDS market must be responsible for tallying each firm's net exposure in the CDS market and limits of total risk exposure must be set. No firm should be allowed to have net CDS exposures across all of its investments greater than say 10 percent of its book equity. The days of a billion-dollar hedge fund guaranteeing $10 billion of defaults in the CDS market must be stopped. Similarly, Goldman Sachs with $40 billion of equity will not be allowed to have exposures to hundreds of billions of dollars of positions in the CDS market. It is destabilizing and it is unethical because these contracts cannot all be honored in bad times. The government must step in and be sure that given even the worst-case scenario, all CDS contracts can be honored.

There is a second problem with the CDS market. By its very existence, the CDS market makes security and investor analysis of individual companies almost impossible. Imagine the frustration of a Warren Buffett who would like to make an investment in the financial institutions sector and has his analyst review financial information filed with the SEC by Citibank, Goldman Sachs, and Bank of America. Although the firm's assets and liabilities are stated, the exposures each firm faces in the CDS market are not explained. As a matter of fact, they are so complex and so numerous as to be almost impossible to explain in a simple reporting format. When you buy Citibank stock or debt, you think you are buying the risk of Citibank going bankrupt, but because of Citibank's participation in the CDS market, you might be buying the risk of Goldman Sachs going bankrupt. Citibank, with $50 billion of equity, may have guaranteed $500 billion of Goldman Sachs debt in the CDS market. In other words, if Goldman Sachs goes bankrupt, so does Citibank by paying off its CDS contracts. What is Warren Buffett to do?

It is an important question. The whole idea of capital markets disintegrates if individuals and companies cannot properly value risk. If I cannot properly analyze the risk exposure a company faces, I cannot make an intelligent interpretation of the price that I will charge them for capital. The CDS market, which originally grew out of an honest attempt at diversifying risk, became so big and so successful that it socialized collective risk. In other words, the CDS market so spreads risk across all institutions that there is no variance in risk by company. They all hold each other's risk. They are a collective. They are no longer competitors. They are all too big to fail, therefore it is not a capitalist system.

So, when regulators begin to do their analysis of the CDS market and the risk inherent in it, they may conclude that the systemic risks it poses are not worth whatever hedging services it manages. Regulators may decide to shut down the entire CDS market. This appears to be a good idea. The CDS market has made the measurement of risk impossible and the proper allocation of capital nearly impossible. If Karl Marx said that capitalists will manufacture the rope that hangs them, the CDS market is as close to such rope as I have seen. Under the disguise of a risk-hedging tool, the CDS market has been allowed to grow into a threat to the entire global financial system and the capitalist system because it is impossible to price risk of CDS market participants.

This crisis has put the capital markets and this entire country at risk. The short-term solution to many of the problems has been to offer government guarantees, taxpayer support, or to nationalize industries. As a result of this crisis, the government has nationalized the mortgage-lending process, the mortgage-packaging and securitization business, has extended deposit insurance to not only commercial banks but investment banks, now owns one of the largest insurance companies in the world, has guaranteed investments in money market funds, has guaranteed certain municipal bond funds, provides guarantees to the commercial paper market, and prevents the failure of many financial institutions across the country. The government has nationalized the American financial system and the capital markets thus ending the greatest experiment in free-market capitalism the world has ever seen. In effect, the village was burned to save it.

This should scare you. In the short run, everyone feels better. All investments seem safe and secure. Deposits in commercial banks are safe because the government guarantees them. Money market investments are guaranteed by the government. But there are limits.

Throughout this crisis, analysts and commentators referred to the benefit that commercial banks have relative to investment banks because of the stability of their deposits. They fail to mention that the reason their deposits were more stable, and less likely to flight, was because the government guaranteed deposits up to $100,000 and now,

$250,000. They went so far as to suggest that the bigger commercial banks should buy up the riskier investment banks because of their stable deposit bases. What they were proposing, and what happened to a great degree, was that commercial banks with guaranteed deposit bases got back into some risky businesses such as the underwriting of securities, the merger and acquisition business, and the leverage buyout and private equity business at a time when they were overleveraged and at great risk themselves. Isn't this exactly what caused part of the mortgage crisis? Didn't Fannie Mae and Freddie Mac ignore the risks in their business because they knew their cost of debt capital would never increase because of the implicit government guarantees they enjoyed? In the short run, government guarantees to financial institutions will distort their operations and encourage unusual risk-taking for which all will be punished in the future. In the long run, it threatens the entire country as there are limits to how much capital and how much financial risk even a country as great as the United States can shoulder.

So a great deal of work has to be done in Washington to reinstitute meaningful and effective legislation and regulation on Wall Street and the financial markets. But Washington itself needs reform. It was Washington who looked the other way when asked to more closely supervise Fannie Mae and Freddie Mac, to better regulate overly aggressive mortgage lenders, to allow a $65 trillion CDS market to develop from scratch, and to ignore that major financial players like hedge funds had no reporting requirements at all. Elected representatives are not stupid. It is inconceivable that they didn't have prior warnings about the weaknesses in the system prior to October 2008 or that they didn't realize that their lack of regulation and supervision was causing great problems to the financial system and the economy. Their inaction is testimony to the fundamental underlying problem behind all of this. A system of lobbying and campaign contributions from corporations and banks assured that congressional representatives never took action on the behalf of the voters. Elected representatives were being paid to dismantle laws and regulations that their clients on Wall Street found offensive.

In 2007 financial service companies spent more than $402 million on lobbying expense. This is a record for annual gift giving by the financial services industry, with the exception of the $417 million they spent on lobbying in 1999 to repeal the Glass–Steagall Act. Of course, the repeal of the Glass–Steagall Act allowed commercial banks to package and sell mortgage securities globally, which was a prime reason for the current crisis. They were able to get troubled loans off their balance sheet and thus lost most of their incentive for tough credit analysis of borrowers.

The same elected representatives whose lack of regulation during the housing boom and crash and the meltdown of the financial system are asked to now ignore their biggest corporate and bank contributors and reregulate these industries. It simply is not going to happen without lobbying and campaign finance reform. To see this clearly, you need only examine congress's actions during the debate on the recently passed $700 billion Paulson bailout. Congress was in a rush to give away $700 billion of taxpayer money to the very institutions that caused this mess. Not only were these institutions bribing congresspeople, but by quickly brushing the problem under the rug, Congress may itself avoid any future investigation that would lead to an exposure of their compliance in the tragedy. The fact that Congress would so quickly give hard-earned tax money to their corporate contributors, even after the problems faced in this crisis, assures me that they have not learned their lesson and that day will never come when they might enact the reforms necessary and regulation needed to properly supervise this industry area.

So you have to attack the root cause of the problem, the big issue, first. Without lobbying reform, it is a mistake to talk about regulatory reform. It won't be easy. Wall Street and the biggest corporations are extremely powerful and have their hands deep into Washington. Every congressperson and senator is guilty of taking money from these organizations and their employees.

As if this mortgage and banking crisis were not big enough, let me assure you that lobbyist control of government representatives is a far bigger problem than just this financial crisis. Lobbyists get in the way of solving almost every single problem America faces today. Elected representatives are being paid by corporate lobbyists to avoid solving the problems that are of utmost importance to the American people.

For example, Americans are concerned about high pharmaceutical prices, but congresspeople regularly take hundreds of millions of dollars from pharmaceutical companies when writing laws that determine to a great degree those prices. Americans are concerned about the cost of medical insurance, but congressmen are taking huge amounts of money from HMO lobbyists. Americans are concerned about the price of gasoline and wish to see alternative energies developed, but congresspeople are in the bag and employ of the largest oil and gas companies. Americans wish to see global warming explored and addressed, and yet the coal lobby and the electric utility lobby prevent congresspeople from taking any action. Most Americans would like to see action on immigration and the minimum wage to assure that no working American must live in poverty and yet the business lobby pays congresspeople to avoid addressing the issue. Big defense company lobbyists request hundreds of billions of dollars for new weapons systems development while troops and their families and veterans struggle on low-income wages and benefits.

And it is not just corporate lobbying that is to blame. The AARP prevents an intelligent discussion about how to solve Social Security and Medicare shortfalls, the NRA prevents an intelligent discussion of what to do about gun violence in inner cities, and lobbyists hired by teachers unions slow any discussion about needed education reform.

No one president will be able to accomplish lobbying reform on his own. Lobbying is not a Democratic or Republican function. It is an incumbent function. Incumbents benefit from campaign contributions because it is the incumbent that can return the quid pro quo legislative benefits to businesses that justify their campaign contributions. This is why 98 percent of incumbents win reelection in Congress. Because of these illicit campaign contributions from big corporations they can outspend almost any competitor from the outside.

So if all incumbents are in favor of continuing the present campaign finance system because it assures their reelection, how is needed reform ever to pass? It must come from the people. Washington is broken, but there is no one person Americans can elect who can straighten it out on his own. The president needs everyone's support if he decides to try to stop the lobbying express. In no unflinching terms Americans must tell Congress and the president that they believe any corporate campaign contribution they accept and any substantial campaign contributions they accept from an employee of a corporation must be considered a bribe and Americans will hold them accountable. The information is available on the Internet as to who is receiving these bribes and it is up to the American people to act. The American people do not deserve good government, good regulation, and a resulting strong and prosperous economy if they reelect representatives who so obviously and willingly accept bribes from big business.

It should not surprise you that the root underlying cause of the near collapse of the entire financial system is itself a serious and large problem. It's not easy to take down an entire financial system the size of the United States or the world. It cannot happen by accident. It had to result from collusion between the two most powerful forces in this country, the business community and the government. The power of the people, while great, is too diffuse to cause such immediate problems. No, this was done the old-fashioned way. People were paid to look the other way as people ripped off their fellow citizens. There is no other explanation.

Chapter 16

A Warning Shot
Across the Bow

A problem of this magnitude could not have occurred unless there was something fundamentally wrong with the way this country is organized as a society. Simply blaming Wall Street or Washington D.C. for the problem won't cut it. It assumes complete ignorance on the part of average citizens. If Americans are indeed ignorant of the greatest problems facing the economy and the government, then that is a major problem for which Americans all bear responsibly. And if the people are not ignorant of these problems and do nothing to resolve them, that also is a problem that finger pointing cannot resolve. And the problem did not reside solely on Wall Street and Washington. Main Street has its fair share of blame also.

Many far from Wall Street and Washington have been living far beyond their means on borrowed funds. Americans legally and morally committed to mortgage contracts with no intention of repaying them if things went bad. Some citizens were the realtors and appraisers and mortgage brokers who unethically pushed larger and larger mortgages on people. Some were the bankers who did unscrupulous work to maximize the value of stock options. When the government acted unethically, citizens looked the other way. When told congresspeople were taking bribes from corporations they never got involved. When they heard the government was torturing prisoners they never got up out of their recliners and protested. When told that inequality in the country was exploding and that opportunity was disappearing for the middle class they never reacted. They didn't respond when the scientific community warned them they were harming the planet. They ran up government debts and unfunded Social Security and Medicare liabilities with no regard for how their children would repay them.

Newscaster and author Tom Brokaw describes an earlier generation of Americans as "The Greatest Generation," many of whom were the sons and daughters of immigrants. They had next to nothing when they were growing up, and this situation was only aggravated by the Great Depression. What made them great was a genuine concern for each other that extended far beyond simple self-interest.

Many far from Wall Street and Washington have been living beyond their means on borrowed funds.

And what miracle brought this country out of that depression? A military buildup in preparation for World War II. In what must be the ultimate example of going from the frying pan to the fire, this generation's youths left the Depression behind only to find themselves fighting in the war. Plans for college were deferred in order to enlist. This was no regional conflict or police action. The entire world was at war. More than 50 million military and civilian casualties. More than 400,000 American military dead, but that pales in comparison to the estimated 20 million Soviets, 10 million Chinese, 6 million Poles, 5 million Germans, and 2 million Japanese military and civilians who perished in the war.

Enter the baby boom generation. Although not enormously spoiled with material things while growing up, they did have relatively stable home lives. Many boomers experienced rather self-absorbed child-hoods involving binge drinking, experimenting with drugs, and yes, listening to rock-and-roll. And yet the 1960s were this generation's brightest light as it was an attempt by the nation's youth to show con-cern for others. Young people organized and fought hard for the rights of women, minorities, the environment, and to stop the killing of the Vietnam War.

At the time, many people thought that the torch had been passed to a new generation as John F. Kennedy suggested. Although the great-est generation was extremely hard working and tough, here was a new generation that was born after the Depression and World War II and so it was assumed would have a natural optimism about them. Many of this new generation attended at least some college, gaining some enlightenment about other cultures, human rights, and human dignity. It was a heady optimistic time.

Most baby boomers are now in their fifties and are at the peak of their lifetime earnings capacity. And what have they seen fit to do with their new-found wealth and status? They have bought bigger and bigger homes, have invested in second vacation homes, have multiple cars and SUVs at their disposal, and spend huge sums on fashion, res-taurants, vacations, and other self-indulgences. Rather than contribut-ing more so that others might suffer less, they have pushed through the largest tax cut in history, more than $4 trillion, the great major-ity of which goes to the richest Americans. They have run up govern-ment deficits, which when you exclude the illusionary Social Security surplus, exceed $500 billion annually and could quickly in the coming recession top $1 trillion annually.

This generation of Americans has shown little to no concern for other people around the world. Total foreign aid as a percentage of the U.S. GDP is less than 0.1 percent as billions suffer in poverty. AIDS is at the epidemic stage in Africa with some countries there reporting infection rates as high as 30 percent of their total adult population, and more than 25 million dead already. Although China is indeed growing, it is the free market's infatuation with $1 a day labor that is the driving force. There has been no effort on behalf of the American consumer to reduce purchases of Chinese goods in order to properly address concerns there such as religious persecution, the illegality of union organizing, human rights violations, and consumer rights and environmental issues.

This generation has sat idly by while the American government has pursued a foreign policy that ignores the pleas of the developing world to lift subsidies to American farmers, invades foreign countries without allies' support, and tortures its captives.

This generation of American consumers is using more energy and creating more waste per person than any country in history. Oil prices are up considerably, world oil production is forecasted to peak and then decline in the near future, and this generation continues to drive gas-guzzling SUVs and generously air condition their enormous homes. There is no effort to conserve energy or to actively develop alternative sources of energy like wind or solar power. In the most contemptuous act, Americans subsidized ethanol production, a means of stuffing food needed for the world's hungry into their gas tanks in order to take them to the mall.

Many people of this generation are retiring early to take advantage of generous pension plans and grab as many Social Security's benefits as they can before the system collapses. They continue to vote to increase payroll taxes on the nation's youth, crippling the future economy, just to continue to pay retirement benefits to themselves that no other future generation will ever see.

There is little chance that global warming will accelerate such that the baby boomer generation has to worry about it in its lifetime. It is a problem for future generations. Baby boomers don't have to worry about the education system declining, their kids go to private school or have already graduated high school. There is no chance that the boomers will wake up tomorrow in poverty, and thanks to the repeal of inheritance taxes, there is no likelihood that their children or grand-children will either. Hopefully, it is a small probability that a boomer would find himself in prison, and if so it would most likely be a mini-mum security facility for white collar criminals. If gasoline goes to $6 a gallon—good—maybe the boomer's commute time will be faster once the poor get off the highways.

And so, most of these problems are being ignored by this generation because they realize it is unlikely that they will be directly affected. The self-centered nature of this generation prevents them from applying energy and time to issues that do not immediately benefit themselves. They end up under-investing in societal solutions to global problems that at first blush appear to benefit others, but have solutions that will create a better functioning society that protects the rights of all.

Somewhat surprisingly, ethical concern for a fellow man is the missing ingredient preventing people in this country from solving their most pressing problems. If Americans can look to help others, society benefits, and surprisingly ends up helping everyone. In what may sound confusing, it is in their self-interest to begin to care about the wel-fare of others as only then will major societal problems affecting them directly be resolved.

Market and governmental power have been the weapons of choice to date in addressing threats to prosperity and well-being, but they by themselves are not enough. Economic markets are ill suited for solving many of the complex problems facing us that require more cooperation than competition and world governments have enormous shortcomings that prevent these issues from being properly addressed. In addition to

The self-centered nature of this generation prevents them from applying energy and time to issues that do not immediately benefit themselves.

business and government involvement, civil society must begin to take a more active and ethical role to ensure a proper productive balance of this truly holy triangle. Government corruption and corporate lobbying power may be the most visible problem, but wars, poverty, environmental degradation of the planet, human rights violations, education problems, energy self-sufficiency, world health, and the commercialization of the media will not be addressed and cannot be solved without direct citizen involvement.

Ethical action is not limited to just finding a way to get politicians to stop lying and businesspeople to stop cheating. It also means that the people themselves must elevate ethical concerns in all their decision making. Simply speaking, acting ethically can be thought of as just doing the right thing and showing as much concern for others as we have shown to date for ourselves. Hopefully, there can be a discussion about proper ethical action even if Americans are not ethically perfect—or else I would have to stop right here.

First and foremost, it is the people who have to lead on this front by acting ethically and behaving morally before I can expect the world situation to improve. With no moral outrage on behalf of the people there can be no progress in addressing concerns on how businesses and government act. Unless people elevate their concern for others and the health of the group, these problems will continue to languish. And without firm ethical accountability of elected representatives and business leaders, suggested solutions will never translate into implementable programs.

Somewhat magically, if the people do find a new moral voice and begin to act in the public good, not only will general society improve, but problems directly threatening them and their families will quickly

begin to disappear. Fears about their retirement plans, the proper education of their children, adequate health care for their family, their own self-worth, and a general worry that the world is headed to hell in a hand-basket will all begin to subside. Most importantly, people will start feeling good about themselves again as they will realize they are not alone, but rather important and integral parts of a world community. Their work, their ideas, and their lives will have meaning again. As opposed to worrying about home mortgage rates, the latest fashion craze, music video news, and the latest political corruption scandal, people will start devoting their time to real problems the world faces knowing that solutions are achievable and real people, including themselves, will benefit.

The key to uncovering this true path to greater prosperity and societal well-being lies in marrying knowledge of government, economics, and ethics. One would not be surprised to learn that politicians and ethics are a bad mix, but there must be a way of transferring this new-found ethical action on behalf of a people through their government representatives and into practical governmental programs.

Economics and the free market have also made strange bedfellows with ethics over time as Adam Smith's free-trade theories are based on people acting narrowly in their self-interest and yet society still benefiting. This is not to suggest that acting in one's self-interest is inherently unethical. But, depending on circumstances, ignoring the public interest or the effects of your actions on others can indeed be unethical. Proved as an effective system for providing many traditional goods and services, free-market economics has little to offer in the study of problems for which self-interested action exacerbates rather than alleviates the situation. Are these type of problems highly prevalent in society? The answer is definitely yes!

It should disturb everyone that the fundamental premise on which all modern economic theory is based is that people are assumed to always act rationally—and rational action is partly defined as people

acting solely in their self-interest. How could such a self-centered theory explain young soldiers selflessly volunteering to die for the love of their country, international aid workers risking their lives for little to no income to assist the sick and dying of the world, mothers sacrificing exciting business careers to spend more time at home with their children, people shortening their lives by smoking tobacco and drinking alcohol, the poor wasting their few precious dollars on lotteries with little chance of winning, and teachers and professors accepting less pay than they might earn elsewhere simply because they just feel good about helping the next generation learn.

Global free markets are so pervasive and powerful in the world today that you would expect that if free markets acting alone could have solved these problems, the problems would have already been solved. In other words, it should not be surprising that many, if not all, of the major threats and problems that remain unsolved and continue to imperil an individual's well-being today are those that the traditional free market allocation of economic goods and services could not easily handle. In fact, they are. Almost universally, they share common characteristics that make them exceedingly difficult for the free market to address.

It as if billions of self-interested free-market profit-oriented entrepreneurial businesspeople have raced about the planet for centuries solving every problem and satisfying every consumer need they could, so long as they themselves also benefited. As a result many traditional goods and services allocation problems have indeed been solved. And thanks to the beauty of the properly regulated free market, most of this activity has happened almost automatically with little central planning or government interference. But, these same free-market participants have put little energy into solving those problems that provide little direct benefit to themselves and yet are critical for the proper overall functioning of society.

This class of societal concerns such as corrupt government and proper regulation of business are known generally as collective action

problems. They are representative of a special class of economics and societal problems that are better solved through cooperative collective action of the group than by having each participant acting solely in his narrow self-interest.

A system of property rights, a well-managed currency, a constitutional system for controlling concentrated government and economic power, the rule of law and even democratic voting rights can all be thought of as partial solutions to collective action problems that successful societies have enacted. That is why regulation is not a dirty word. Proper rule making and regulation is the foundation of any civil society and free market. But, as many libertarians argue, too much regulation can be inhibiting to individualism and free spirit and itself must be rigorously guarded against. The proper amount of regulation itself is a collective action problem that needs addressing by all the citizens of the world.

Free-market libertarians should realize that their beloved markets could not operate at all if not for prior government action that provided essential contract enforcement, dispute resolution, punishment for transgressors, limitations on monopoly formation, and other restrictions on the coercion of market participants. One of the major reasons that the spread of free markets has failed to catch on in many developing countries is the failure of the market proponents to recognize the importance, no, the absolute necessity of having vital rules and laws in place before trading and commerce can begin. These rules and laws of society, government, and business result directly from a successful cooperative effort of people to solve collective action problems, which result when individuals begin to interact and trade with each other.

It just so happens that these economic and governmental institutions while critically important to a society's proper development and the growth of a healthy economy are not the most important collective goods that a society possesses. An independent judiciary is an important component of the extremely critical institution broadly referred to as the rule of law. But the court system would have little value to a society unless it properly reflected the society's values of justice and fairness. These higher order societal values include justice, fairness, equality of opportunity, liberty, basic human rights, the sanctity of life, and the freedom to lead lives in pursuit of happiness.

Incredibly, each of these higher order societal values creates another extremely important collective action problem as to how these values should be distributed among the population. Most civilized societies strive for an egalitarian distribution of these values, but do not necessarily attain egalitarian results. For example, most people would agree that justice should be equally available to all and yet court systems that allow high-priced defense attorneys for the rich and poorly trained public defenders for the poor can hardly be seen as providing justice to all equally. Surely, allowing people to bid for any of these universal values with dollars is an unfair and unequal distribution method as different people have varying amounts of wealth with which to bid and so the free market should abstain from participating in their distribution. Although this seems inherently obvious, a political campaign system that allows private contributions from corporations and wealthy individuals is rife with examples of favoritism that makes a mess of fairness and justice for all. A corporation that contributes millions to congressional representatives in exchange for billions in corporate tax cuts and subsidies may not be breaking any current law, but it is definitely free riding and unethically corrupting a system established to fairly represent all the people not just its richest and most powerful.

Again, because the free market and dollar bidding is an inappropriate method for allocating these higher order values across the citizenship, an alternative distribution scheme must be adopted. There must be broad discussion of how the system will work, the system must be transparent so that all can observe how it works, it must be unbiased, it must represent the will of all the people, and representative agents must be held accountable to the citizenry. To date, the best vehicle to accomplish these goals is liberal representative democracy with its universal voting rights, freedom of the press, and constitutional guarantees of individual freedom and civil liberties. Ideally, democracy ensures that all participate equally in these most important distribution decisions. But, given the failure of elected representatives to faithfully represent their constituents, more direct democracy alternatives such as expanded polling and national referendums should be considered. It is hard to imagine any system of more direct voting doing a worse job in representing the people's will than the current representative system.

Originally, some geneticists and social Darwinists suggested that such concern for anyone other than one's own gene pool was counter to evolutionary theory and not sustainable in human behavior. They tried to argue that in a world of survival of the fittest, it was greed that was most important to survival. Many of these same socio-biologists are now beginning to recognize that there exists in man and his ancestors many examples of genetic-inspired behavior that encourages cooperation and that this very cooperation aids in survival of the group and thus of the individual's gene pool.

Even if there were no genetic basis for cooperative, unselfish behavior, humans exercising their free will and creative ingenuity would invent it if they deemed it helpful in better organizing and advancing their society and providing greater opportunities for themselves. No one is limited in thought and action by their genes.

It turns out the movie *Spiderman* had it right. "With great power comes great responsibility." The challenge of this definitional approach to moral action is that it puts a heavier burden on the truly talented than it does on the mundane, blissfully ignorant, poorly educated huddled masses. Although a brilliant successful person could claim enormous opportunity costs if she had to forego her personal career to aid society, this same person would be invaluable to organizing and solving many of the world's worst problems. Where can you have greater impact, in a cubicle on the executive floor of a Fortune 500 company or starting a movement to clean up Washington and end corporate lobbying abuse?

For solutions to be found to the world's most pressing problems, people are going to have to wage war on the establishment as it exists today. Through globalization, an elaborate system has been created, led by the United States, which is pushing completely free-market capitalism on the world as the solution to all of its problems. You do not have to be a conspiracy nut to realize that multinational corporations are the most powerful organizing force on the planet today and that their sole objective is the amoral pursuit of increased profits globally. The major benefit to these corporations going global has been their transcendence from any single government's regulation or taxation.

And so, the world today is dominated by a system that favors market solutions to most everything, sees the corporation as the prime vehicle for action, virtually controls many of the world's governments, and emphasizes open markets and globalization as the cure-all to the world's problems.

Free-market capitalism is often blamed for many of the world's ills. But the truth is that capitalism has created greater wealth than the world has ever seen in its history. Capitalist countries often have average incomes that are 10 to 20 times as great as those in communist or dictatorial regimes. There are many reasons for this, but the most important are that free trade and property rights allow people to participate in economic decisions. Properly functioning and properly regulated free markets are to an economy what democracy is to good government.

> *Free market capitalism is often blamed for many of the world's ills. But the truth is that capitalism has created greater wealth than the world has ever seen in its history.*

The major objection to capitalism, namely that it distributes wealth and incomes unfairly and unequally, is just wrong. It turns out that more capitalist, more advanced countries have much better, more equal, distributions of income than the poorer less capitalist countries of the world. So over longer periods of time it must be the case that the poor do relatively better than the rich under industrialization and development.

The problem with capitalism is not that it is a failure, but rather that it has been too successful. Capitalist advanced countries of the world have such large concentrations of wealth and power that they can easily dictate to the poorer countries of the world what their policies ought to be and global corporations often control governments, here and abroad. Properly regulated free markets do indeed effectively create and distribute most of the goods and services in the world. But, as stated earlier, free markets are impotent in finding solutions to collective action problems that require cooperation, not competition.

Somehow capitalism's constructive power must be constrained to operate only in the economic marketplace and avoid manipulation of regulations, governments, politicians, and societal rules. In my book *Where America Went Wrong,* I argue that the first step to ensure this is to prohibit corporations from participating in politics and government— no voter organizing by corporations, no corporate campaign contributions allowed, corporate lobbying must be prohibited, no corporate monies for political advertising, and if private corporations own news media outlets there must be assurances that they have publicly owned news media competitors in each of their markets.

There is a deeper problem with capitalism that is more ephemeral, less well understood, and much less discussed. Advanced capitalist countries, because they emphasize competition instead of cooperation, self-interest rather than public interest, and consumption instead of altruism end up creating a mind set in their people that is distinctly different from the less capitalist, less developed countries. World travelers are always somewhat surprised at how warm and friendly the lesser developed countries of the world are as compared to the advanced countries. It is easy to assume that this lack of killer spirit is the reason that these countries have not developed faster, but the opposite may be true. It may be that all people of the world are cooperative and sharing and compassionate until they adopt capitalism and begin to industrialize. It may be the advanced countries' people who are different and abnormal, not the people in the developing world. It may be that the advanced world has a problem that has gone undiagnosed until now.

In traveling, the first thing you notice about Americans, the British, and people from other advanced countries is that they are obsessed with status. They talk about their material possessions and work accomplishments in an attempt to demonstrate their more dominant position. Such status seekers are inherently insecure and their arrogance is but a defense mechanism. Such people begin to define themselves in terms of their incomes, their jobs, and their material possessions. No wonder they are insecure. If a person's identity is defined by such temporal and material objects then it makes sense that the person will be insecure as to whom he really is.

Second, many people from advanced countries come across as extremely self-centered and greedy when viewed through the eyes of someone who lives in the developing world. The hoarding, gross consumption, and wastefulness of many in the advanced world is disturbing to people in the developing world.

The solution to the major problems facing the United States today is a societal-wide reemphasis on cooperation, compassion, and concern for others. The first step is to better understand how Americans became this greediest of generations to see if there is not an as yet undisclosed path out of the darkness of such self-centered behavior. Unless people's concern for their neighbors can be restimulated, there will never be the true moral outrage by the majority of the population that is required for real cooperative action necessary to address these threats to society.

What happened in one generation to make such a dramatic shift from the greatest to the greediest? A combination of forces were at work, all of which increased the individual's level of insecurity. First, America during this time period of some 50 years became a fairly advanced industrialized country. The frontier was gone and independent living on farms had pretty much ceased to exist. Most Americans had become employees of large corporations rather than independent farmers or business owners. Specialization of labor, the key to value creation under capitalism and industrialization, also meant that workers performed a single task, thousands of times, and with little intellectual stimulation or pride in a finished product they could call their own. Although not necessarily outright humiliating, the hierarchical dictatorial top-down structure of most corporations leads to a general feeling of passivity on behalf of many employees.

Such a hierarchical organizational structure prevalent in most of today's corporations assures a continuing fight for status and recognition. Corporations breed insecurity because they feel that fear is a great motivator and because there is no better way to demonstrate status in any organization than by abusing those under you. Control isn't absolute unless you can cause pain, as the novel *1984* reminds us. How many of you really like your boss? And the ultimate threat of being laid off carries much greater significance today in a world where many are just barely making their mortgage payments.

Faster and wider communications means that any story that threatens or scares you can easily be distributed globally in seconds. As Barry Glasser argues in his book, *The Culture of Fear,* such frightful stories about sickness, guns, homicides, kidnappings, and wars not only keeps us glued to the tube to sell advertising for the media but instills in us a deep sense of fear that breeds insecurity and distrust of fellow citizens and other citizens of the world.

Although rapid innovations in technology have brought the wonders of the computer age, space flight, medical cures, and treatments and other miracles to us, it does come at a cost. By definition, if technology is advancing quickly, it is quickly making other older processes obsolete. How insecure do you think a union type person working at a printing press was when printing was transferred from manual-type placement to computer generation? How insecure do you think English teachers are when they read that computers will be grading the essay portion of standardized tests in Indiana high schools this year?

Finally, globalization, the worldwide movement of goods and services, means that the competitive market has been expanded to cover the entire planet. It is no longer sufficient to be the highest quality, lowest cost producer of a product in your city, your state, or even your entire country. You are now in competition with the entire planet. How secure can you feel as an American supplier to Walmart or General Motors when you know full well that a Chinese company is gearing up to provide your same product for half the price, utilizing $1 a day wages for workers with no worker benefits, inadequate health care, little to no regulation, including environmental protections, and almost no taxation? World markets only allow for one winner. There can only be one low-cost producer in the world for each product. Everybody else is second best, and scared and insecure about losing market share.

Specialization of labor, the hierarchical structure of corporations, greater communication abilities, rapid technological obsolescence, and globalization have all led to greater insecurity on behalf of the individual. Increased insecurity in a fast-moving world is the prime culprit to explain why this generation turned so inward in its greed and self-interest. Until people feel comfortable with their own well-being and identity it is difficult to show concern for others. Greater personal security comes with increased confidence that you are leading a productive and good life, not in greater material possessions.

People who are not sure of their own identity turn to other ways of defining who they are. People often define themselves by the status of their job, what school they went to, what neighborhood they live in, or what kind of car they drive.

Greater prosperity itself may ironically fuel more intense feelings of self-interest rather than satisfy individual needs and wants and thus be an enemy of cooperative effort for the societal good. Experts are studying whether absolute wealth or relative wealth brings greater pleasure to humans. If the answer is relative wealth, it might provide another possible reason why this baby boom generation has gotten so wrapped up in itself. Clearly, this generation has lived a rather charmed life of luxury relative to any other generation and America has enjoyed a material wealth available to few others on the planet. But if relative wealth is the measure, there can be only one person with the nicest car, the biggest house, the best paying job; the rest of us have to suffer in relative despair.

In the book *The Progress Paradox,* Gregg Easterbrook presents startling statistics that the American baby boom generation has a level of wealth, health, and prosperity that others could only envision. The average life expectancy in America has grown from 41 years to 71 years since 1900. Polio, smallpox, measles and rickets all virtually eliminated. Starvation has been eliminated, although hunger still plagues the poorest citizens. Leisure time has expanded. Educational opportunities have exploded. A much greater percentage own their own homes today, most with central air and heating and many with swimming pools.

Surprisingly, Easterbrook also reports that this generation of Americans is much less happy than earlier generations. Surveys structured to measure happiness show a broad trend that people are significantly less happy today than people of 40 years ago. Reported cases of depression are up tenfold in 40 years, a statistic that is probably biased upward by better diagnostic techniques today.

Easterbrook has done a great service in demonstrating that greater material wealth and incomes do not automatically translate into greater happiness. He even provides a per capita inflection point of $10,000, below which greater personal incomes in countries around the world seem to provide greater happiness and above which happiness seems to decline with greater income. Below $10,000 of income, any increased earnings go to providing real necessities such food, clothing, shelter, education, and medical care, and thus alleviate real suffering and allow for the provision of basic human rights. Above $10,000, something strange happens. People earn more, have more disposable income, more leisure time, bigger homes, more cars and boats, longer and more luxurious vacations, and yet, the more they make and spend the less happy they are.

Easterbrook is joined by George Will, Milton Friedman, and other conservative scholars who make a fundamental error in trying to explain this apparent dichotomy that greater material welfare does not necessarily bring greater happiness. In their heart they believe that greater incomes and material wealth should make people happier because that is the basis for supposedly rational economics. Namely, that market participants are not only self-interested, but that they will always value more of good things. Two houses are better than one, three ski boats are better than two and four-wheel drive is better than two. The belief that more is better is so endemic to their theory of economics and human behavior that it leads them to the following mistaken conclusion with regard to the dichotomy.

Above $10,000, something strange happens. People earn more, have more disposable income, more leisure time, bigger homes, more cars and boats, longer and more luxurious vacations, and yet, the more they make and spend the less happy they are.

They reason, "If humans are much better off materially and are less happy it must be because humans just don't know how good they have it." These same people who insist that humans are rational and informed enough to make complex pricing, purchasing, and investing decisions in the economic marketplace suddenly turn out to be so dumb as to not even be able to judge how well off they are. Whenever you hear an argument that the people would be in favor of their theory or proposal but they just don't understand it—watch out! This is the clarion call for the people to be abused by other self-interested types who don't have a clue what will benefit the public. The public is the best judge of what is good for them and what might improve their welfare, and it is this fundamental premise that is the basis of democratic government.

What is wonderful is that Americans, as well the other advanced countries of the world, have incomes that satisfy basic survival and human rights needs, and so are perfectly positioned to adopt a more societally-friendly posture to helping solve the really big problems the planet faces. And it turns out it doesn't look like you will be losing any happiness by turning your attention outward; as a matter of fact you may help others experience greater happiness and in turn find your own lives more fulfilled, more meaningful, oh, and yes, perhaps more happy.

Obviously, not all members of the American baby boom contributed to being the world's greediest. There are some who have not bought into this age of rampant consumerism and joined the me generation. Surely, some baby boomers led the efforts to create the environmental movement, fought for woman's rights, fought for minorities' civil rights, led the charge on the consumer protection front, fought for world peace, demonstrated against globalization's abuses of workers' rights, and tried to protect the human rights of indigenous people around the world. But, those involved were a clear minority. The same people who tried to end the war in the 1960s were the ones who fought to clean up the environment in the 1970s, marched for women's rights in the 1980s, demonstrated in support of animal rights in the 1990s, and are forming nongovernmental organizations (NGOs) today to address the abuses of globalization.

This generation had it all, prosperity, education, security, family, friends and global access to information and markets, but they failed to deliver. The most important problems facing the earth were not addressed, not because they were not fully understood, but because this generation didn't have time as they were too busy clothing their children in designer outfits, furnishing their second homes, and seeing that their pools got cleaned.

The problems in Washington and on Wall Street, and for that matter, in Africa as well as rural poor America, begin with us on Main Street. The housing boom and bust was a symptom of a broken regulatory system that was allowed to fester because of the corruption of corporate lobbying and campaign bribes to elected representatives. But it is not the only symptom that society needs changing. Corporate lobbyists have prevented health-care reform, energy reform, global warming initiatives, minimum wage legislation, social security reform, and peaceful resolution of conflicts around the world.

After people in this country clean up Washington, throw the lobbyists out, and properly regulate Wall Street, hopefully there will be time for some self-reflection. Have Americans become consumed by status seeking? Are they truly any happier with their enormous consumption and debts? Is there something to life beyond satisfying self-interest? If this crisis was a shot across the bow, maybe it will be the clarion call needed to make people rethink how they wish to live their lives, to decide what is truly important in life, and what ultimately they hope to accomplish with their short time here on the planet.

References

Ackman, Dan. Fresh Pricks in the Housing Bubble. *Forbes* (March 2, 2005).

Agence France-Presse. Ireland faces recession after Celtic Tiger era. (June 30, 2008).

Agence France-Presse. Spain facing worse economic slowdown than expected. (August 8, 2008).

Agence France-Presse. Japan economy contracts by most in seven years. (September 12, 2008).

Altman, Roger C. How the Fed Can Fix the World. *The New York Times* (September 2, 2008). Available at www.nytimes.com/2008/09/03/opinion/03altman.html.

Andrews, Edmund L. Report Finds Tax Cuts Heavily Favor The Wealthy. *New York Times* (August 13, 2004). Available at http://query.nytimes.com/gst/fullpage.html?res=9A03E2D6173FF930A2575BC0A9629

Andrews, Edmund L. Vast Bailout by U.S. Proposed in Bid to Stem Financial Crisis. *The New York Times* (September 18, 2008).

Andrews, Edmund L. Bush Officials Urge Swift Action on Rescue Powers. *The New York Times* (September 19, 2008).

Andrews, Edmund L. House Republicans Support a Plan That Would Insure Troubled Mortgages. *The New York Times* (September 26, 2008).

Appelbaum, Binyamin, Carol D. Leonnig, and David S. Hilzenrath. How Washington Failed to Rein In Fannie, Freddie. *The Washington Post* (September 14, 2008). Available at www.washingtonpost.com/wp-dyn/content/article/2008/09/13/AR2008091302638.html?hpid=topnews

Asian Week. No Bailing Out the Bad Guys. (September 25, 2008).

Bagley, Nicholas. Crashing the Subprime Party: How the feds stopped the states from averting the lending mess. *Slate* (February 14, 2008).

Bajaj, Vikas and Jonathan D. Glater. S.E.C. Issues Temporary Ban on Short-Selling. *The New York Times* (September 19, 2008).

Bajaj, Vikas. Plan's Mystery: What's All This Stuff Worth? *The New York Times* (September 24, 2008).

Baker, Dean. There has never been a run up in home prices like this. The bubble question: How will rising interest rates affect housing prices? CNN. (July 27, 2004).

Barone, Michael. The Wealth of the Nation. *US News &World Report* (March 1, 2006). Available at www.usnews.com/blogs/barone/2006/3/1/the-wealth-of-the-nation.html

Barron's. The No-Money-Down Disaster. (August 21, 2006).

BBC News. New Zealand 'enters recession.' (August 5, 2008).

BBC News. Irish economy goes into recession. (September 25, 2008).

Becker, Gary S., and Kevin M. Murphy. The Equilibrium Distribution of Income and the Market for Status. *The Journal of Political Economy* 113, 2, pp. 282–310. (April 2005).

Bergsman, Steve. The Hispanic Housing Boom. *Mortgage Banking* 65, 4, pp. 48–54. (January 2005).

Bernanke, Ben S. *Financial Markets, the Economic Outlook, and Monetary Policy*. Washington, DC: U.S. Government. (January 10, 2008).

Bernanke, Ben S. Mortgage Delinquencies and Foreclosures Columbia Business School's 32nd Annual Dinner, New York, New York. (May 5, 2008).

Bernanke, Ben S. The Subprime Mortgage Market. Speech in Chicago, Illinois. (May 17, 2008).

References

Bernanke, Ben S. Text of the testimony prepared for delivery before the Senate Committee on Banking, Housing, and Urban Affairs. *The New York Times* (September 23, 2008).

Bernard, Tara Siegel. Money Market Funds Enter a World of Risk. *The New York Times* (September 17, 2008).

Bitner, Richard. *Greed, Fraud & Ignorance: A Subprime Insider's Look at the Mortgage Collapse.* New York: LTV Media. (2008).

Bitner, Richard. *Confessions of a Subprime Lender: An Insider's Tale of Greed, Fraud, and Ignorance.* New York: Wiley. (June 30, 2008).

Blanton, Kimberly. Adjustable-rate loans come home to roost: Some squeezed as interest rises, home values sag. *The Boston Globe* (January 11, 2006).

Bloomberg. Bernanke Says 'Substantial' Housing Downturn Is Slowing Growth. (October 4, 2006).

Bloomburg. New Zealand Building Approvals Fall to 22-Year Low. (July 29, 2008).

Bloomberg. Canada GDP Unexpectedly Shrank in May on Gas, Cars. (July 31, 2008).

Bloomberg. U.S. may be in 'Very Long' Recession, Harvard's Feldstein says. (July 31, 2008).

Bloomburg. Italy's Economy Unexpectedly Shrinks; Nears Recession. (August 8, 2008).

Bloomberg. Japan, Australia Inject $33 Billion to Soothe Markets. (September 17, 2008).

Board of Governors of the Federal Reserve System. Joint Press Release: Agencies Issue Credit Risk Management Guidance for Home Equity Lending. (May 16, 2005).

Bonner, Raymond. Hole in the Housing Bubble. *The New York Times.* (July 5, 2005).

Brownell, Charles. *Subprime Meltdown: From U.S. Liquidity Crisis to Global Recession.* New York: CreateSpace. (July 16, 2008).

Bruner, Jon. Bear Stearns: What the Candidates Say. *Chicago Tribune* (March 2008). http://blogs.forbes.com/trailwatch/2008/03/bear-stearns-wh.html

Budget of the United States Government. Fiscal year 2008, Table S–7. Budget Summary by Category, Office of Management and Budget, www.whitehouse .gov/omb/budget/fy2008/summarytables.html

Buffett, Warren. *Berkshire Hathaway Inc. Annual Report 2002.* Berkshire Hathaway. (February 21, 2003).

Bureau of Labor Statistics. Consumer Price Index. U.S. Department of Labor. (March 14, 2008). ftp://ftp.bls.gov/pub/special.requests/cpi/cpiai.txt

BusinessWeek. The Mortgage Mess Spreads. (March 7, 2007).

BusinessWeek. The Fed Bails Out AIG. (September 16, 2008).

Calbreath, Dean. Americans addiction to borrowing root of crisis. *The San Diego Tribune* (September 21, 2008). Available at http://www.signonsandiego.com/news/business/20080921–9999–1n21debt.html

Case, Karl E., and Robert J. Shiller. The Efficiency of the Market for Single Family Homes. *American Economic Review.* 79 (March) 125–137. (1989).

Case, Karl E., and Robert J. Shiller. A Decade of Boom and Bust in Single Family Home Prices: Boston and Los Angeles, 1983–1993. *Revue D'Economie Financiere* (December 1993), pp. 389–407. Reprinted in *New England Economic Review* (March/April 1994) 40–51. (1993).

Case, Karl E., and Robert J. Shiller. Mortgage Default Risk and Real Estate Prices: The Use of Index-Based Futures and Options in Real Estate. *Journal of Housing Research* (1996), 7(2): 243–258. (1996).

Case, Karl E., and Robert J. Shiller. Is There a Real Estate Bubble? *Brookings Papers on Economic* Activity, 2004-I. (2004).

Case, Karl E., John M. Quigley and Robert J. Shiller. Comparing Wealth Effects: The Stock Market Versus the Housing Market. *Cowles Foundation Discussion Paper* No. 1335. (2001).

Case, Karl E., John M. Quigley and Robert J. Shiller. Home-Buyers, Housing, and the Macroeconomy in Anthony Richards and Tim Robinson, eds., *Asset Prices and Monetary Policy* Reserve Bank of Australia, 2004, 149–188. (2004).

CBS News. FBI Cracks Down On Mortgage Fraud. (June 19, 2008).

Census Bureau Reports on Residential Vacancies and Homeownership. U.S. Census Bureau. (October 26, 2007).

Center for Responsive Politics. Charles E. Schumer (D-NY) Detailed Contributor Breakdown, 2000 Election Cycle. (2000). Available at www.opensecrets.org/politicians/detail.asp?CID=N00001093&cycle=2000

Christie, Les. No help for 70% of subprime borrowers, *CNNMoney.com* Cable News Network. (April 4, 2008).

References

Clark, Kim. Through the Roof. *U.S. News and World Report* 138, 21, p. 46. (June 6, 2005).

CNN. Worries grow of deeper U.S. recession. (March 21, 2008).

CNNMoney.com PIMCO's Gross. (June 27, 2007).

Cooper, James C. Pop Goes the Housing Bubble. *Business Week* 3908, 36. (November 15, 2004).

Counterparty Risk Management Policy Group. CRMPG III Releases Report. (August 6, 2008). Available at www.crmpolicygroup.org/press-release.html

Cowley, Geoffrey. Why We Strive For Status. *Newsweek* Vol. 141, Issue 24, p. 66. (June 16, 2003).

Coy, Peter. Locating Affordable Luxury Homes. *Business Week Online* (May 23, 2005). www.businessweek.com

Coy, Peter. Is a Housing Bubble About to Burst? *Business Week Online* (July 19, 2004). www.businessweek.com

Crichton, Michael. *State of Fear* New York: Avon Books. (2005).

Cutler, David M. *Your Money or Your Life: Strong Medicine for America's Health Care System* London: Oxford University Press. (2004).

Darlin, Damon. Do Try This At Home: Assess Your Area's Real Estate Bubble. *The New York Times* (August 13, 2005).

Das, Satayjit. CDS market may create added risks. *Financial Times* (February 5, 2008).

Demyanyk, Yuliya (FRB St. Louis), and Otto Van Hemert (NYU Stern). Understanding the Subprime Mortgage Crisis. Working paper published at Social Science Research Network. (August 19, 2008).

DiLorenzo, Thomas J. The Government-Created Subprime Mortgage Meltdown. (September 6, 2007). LewRockwell.com

Draffan, George. Facts on the Concentration of Wealth. (April 2008). Available at www.endgame.org/primer-wealth.html

Draft Proposal for Bailout Plan. *The New York Times* (September 21, 2008).

Duhigg, Charles. Loan-Agency Woes Swell From a Trickle to a Torrent. *The New York Times* (July 11, 2008).

Easterbrook, Gregg. *The Progress Paradox: How Life Gets Better While People Feel Worse.* New York: Random House. (2004).

Economic Times (India). Are emerging economies causing inflation? (July 7, 2008).

Economist. Going Through the Roof. (March 28, 2002).

Economist. A Boom Out of Step. (May 31, 2003).

Economist. Faltering Meritocracy in America. (December 29, 2004).

Economist. After the Fall. (June 16, 2005).

Economist. In Come the Waves. (June 16, 2005).

Economist. Full speed ahead. (January 24, 2008).

Economist. Britain's Economy: How Bad is It? (September 4, 2008). Available at www.economist.com/opinion/displayStory.cfm?source=hptextfeature&story_id=12070800

Economist. Investment banking: Is there a future? (September 18, 2008). Available at www.economist.com/finance/displayStory.cfm?source=hptextfeature&story_id=12274054

Economist. Financial crisis: Carping about the TARP: Congress wrangles over how best to avoid financial Armageddon. (September 23, 2008).

Economist. The doctors' bill. (September 25, 2008).

Elliott, Larry. Credit crisis—how it all began suddenly, one August day last year shook the world, turning an Edwardian summer of prosperity into a grim financial crisis. *The Guardian* (August 5, 2008).

England, Robert. Assault on the Mortgage Lenders. *National Review* (December 27, 1993).

Evans, David. Hedge Funds in Swaps Face Peril With Rising Junk Bond Defaults. *Bloomberg* (May 20, 2008).

Expat Focus. India—Currency and Cost of Living. (March 2008). Available at www.expatfocus.com/expatriate-indiacurrency-costs

Fahey, J. Noel. The Pluses and Minuses of Adjustable-Rate Mortgages. *Fannie Mae Papers* Vol. III, Issue 4. Fannie Mae. (December 2004).

Fernandez, Manny. Study Finds Disparities in Mortgages by Race. *The New York Times* (October 15, 2007).

Financial Times. Early Easter puts Danish economy in recession. (July 17, 2008).

Financial Times. Estonia becomes first victim of Baltic recession. (August 14, 2008).

Financial Times. Recession to hit Germany, UK and Spain. (September 10, 2008).

References

Finfacts Ireland. Eurozone GDP fell 0.2% in the second quarter of 2008: EU27 GDP fell 0.1%; Economies of Eurozone's Big 4—Germany, France, Italy and Spain all shrank. (August 14, 2008).

Fischel, William. An Economic History of Zoning and a Cure for Its Exclusionary Effects. *Urban Studies* (2004) 41(2): 317–340.

Fortune. Welcome to the dead zone: The great housing bubble has finally started to deflate, and the fall will be harder in some markets than others. (May 4, 2006).

Fox, Justin. Betting Against the House. *Fortune* 151, 12, p. 25. (June 13, 2005).

Fox, Justin. Why the Government Wouldn't Let AIG Fail, *TIME*, Time Inc. (September 16, 2008).

Frank, Robert. *Luxury Fever: Why Money Fails to Satisfy in an Era of Excess* New York: Free Press. (1999).

Frank, Robert. Making Waves: New Luxury Goods Set Super-Wealthy Apart From Pack. *The Wall Street Journal* (Eastern Edition) A.1. (December 14, 2004).

Gladwell, Malcolm. *The Tipping Point: How Little Things Can Make a Big Difference.* New York: Back Bay Books. (2002).

Glaeser, Edward, and Albert Saiz. The Rise of the Skilled City. *Brookings-Wharton Papers on Urban Affairs 5* (2004) 47–94. (2004).

Glaeser, Edward and Joseph Gyourko. The Impact of Zoning on Housing Affordability. *Economic Policy Review* 9(2): 21–39. (2003).

Glaeser, Edward, and J. Shapiro. The Benefits of the Home Mortgage Interest Deduction. *Tax Policy and the Economy* 17 (2003) 37–82. (2003).

Glaeser, Edward, and Jed Kolko and Albert Saiz. Consumer City *Harvard Institute of Economic Research.* Working paper. (2000).

Glaeser, Edward, Joseph Gyourko and Raven E. Saks. Why Have Housing Prices Gone Up? *American Economic Review*, forthcoming. (2005).

Glaeser, Edward, Joseph Gyourko and Raven E. Saks. Why is Manhattan So Expensive? Regulation and the Rise in House Prices. *Journal of Law and Economics* (2005).

Glasser, Barry. *The Culture of Fear: Why Americans are Afraid of the Wrong Things.* New York: Basic Books. (2000).

Goodman, Peter S. Credit Enters a Lockdown. *The New York Times* (September 25, 2008).

Gordon, Robert. Did Liberals Cause the Sub-Prime Crisis? *The American Prospect.* (April 7, 2008).

Gray, Michael. Almost Armageddon: Markets Were 500 Trades from a Meltdown. *New York Post.* (September 21, 2008).

Greenspan, Alan. We will never have a perfect model of risk. *Financial Times* (September 22, 2008).

Griswold, David, Stephen Slivinski and Christopher Preble. Six Reasons to Kill Farm Subsidies and Trade Barriers, The Cato Institute. (February 1, 2006). www.freetrade.org/node/493

Gullapalli, Diya. Muni Money-Fund Yields Surge. *The Wall Street Journal* (September 27, 2008). Available at http://online.wsj.com/article/SB122247111922280837.html?mod=testMod

Gyourko, J., and Albert Sinai. Superstar Cities. Zell/Lurie Real Estate Center at Wharton. Working paper, University of Pennsylvania. (July 2004).

Gyourko, J., and Albert Saiz. Construction Cost and the Supply of Housing Structure. Working paper. (May 25, 2005).

Hagerty, James R., and Ruth Simon. Fannie Sees Higher Odds of Regional Housing Bust. *The Wall Street Journal* (Eastern Edition) A.8. (June 20, 2005).

Hagerty, James R. S&P, Citing Option ARM's, Sees Growing Risks for Home Loans. *The Wall Street Journal* (Eastern Edition) A.8. (June 22, 2005).

Hagerty, James R., Dawn Kopecki and John D. McKinnon. White House Seeks Tougher Bill in Push to Rein in Fannie, Freddie. *The Wall Street Journal* (Eastern Edition) A.1. (June 15, 2005).

Herszenhorn, David M., and Carl Hulse. Breakthrough Reached in Negotiations on Bailout. *The New York Times* (September 27, 2008).

Herszenhorn, David M. Congressional Leaders Were Stunned by Warnings. *The New York Times* (September 19, 2008).

Herszenhorn, David M. $700 Billion Is Sought for Wall Street in Vast Bailout. *The New York Times* (September 20, 2008).

Hevesi, Dennis. Which Mortgage? A Complicated Tale. *The New York Times* (July 17, 2005).

References

Holden, Karen C., and Timothy M. Smeeding. The Poor, the Rich, and the Insecure Elderly Caught in Between. *Milbank Quarterly*, vol. 68, no. 2, 1990, 191–219. (1990). www.ncbi.nlm.nih.gov/pubmed/2122199

Hopkins, Jamie Smith. Out without warning. *The Baltimore Sun* (May 15, 2008).

HousingWire.com. Will the Bailout Plan Work? Economists Weigh In. (September 26, 2008). Available at www.housingwire.com/

Hulse, Carl. Conservatives Viewed Bailout Plan as Last Straw. *The New York Times* (September 26, 2008).

Husock, Howard. The Trillion-Dollar Bank Shakedown That Bodes Ill for Cities. *City Journal* (January 1, 2000).

Ibrahim, S.A. Alarm Over Interest-Only ARM's: Much Ado About Nothing. *Mortgage Banking* 65, 8, p. 20. (May 2005).

Infoplease. World Energy Consumption and Carbon Dioxide Emissions, 1990–2025. (March 2008). Available at www.infoplease.com/ipa/A0776146.html

International Herald Tribune. Global inflation climbs to historic levels. (February 12, 2008).

International Herald Tribune. UK economic data points to recession. (August 1, 2008).

International Herald Tribune. Asian central banks spend billions to prevent crash. (September 9, 2008).

International Herald Tribune. Ban on short-selling won't fix markets on its own. (September 9, 2008).

Investor's Business Daily. Congress Tries To Fix What It Broke. (September 17, 2008).

Ip, Greg. Greenspan Again Plays Down Fear of Housing Bubble. *The Wall Street Journal* (Eastern Edition) A.2. (October 20, 2004).

Ip, Greg. Side Effects: In Treating U.S. After Bubble, Fed Helped Create New Threats. *The Wall Street Journal* (Eastern Edition) A.1. (June 9, 2005).

Ip, Greg. What Happens if Real Estate Goes Bust? *The Wall Street Journal* (Eastern Edition) 1. (June 12, 2005).

Ip, Greg. Crash Test: Does a Housing Bust Hurt More Than a Stock Collapse? *The Wall Street Journal* (Eastern Edition) D.2. (June 14, 2005).

Ip, Greg. Booming Local Housing Markets Weigh Heavily on Overall Sector *The Wall Street Journal* (Eastern Edition) A. 1. (June 20, 2005).

Irish Times. House sales in North decline by about half. (August 6, 2008).

Jaffe, Chuck. The Risks From Falling Home Prices. *Market Watch from Dow Jones.* (April 8, 2005). www.marketwatch.com

Kaiser, Emily. Lehman fallout threatens deeper, wider recession, *Reuters* (September 16, 2008).

Kelleher, James B. Buffett's 'time bomb' goes off on Wall Street. *Reuters* (September 18, 2008).

Kotlikoff, Laurence J., and Scott Burns. *The Coming Generational Storm: What You Need to Know About America's Economic Future.* Boston: MIT Press. (2005).

Krugman, Paul. Safe as Houses. *The New York Times* (August 12, 2005).

Lahart, Justin. Egg Cracks Differ In Housing, Finance Shells, *WSJ.com, Wall Street Journal.* 2008–07–13. (December 24, 2007).

Lahart, Justin. Ahead of the Tape. *The Wall Street Journal* (Eastern Edition) C.1. (May 24, 2005).

Laing, Jonathan R. The Bubble's New Home. *Barron's.* (June 20, 2005).

Landers, Kim. Lehman tumbles, Merrill Lynch totters on Meltdown Monday, *ABC News* (September 16, 2008).

Lasch, Christopher. The Culture of Consumerism. *Consumerism.* Smithsonian Center for Education and Museum Studies. (September 15, 2008).

Leonhardt, David, and Motoko Rich. The Trillion Dollar Bet. *The New York Times* (June 16, 2005).

Lereah, David. *Are You Missing the Real Estate Boom?: Why Home Values and Other Real Estate Investments Will Climb Through The End of The Decade.* New York: Currency Books. (2005).

Levy, Ari, and Elizabeth Hester. JPMorgan Buys WaMu Deposits; Regulators Seize Thrift. *Bloomberg* (September 26, 2008).

Lewis, Holden. 'Moral hazard' helps shape mortgage mess. (April 18, 2007). Bankrate.com

Liu, David. Interest-Only and Jumbo Mortgage Data. Mortgage Strategy Group, UBS. New York. (2005).

Lobbying Overview. opensecrets.org Lobbying Database. (April 2008). Available at www.opensecrets.org/lobbyists/overview.asp?showyear=a&txtindextype=s.

References

Madigan, Keith, Ann Therese Palmer and Christopher Palmieri. After the Housing Boom. *Business Week* (April 11, 2005).

Market Watch. U.S. mortgage, housing markets seen caught in 'vicious cycle.' (May 19, 2008).

Market Watch. Moody's says South Africa may slip into recession. (July 7, 2008).

Market Watch. White House says U.S. avoided recession. (July 31, 2008).

Maulden, John. Thoughts on the Housing Bubble. *Forex Rate—Currency News* (July 2, 2005). www.forexrate.co.uk/news

Moffett, Sebastian. The Japanese Property Bubble: Can It Happen Here? *The Wall Street Journal* (Eastern Edition). (July 11, 2005).

Molotch, Harvey. The City as a Growth Machine. *American Journal of Sociology* 82(2) (1976) 309–330.

Morgenson, Gretchen. Arcane Market Is Next to Face Big Credit Test. *The New York Times* (February 17, 2008).

Morgenson, Gretchen. First Comes the Swap. Then It's the Knives. *The New York Times* (June 1, 2008).

Morris, Charles R. *The Trillion Dollar Meltdown: Easy Money, High Rollers, and the Great Credit Crash*. New York: Public Affairs. (March 3, 2008).

Mortgage Bankers Association. Delinquencies and Foreclosures Increase in Latest MBA National Delinquency Survey. Press release. 2008–07–13. (June 12, 2007).

Mozilo, Angelo. Countrywide Financial putting on the brakes. *Wall Street Journal* (August 9, 2006).

MSN Money. Next: The real estate market freeze. (March 12, 2007).

msnbc.com. How severe is subprime mess? *Associated Press* (July 13, 2007).

Mullen, George. The Coming Financial Tsunami. *The San Diego Union Tribune* (June 9, 2005).

Muolo, Paul, and Mathew Padilla. *Chain of Blame: How Wall Street Caused the Mortgage and Credit Crisis*. New York: Wiley. (July 8, 2008).

Murphy, Kevin. What Excessive Pay Package? *Portfolio*. (June 6, 2007). Available at www.portfolio.com/interactive-features/2007/06/salary_comparison

NationMaster. Municipal Waste Per Capita by Country. (March 2008). www.nationmaster .com/graph/env_pol_mun_was_per_cap-pollutionmunicipal-waste-per-capita

Norris, Floyd. A New Kind of Bank Run Tests Old Safeguards. *The New York Times* (August 10, 2007).

Obama, Barack. *The Audacity of Hope: Thoughts on Reclaiming the American Dream.* New York: Crown Publishing Group and Three Rivers Press. (2006).

Obama, Barack. Renewing the American Economy, Speech given at Cooper Union. (March 27, 2008). Available at www.barackobama.com/2008/03/27/ remarks_of_senator_barack _obam_54.php

O'Driscoll, Jr., Gerald P. Fannie/Freddie Bailout Baloney, *New York Post* (September 9, 2008).

Onaran, Yalman. Subprime Losses Top $379 Billion on Balance-Sheet Marks: Table, *Bloomberg.com* Bloomberg L.P. (May 19, 2008).

Paletta, Damian and Elizabeth Williamson. Lobbyists, Small Banks Attack Plan For Markets, *Wall Street Journal* (April 1, 2008).

Paulson Jr., Henry M. Text of the testimony prepared for delivery before the Senate Committee on Banking, Housing, and Urban Affairs. *The New York Times* (September 23, 2008).

Peterson, Peter G. *Running On Empty: How the Democratic and Republican Parties Are Bankrupting Our Future and What Americans Can Do About It.* New York: Picador. (2005).

Phillips, Kevin. *Bad Money: Reckless Finance, Failed Politics, and the Global Crisis of American Capitalism.* New York: Viking Adult. (April 15, 2008).

Poirier, John, and Patrick Rucker. Government plan for Fannie, Freddie to hit shareholders, *Reuters*, Yahoo! Finance. (September 6, 2008).

Poterba, James M. Stock Market Wealth and Consumption. *Journal of Economic Perspectives* Vol. 14, No. 2. (2000).

Powell, Robert. Home is where the nest egg is. *MarketWatch* (September 17, 2008). Available at www.marketwatch.com/News/Story/Story.aspx?guid= a2f51c1bf155453d9bb89f7a925fa041&siteid=nwhreal&sguid=1EjmfkpIvkiCi C2kpqp9zw

Pulliam, Susan, and Serena Ng. Default Fears Unnerve Markets. *Wall Street Journal* (January 18, 2008).

Rajan, Raghuram G., and Luigi Zingales. *Saving Capitalism from the Capitalists.* New York: Random House Business Books. (April 3, 2003).

References

Randall, Maya Jackson, and Andrea Thomas. Paulson: 2008 to Be Difficult Year. *Wall Street Journal* (April 13, 2008). Available at http://online.wsj.com/article/SB120800396896310415.html?mod=hps_us_whats_news

Rawles, James Wesley. Derivatives–The Mystery Man Who'll Break the Global Bank at Monte Carlo. www.survivalblog.com/derivatives.html. (2007).

Reinhart, Carmen M., and Kenneth S. Rogoff. Is the 2007 U.S. Sub-Prime Financial Crisis So Different? An International Historical Comparison. (February 5, 2008).

Reuters. Japan exports shrink as global downturn hits Asia. (July 24, 2008).

Reuters. Global slowdown may put U.S. in recession: Greenspan. (July 31, 2008).

Reuters. Japan ruling party's Aso: Economy in a recession. (August 5, 2008).

Reuters. Greenspan sees turmoil similar to 1987: report. (September 7, 2007).

Ricardo, David. *Principles of Political Economy and Taxation.* New York: Cosimo Classics. (2006).

Roll, Richard, and John R. Talbott. Political Freedom, Economic Liberty, and Prosperity. *Journal of Democracy.* 14, 3 (July) 75–89. (2003).

Roll, Richard, and John R. Talbott. Revenu Inegal et Lutte des Classes: L'Angle Positif *FINECO Journal.* Vol. *15*. English Translation: Income Inequality and Class Warfare: The Positive Approach. (2005).

Roubini, Nouriel. Recession will be nasty and deep, economist says. *MarketWatch* (August 23, 2006).

Saks, Raven E. From New York to Denver: Housing Supply Restrictions Across the United States, Economics Department. Working Paper, Harvard University. (2003).

Saks, Raven E. Job Creation and Housing Construction: Constraints on Employment Growth in Metropolitan Areas. Working Paper. (2004).

Saporito, Bill. Getting Suckered by Wall Street—Again, *TIME*, Time Inc. (September 16, 2008).

Scherer, Ron. House Not Home: Foreigners Buy Up American Real Estate. *The Christian Science Monitor* (July 15, 2005).

Schroeder, Robert. Housing Markets Show Signs of Bust: Fannie. *Market Watch from Dow Jones* (June 24, 2005). www.marketwatch.com

Schwartz, Nelson D., and Carter Dougherty. Foreign Banks Hope Bailout Will Be Global. *The New York Times* (September 22, 2008).

Schwartz, Nelson D., and Julie Creswell. Who Created This Monster? *The New York Times* (March 23, 2008).

Seidman, Ellen. No, Larry, CRA Didn't Cause the Sub-Prime Mess. *New American Foundation*. (April 15, 2008).

Shaw, Richard. Time to Change Country Mix in World Market-Cap. *Seeking Alpha* (June 22, 2008). Available at http://seekingalpha.com/article/82244 -time-to-change-country-mix-in-world-market-cap

Shenn, Jody. Amid Housing-Bubble Din, Something Different? *American Banker* 170, 69 (April 12, 2005) 1–3.

Shiller, Robert J. *Irrational Exuberance: Second Edition* New Jersey: Princeton University Press. (2005).

Shiller, Robert J. *The Subprime Solution: How Today's Global Financial Crisis Happened, and What to Do about It*. Princeton, NJ: Princeton University Press. (August 24, 2008).

Shiller, Robert J. People Are Talking…; *The Wall Street Journal* (Eastern Edition) p. A.12. (June 2, 2005).

Shiller, Robert J. The Bubble's New Home, *Barron's* (June 20, 2005).

Showley, Roger M. Housing Bubble Blip. *San Diego Union Tribune* (June 15, 2005).

Simon, Ruth. Mortgage Lenders Loosen Standards. *The Wall Street Journal* (Eastern Edition) D.1. (July 26, 2005).

Skousen, Mark. Ride out Wall Street's hurricane—The real reasons we're in this mess—and how to clean it up. *Christian Science Monitor* (September 17, 2008).

Social Security Online. Social Security Basics. Social Security Administration Press Office. (March 28, 2008). Available at www.ssa.gov/pressoffice/basicfact.htm.

Sorkin, Andrew Ross. Lehman Files for Bankruptcy; Merrill Is Sold. *The New York Times* (September 14, 2008).

Sorkin, Andrew Ross. Goldman, Morgan to Become Full-Fledged Banks. *The New York Times* (September 21, 2008).

Soros, George. *The New Paradigm for Financial Markets: The Credit Crisis of 2008 and What It Means*. New York: Public Affairs. (May 5, 2008).

References

Sowell, Thomas. Cross Country: Froth in Frisco or Another Bubble? *The Wall Street Journal* (Eastern Edition) A.13. (May 26, 2005)

Statistics Bureau-Ministry of Internal Affairs and Communications. *Japan Statistical Yearbook.* Table 2.1. (2005).

Stiglitz, Joseph. Stiglitz Says U.S. May Have Recession as House Prices Decline. *Bloomberg* (September 8, 2006).

Stockholm News. Sweden heading for recession. (August 8, 2006).

Stout, David. Paulson Argues for Need to Buy Mortgages. *The New York Times* (September 19, 2008).

Swibel, Matthew. Retire? Not so Fast. *Forbes* 175, 12, p. 100. (June 6, 2005).

Talbott, John R. *Obamanomics: How Bottom-Up Economic Prosperity Will Replace Trickle-Down Economics.* New York: Seven Stories Press. (August 2008).

Talbott, John R. *Sell Now! The End of the Housing Bubble.* New York: St. Martin's Press. (February 2006).

Talbott, John R. *Slave Wages: How the Rich and Powerful Play the Game.* New York. (February 1999).

John R. Talbott. *The Coming Crash of the Housing Market.* New York: McGraw Hill. (May 2003).

John R. Talbott. *Where America Went Wrong: And How to Regain Her Democratic Ideals.* New York: Financial Times/Prentice Hall. (May 2004).

Talbott, John R. Yes, the Market is Ripe for a Crash. *The Boston Globe.* Boston, MA: The New York Times Company. (July 27, 2003).

Talbott, John R. Home Investments Report: The Housing-Price Run-Up Can't Last; The Housing-Price Run-Up Will Go On; Two Experts Debate the Issue. *The Wall Street Journal.* New York: Dow Jones & Company, Inc. (June 14, 2004).

Talbott, John R. Turn Out the Lights—The Housing Party is Over. *The Financial Times.* London: The Financial Times Limited. (July 26, 2004).

The Center for Responsive Politics. Federal Election Commission. Contributions from Selected Industries. (March 20, 2008). Available at www.opensecrets. org/pres08/select.asp?Ind=K02

The Chosun Ilbo. Autos, Electronics Face Slumps at Home and Abroad. (July 7, 2008).

The Daily Telegraph. European recession looms as Spain crumbles. (July 18, 2008).

The Daily Telegraph. Spain drops reassuring gloss as crisis deepens. (July 18, 2008).

The Daily Telegraph. The global economy is at the point of maximum danger. (July 21, 2008).

The Daily Telegraph. Australia faces worse crisis than America. (July 29, 2008).

The Guardian. German finance ministry writes off Q2 GDP. (July 21, 2008).

The Guardian. The Italy business morale hits 7-yr low, recession seen. (July 24, 2008).

The Guardian. German June retail sales fall adds to economic gloom. (August 1, 2008).

The Guardian. Latvia joins Estonia in recession. (September 8, 2008).

The Herald. Recession fears are stoked as UK economy grinds to a halt. (August 23, 2008).

The Market Oracle. US in Recession Despite Manipulated Employment and Inflation Statistics. The Market Oracle. (May 3, 2008).

The National Coalition on Health Care. Health Insurance Costs. (2008). Available at www.nchc.org/facts/cost.shtml.

The New York Times. Ratios of Home Prices to Rental Prices in Selected Metro Areas. (May 27, 2005).

The New York Times. Rescue Plan Seeks $700 Billion to Buy Bad Mortgages. (September 20, 2008).

The New York Times. How Three Economists View a Financial Rescue Plan. (September 26, 2008).

The Sunday Times. UK economy heads for 'horror movie.' (July 20, 2008).

The Times. Nationwide warns of recession as house price drop doubles. *The Times* (July 31, 2008).

The Times. Japan heads towards recession as GDP shrinks. (August 13, 2008).

The Wall Street Journal. Homebuilders: Get Ready to Raise Roof Beams. WSJ (Eastern Edition) A.13. (August 31, 2004).

Timmons, Heather. Shoddy Building in the Housing Boom? *Business Week Online* (April 25, 2003).

References

Toll, Robert. Housing Slump Proves Painful For Some Owners and Builders: 'Hard Landing' on the Coasts Jolts Those Who Must Sell; Ms. Guth Tries an Auction; 'We're Preparing for the Worst'. *Wall Street Journal* (August 23, 2006).

Tracy, Joseph, Henry Schneider and Sewin Chan. Are Stocks Overtaking Real Estate in Household Portfolios? *Current Issues in Economics and Finance*. Federal Reserve Bank of New York. (April 1999).

Tully, Shawn. The New King of the Real Estate Boom. *Fortune* 151, 8, p. 124. (April 18, 2005).

U.S. Bureau of the Census. Statistical Abstract of the United States—2004–2005. U.S. Government Printing Office. (2005).

U.S. Census Bureau. United States Aging Demographics, UNC Institute on Aging. (October 2006). Available at www.aging.unc.edu/infocenter/slides/usaging. ppt#259.

US News and World Report. Housing bubble correction could be severe. (June 13, 2006).

Van Duyn, Aline. Moody's issues warning on CDS risks. *Financial Times* (May 28, 2008).

Veblen, Thorstein. *The Theory of the Leisure Class: An Economic Study of Institutions.* New York; Modern Library. (1934).

Wall Street Journal. Carlyle Capital's Comeuppance: High Leverage Proves Onerous. (March 7, 2008). Available at http://online.wsj.com/article/SB120484590324917929.html?mod=googlenews_wsj

Wallace-Wells, Benjamin. There Goes the Neighborhood: Why Home Prices Are About to Plummet and Take the Recovery With Them. *Washington Monthly* (April 2004).

Weiner, Eric. Subprime Bailout: Good Idea or 'Moral Hazard. (November 29, 2007). NPR.org

Wessel, David. Capital: The Fed Starts to Show Concern Signs of a Bubble in Housing. *The Wall Street Journal* (Eastern Edition) A.1. (May 19, 2005).

White, Ben and Eric Dash. Wachovia, Looking for Help, Turns to Citigroup. *The New York Times* (September 26, 2008).

White, Ben, and Eric Dash. As Fears Grow, Wall St. Titans See Shares Fall. *The New York Times* (September 17, 2008).

Wolk, Martin. Feds No Longer Dismiss Talk of Housing Bubble. *MSNBC* (July 11, 2005). www.msnbc.msn.com

Xinhua. New Zealand considered to be in recession. (July 9, 2008).

Zandi, Mark. *Financial Shock. A 360° Look at the Subprime Mortgage Implosion, and How to Avoid the Next Financial Crisis.* New York: FT Press. (July 19, 2008).

Zibel, Alan. Report: More Foreclosures Than Workouts, *Associated Press, International Business Times* (January 17, 2008).

Zumbrun, Joshua. Technically, No Recession (Feel Better?). *Forbes* (May 30, 2008).

About the Author

John R. Talbott is a former top investment banker for Goldman Sachs in New York. In 2003 he was a visiting scholar at UCLA's Anderson School of Management. For the last decade he has been writing full time as an author, publishing six books and numerous peer-reviewed academic journal articles on economics and politics. His first book, *Slave Wages* (1999) describes the threat that increased income and wealth inequality poses to America's societal foundation. *The Coming Crash of the Housing Market* (McGraw Hill, 2003) was an amazon.com and *BusinessWeek* bestseller that accurately foretold the current problems in the U.S. housing, mortgage, and credit markets.

In *Where America Went Wrong and How to Regain Her Democratic Ideals* (Financial Times/Prentice Hall, 2004), John examines the importance of democratic institutions, both in the United States and abroad, in promoting and maintaining a prosperous economy. *Sell Now! The End of the Housing Bubble* (St. Martin's Press, 2006) accurately called the peak of home prices, placing the blame on unregulated lending institutions and lobbyists. *Obamanomics* (Seven Stories Press, 2008) shows how Barack Obama's economic policies will right the U.S. economy, bring about housing, banking, and energy reform, and instigate social change.

John has served as an economic adviser to a number of developing countries, including Jordan and Russia. He has appeared live on CNN, Fox News, CNNfn, CNBC, Fox, MSNBC, and CBS, and has published articles in the *Wall Street Journal,* the *Boston Globe,* the *Philadelphia Examiner,* the *San Francisco Chronicle,* and the *Financial Times.* John graduated from Cornell University with a BS in Civil Engineering, worked for two years for Bechtel Corporation, and received his MBA from the Anderson School at UCLA, where he majored in finance. He can be reached at johntalbs@hotmail.com.

Index